Timeless

LIVING EVERY DAY IN THE TIMELESS TRUTHS OF HIS GRACE

Introduction

Last week I had a conversation with a psychology professor from an eastern university whose special area of interest is people's attitudes and thought processes regarding physical fitness. "What do you think is the number-one reason people give for not exercising?" he challenged me. I offered several answers. "Wrong, wrong, and wrong," he replied. "By far the biggest reason we hear is that people say they don't have time."

I guess I should have thought of that, since it's my favorite excuse. And to be honest, it's an excuse, not a real reason. Truthfully, I can find time for anything I think is important. I never have trouble finding or making time for things I like.

Why don't people read their Bibles or devotional materials? You know the answer—it's the same. God's wonderful Word won't jump into your brain. His book lies quietly where you put it last, and it won't open up and yield its treasures of wisdom, guidance, and strength until you choose to pick it up.

How can you change your personal life patterns to have more God in your day? Here are some simple choices: (1) Put your Bible next to your favorite chair. (2) Use the buddy system. Just as you're more likely to work out if you have a partner, having a devotion partner cuts in half the likelihood that you'll forget your devotion or procrastinate. (3) Keep the Bible readings or devotions short as you're building the habit.

I hope that's why you like Grace Moments—they are Scripture-based, down-to-earth, and short. It is my great pleasure, and the pleasure of our contributing writers, to provide you with devotions for another year of God's grace.

Pastor Mark Jeske

January

"THE LORD HIMSELF GOES BEFORE YOU
AND WILL BE WITH YOU; HE WILL NEVER LEAVE
YOU NOR FORSAKE YOU.
DO NOT BE AFRAID; DO NOT BE DISCOURAGED."
DEUTERONOMY 31:8

January 1

What did you do right?

Pastor Mark Jeske

Did you do anything right last year?

No, really. I'm serious. It's good to push yourself to improve, and the beginning of January is the best time for personal tune-ups, but you can overdo self-criticism to the point where you focus only on your weaknesses and failings.

You are *not* a loser. God did not make a piece of junk when he made you. As we stand on the crack between two years, it's a great time to reflect on what God did for you in the past year, but you might also recall the things you did right. The Spirit of the Lord who planted faith in your heart will also produce righteous fruits. **"God did not give us a spirit of timidity, but a spirit of power, of love and self-discipline"** (2 Timothy 1:7).

Itemize five things that you're proud of doing—kindness shown to a struggler, gifts given freely, a listening ear and open heart to a friend in trouble, patience and a tight lip with a cranky coworker, or words of praise to one who hears little of that kind of talk. You are called to be salt and light in a dark and unsavory world. But get this—God promises to infuse you with the wisdom and strength of his Spirit to get 'er done.

I'm afraid of death

Pastor Mark Jeske

Death is creepy. Every film that calls itself a *horror* movie has death in it. A casket is not a happy symbol in our culture, is it?

When people shuffle in line past a grieving family at a wake, their words usually sound sad. "I'm so sorry." "My deepest sympathy." "How hard this must be for you." People put on black clothes to show how sad they are. We look grave because we're thinking of the grave. How can we not dread this experience for our loved ones or for ourselves?

David was a brave man, maybe the bravest in the whole Bible. But death scared him too: **"My heart is in anguish within me; the terrors of death assail me"** (Psalm 55:4). Death seems to make it certain that the body will never move again, that the heart will never beat nor the lungs breathe again. The mind will never think again nor feel any emotion again. Death seems final, the final blow, Satan's last laugh.

Only the events of Holy Week can change that fear into confidence. Jesus' death fixed everything that is wrong in the world as he accepted the blame and consequences for a world of evil. His resurrection demonstrated that his atoning death was successful and that life and immortality now belong to all believers.

He won. We win too. Fear, begone!

Giving gentleness a try

Pastor Mark Jeske

When you feel wounded by your spouse, it sure is hard to manage the adrenaline rush. Who can resist "payback time"? Who can resist "teaching her a lesson" or "I'll show him"? If you catch yourself thinking (or saying) things like this, realize that very little teaching and learning happen with anger.

You can't control your partner's mouth. But you can control your own. **"As God's chosen people, holy and dearly loved, clothe yourselves with . . . gentleness"** (Colossians 3:12).

Gentleness means that you will not allow stress in the relationship to escalate. It takes two to fight. You will not allow a misunderstanding to morph into sharp words. You will not let sharp words morph into the silent treatment, the silent treatment into an argument, an argument into a verbal fight, or a fight into something physical.

Gentleness means that the level of stress stops right here. It means clamping your lips shut so that angry things can't get out. It means keeping your voice soft. It means asking questions of clarification, assuming that your partner couldn't have meant anything so hurtful. It means taking a walk around the block before blurting things you will regret later.

A gentle spirit in your heart comes from your joy in realizing how gently God has treated a sinner like you.

It can't be undone

Jason Nelson

You are forgiven! There. I said it. And I can't unsay it. And you can't unhear it. That unequivocal announcement is the good news. **"In him we have redemption through his blood, the forgiveness of sins, in accordance with the riches of God's grace"** (Ephesians 1:7). We are not somewhat forgiven. We are forgiven. There are no contingencies. God's grace is rich, and Jesus' blood scrubbed us completely clean.

Then why do we pester God to reconsider? Because we can't let go of what he has forgiven. *But Lord, what about the time I . . .? And remember when I . . . ?* God doesn't have any exceptions, but we do. Satan uses those exceptions to create the doubt that he wants to leverage into unbelief. Forgiveness means nothing if we don't believe it.

So, I will say it again. You are forgiven. And so am I. We are forgiven of indiscretions and unspeakable sins. We are forgiven of things we have laughed off and things that we are ashamed to discuss with anyone. We are forgiven of lapses in judgment and shameful lifestyles. It is all forgiven, and that changes everything about us.

I can't hear it often enough. Can you? You are forgiven. So let it go. Whatever it is that haunts you with relentless guilt, please let it go. It's time to move on because God's forgiveness can't be undone.

January 5

Create a servant culture

Pastor Mark Jeske

A congregation is not only a place where you can find, develop, and use *your* gifts. God has gifted you to mentor and influence other people, especially the young.

Church is a retreat from the street. It is a place where the *contrarian* philosophy of Christ can be taught and modeled. Mass media, hip-hop culture, and the streets adore and reward boasting, selfishness, and ego. A church can help people see that being gentle doesn't mean you become a doormat; that serving doesn't mean you'll just get used; that strength in a man shows itself in self-restraint, not violence; that giving is more noble than taking.

A church culture influenced by Christ helps people, especially young people, to see that yielding to others is not weak. It is in fact Christlike power, world-changing power. **"Young men, in the same way be submissive to those who are older. . . . Clothe yourselves with humility toward one another, because, 'God opposes the proud but gives grace to the humble'"** (1 Peter 5:5).

Many young men will not learn this in their own homes, and they sure won't learn it on the street. Will you help them learn joy in serving in your church? Letting yourself be guided by the mature shows respect for their sacrifices; it helps you learn from their wisdom and their mistakes; it helps you cultivate the humble spirit that God finds so pleasing in his children.

Everybody up!

Pastor Mark Jeske

What is it about the human condition that makes adults such light sleepers and teenagers able to stay comatose till noon? My father used to come into my bedroom, roll up the shades, and boom out cheerfully, "Rise and shine!"

The Epiphany message has that same effect. Everybody up! The glory of God himself can be seen in the words and deeds of Jesus of Nazareth (*epiphany* actually means a "shining through"). **"Arise, shine, for your light has come, and the glory of the Lord rises upon you"** (Isaiah 60:1). A powerful special light in the heavens guided Magi from the East to the very house where the holy family was resting. It changed their lives, gave them hope, and set them in motion to worship the King.

The glory of our Lord Jesus shines from the pages of Scripture and warms your face as well. Everybody up! The Slayer of the old dragon, the Crusher of the serpent's head, is here to go to war for us. The promises have been kept. The prophecies have been fulfilled. Through faith in him your sins are forgiven. Through faith in him you have become immortal.

No more slouching or dozing, no more self-pity or depression. Rise and shine! With Christ you can survive and overcome every obstacle. With Christ you too will shine in heavenly glory.

Praying a scary prayer

Linda Buxa

I like to pray easy prayers. You know the ones: "Please bless me. Forgive me for the things that are technically a sin but really aren't *that* bad. Send your angels to watch over my family. And help the persecuted people all over the world. Amen."

I'm not so good at praying a prayer like David prayed in Psalm 139:23: **"Search me, O God, and know my heart; test me and know my anxious thoughts."**

Asking God to search, to test, and to know my thoughts? Well, yikes, that's a little scary. It's getting a little personal. I'm not sure I really want God to be that involved in my head and heart, to truly know me. I don't want him to see the yucky stuff. I don't want him to think less of me.

What's really strange about that line of thinking is that it means I've somehow deluded myself into thinking that God doesn't already know what's in my mind. When, I know for a fact, that he does.

Because Jesus is my Savior *and* my Lord, I'm admitting that he has an intense interest in not only my eternal life but also my earthly life—even the secret part that I like to gloss over or hide or downplay. I'm confessing that I struggle and I need the peace that only he can give.

I bet you might need that kind of prayer too. So pray it with me: "Search me, know me, test me, Lord."

Be a good manager for God

Pastor Mark Jeske

You know, in all honesty we'd have to admit that in our prayers we probably do a lot of asking for more *things*. What we don't do enough of is asking for wisdom and strength to take better care of the things we already have. We're all custodians and managers of God's generosity, and let's face it, it's easy to take our possessions, our jobs, and our families for granted and to neglect them as we dream about an upgrade.

"Be sure you know the condition of your flocks, give careful attention to your herds" (Proverbs 27:23,24). Livestock in the ancient world was like money in the bank—it was how wealth was stored and power measured. A herd needs careful tending or it won't reproduce at the right time. A herd that isn't reproducing will simply die off in a few years.

Most of us don't own cattle. But we can take inventory of what we are managing for God. We can take pride in our stewardship. We can seek Christ's healing forgiveness for the messes we've made and damage that we've done. And we can seek and expect wisdom and strength from the Holy Spirit to get better at our management.

It is liberating to see ourselves more and more as employees in God's huge, wonderful company. He loves it when we take care of our part of the business.

____

____

____

____

____

You know enough right now

Pastor Mark Jeske

We pastors may be doing you a disservice if we overdo our constant encouragement to become better Bible readers. We mean well—really we do—but we can make you feel too ignorant, too incompetent, and too sinful to exercise a ministry for the Lord.

In fact, you are God's royal priests. You have royal status and a call to ministry that come with your baptismal certificate. You do indeed need to stay in the Word your whole lifetime and never settle for yesterday's level of understanding. But—*you know enough right now* to be useful to God. Paul writes, **"I myself am convinced, my brothers, that you yourselves are full of goodness, complete in knowledge and competent to instruct one another"** (Romans 15:14).

Paul trusted their motives—the Christians in Rome had good hearts. You do too. Paul respected their biblical knowledge—they didn't know everything but they knew enough. You do too. Paul encouraged them to feel competent to do with the Word what God intended—believe it first for yourself *and then use it to help other people.* You can too.

Not everyone in the church is a pastor. But all are priests with a holy, priestly ministry, i.e., opportunities to encourage other fools, strugglers, and sinners with the good news that there is hope for them in Christ Jesus.

January 10

Assertive gratitude

Jason Nelson

Along the way, expressing appreciation became a passive activity. It's how we were raised. Grandpa gave us a quarter and Mom said, "Now, what do you say?" We were conditioned to say thanks in reaction to kindness. I am proposing that we become proactive and put gratitude ahead of the curve. That we express appreciation as a way of signaling to others that we anticipate good things from them.

Assertive gratitude is the response of people made alive in Christ. **"Let the peace of Christ rule in your hearts, since as members of one body you were called to peace. And be thankful"** (Colossians 3:15). When Christ is at the heart of our sentiments, thankful is what we be.

We tend to forego expressing appreciation to people we take for granted or for things we view as someone's responsibility, especially if they're getting paid for it. It's their job. They shouldn't need a pat on the back. But if we withhold our gratitude from them, we fail to thank God for them. They are his agents to us through their efforts.

So, I've been practicing.

Thanks for being my friend.

Thanks for your courage in marrying my son.

Thanks for taking my call.

Thanks for taking my pulse.

Thanks for squeezing my car in, again.

Thanks for staying with me for all these years.

Thanks for coming to church today.

And thanks a lot for reading this. I really appreciate it.

Whose approval do you crave?

Pastor Mark Jeske

Who in your life has the most influence over your behavior? The way in which you answer that question will show whom you are really working for. Is it your parents? your friends? your coworkers? your boyfriend or girlfriend? your boss?

I hope you answered, "None of the above." I hope you would say that you crave God's approval most of all. That seems obvious for a Christian, doesn't it? Obvious to say, maybe, but hard to do. We all suffer from occasional spiritual amnesia. We forget that we are *his* workmanship, created in Christ Jesus to do good works. We forget that we are *his* people, bought with the blood of the Son. We forget that it is *he* who will evaluate our lives in the grand judgment at the end of time.

It's never too late to refocus. **"I urge you, brothers, in view of God's mercy, to offer your bodies as living sacrifices, holy and pleasing to God"** (Romans 12:1). Think how patient and forgiving God has been with you. Let his mercy spur you on to give your life back to him, as though you were a fragrant, sweet sacrifice to him, to his agenda, to his glory.

What would God think of how you spent today? Are you hungry for his "Attaboy!" or "Attagirl!"? What are you ashamed of? As you make your plans for tomorrow, what would God like to see in your words and actions? What in your life needs to stop? What in your life needs to increase?

____

____

____

They worshiped the Lord, but . . .

Pastor Mark Jeske

A time-tested destroyer of marriage is when one of the partners wants to be committed and single at the same time. He or she likes some of the aspects of home life with a spouse but craves also the freedom to enjoy romance and sex on the side. "Cafeteria-style" marriage never works. It always leaves the other spouse wounded and angry.

Though attractive to many today, cafeteria-style spirituality also is a disaster. Though it flatters the individual that he or she is discerning enough to pick and choose a belief system and behavior rules, in reality it is an insult to the God who has spoken clearly enough that he will accept no competition.

As many Israelites from the northern kingdom of Israel went off into captivity, their Assyrian conqueror forcibly relocated people from elsewhere in his realm back into Israel. They only partially came to believe in Israel's God. **"They worshiped the Lord, but they also served their own gods in accordance with the customs of the nations from which they had been brought"** (2 Kings 17:33).

People today talk excitedly about their "spirituality," by which they mean they have assembled an eclectic batch of beliefs that they find acceptable and pleasant. The Bible presents a stark choice—worship the Lord God *only*. Anything else is *idolatry*. Any source of revelation other than his Word is a *lie*. Only the blood of the Savior will help you on the day of judgment.

How your story ends

Linda Buxa

So often as I listen to Bible stories, I can't help but be jealous. I mean, almost all of them end well. Ruth and Naomi had no idea how they would survive, yet they ended up being part of Jesus' family tree. Moses was left to drift down a river, but ended up leading God's people out of Egypt.

Then I realize that I get to read their whole story in one sitting. They are considered heroes of faith because they didn't know the whole story. They had to live it day by day—just like I do. They had to trust God—just like you do.

That's why God gives us his Word. He wants us to see the long line of people whom he used for his purpose, to encourage us. He reminds us of the great things he has already accomplished: living a perfect life, dying a painful death, and rising from the dead (so we can be with him forever in heaven).

Because he already accomplished that, we **"do not worry, saying, 'What shall we eat?' or 'What shall we drink?' or 'What shall we wear?' For the pagans run after all these things, and your heavenly Father knows that you need them. But seek first his kingdom and his righteousness, and all these things will be given to you as well"** (Matthew 6:31-33).

The God who has already taken care of our biggest need—bringing us back into a relationship with him—will make sure that our eternal stories end well.

I'm going to be fired

Pastor Mark Jeske

These days when a corporate firing takes place, it's abrupt. No warning. A security guard escorts you to your desk, watches as you clean it out, takes your keys, and escorts you to the parking lot. There's a reason for that seeming coldness. A disgruntled employee can do an incredible amount of damage, either by sabotage or theft, to a company's business in a very short time.

In Jesus' parable of the shrewd manager, the wealthy business owner made a critical mistake. He announced that he would be firing the manager, **"You cannot be manager any longer,"** *but delayed taking away his authority* within the business office.

"The manager said to himself, 'What shall I do now? My master is taking away my job. I'm not strong enough to dig, and I'm ashamed to beg'" (Luke 16:2,3). The first thing the manager did well was to take the threat very seriously. He knew that time was very short, and he made the most of his last hours in office. He racked his brain to come up with a plan to use his resources quickly while he still had them. As it turned out, he used his master's wealth to bribe future friends for himself. Jesus praised the man, not for his embezzlement, but for his accurate sense of the urgency of time.

Sleepy Christians need this wake-up call. Are you alert to the shortness of *your* time? What are you doing with your life to use God's resources for his agenda?

___

___

___

___

January 15

I feel cheated

Pastor Mark Jeske

As you know, when you begin a Monopoly game, everybody gets $1,500 in start-up cash. Everybody's bank account is the same. The score in every major league baseball game since Abner Doubleday's time is always 0-0 at the top of the first inning.

Alas, life is not like board games or sports. Different people have vastly different amounts of "start-up cash." Some are born to wealth. Some are born in happy, stable, loving homes. Some are naturally intelligent and breeze through school. Some are just naturally thin and cute. Many aren't any of the above.

Satan will see to it that you are acutely, intensely aware of all the things you don't have in your life. He will massage a spirit of resentment in your heart to feel cheated, that somehow you are expected to compete at Monopoly with a measly $637.50 in start-up cash. He wants you to brood over your acne, male-pattern baldness, and cellulite.

Here's how to get past those resentments: take inventory of the treasures that you have been given. **"Let them give thanks to the Lord for his unfailing love . . . for he satisfies the thirsty and fills the hungry with good things"** (Psalm 107:8,9). Celebrate God's favor. Believe God's promises. Bask in God's forgiveness. Trust God's providing. We have enough. Rejoice with me—the Lord is not done giving us good things!

Time to confess

Linda Buxa

One of the upsides to growing up with siblings is that you can blame them—especially when they aren't around. The cartoon *Family Circus* captured kids' typical reactions by featuring a little ghost named Not Me.

It's not so cute when we act innocent as adults. Maybe you hint that the project was late not because you procrastinated but because other people lacked commitment. Maybe you try to justify your yelling by saying the kids deserved it. Maybe you keep a second bank account to hide purchases from your spouse.

King David had tried to cover up some of his sins, and he realized it wasn't such a good idea: **"When I kept silent, my bones wasted away through my groaning all day long. Then I acknowledged my sin to you and did not cover up my iniquity. I said, 'I will confess my transgressions to the Lord'—and you forgave the guilt of my sin"** (Psalm 32:3,5).

Here's the thing: God already knew David's sins, the same way he knows yours. Confessing your sins is not something God needs you to do. It's for you. Carrying guilt around makes you feel scared, alone, hopeless, and worthless. It makes you even want to hide from God, the one whose voice speaks forgiveness. When you hide your sins, you hold on to them. When you confess them, you say, "Here, God, Jesus already paid for these, so I don't have to carry them around anymore. Thank you for taking them away."

Appreciate the queen

Pastor Mark Jeske

It has been my experience in life that men tend to be task-oriented and women are wired more for relationships. Do you agree? Think about it—is there male or female handwriting on most of the greeting cards that you receive? Female, of course. What would you say is the female-to-male gender breakdown of gift giving in your circles? 50/50? I doubt it. Try 80/20, and I might believe you.

Everybody needs to grow in cultivating a thankful spirit, but I think I and my fellow males have farther to go. Tending and mending relationships is learned behavior for us, and sometimes we fail. One of the most crushing burdens for a woman to endure, especially one who has sacrificed much to bear and nurture young children, is to go unappreciated by her husband.

TV shows celebrate narcissistic males in an endless quest for a glamorous trophy babe. Husbands, has God blessed you with a woman who has been faithful to you, worked hard, built up your reputation, and poured herself into the lives of your children? Do you have any idea what a prize God gave you? **"A wife of noble character is her husband's crown"** (Proverbs 12:4).

Wear your crown with pride. Have you told her today (hey—I mean *today*—last week doesn't count) how much you appreciate her? Flowers "just because" get you bonus points.

January 18

I'm afraid of all the violence in society

Pastor Mark Jeske

Have you ever had your car broken into? Have you ever been mugged or sexually abused? Has your home ever been broken into? Not only can sad events like those hurt you materially and physically, but they can leave you with more or less permanent fear. They can rob you of your feeling of safety no matter where you are and damage your ability to trust other people.

Our society has too many weapons. Too many unstable people roam the streets. There are too many people whose judgment is distorted by drugs and alcohol. How can you not worry about your safety? How can you not be concerned about the world we are bequeathing to our children?

King David was not always the serene ruler on the throne of a peaceful kingdom. In his early adult life, he spent years on the run in the southern deserts, afraid for his life. In later years he suffered the humiliation of being driven from his throne and capital city by his son Absalom. It must have seemed to him as though the world had gone crazy mad with violence. **"When the foundations are being destroyed, what can the righteous do?"** (Psalm 11:3).

We depend utterly on the Father's protecting hands, on his legions of holy angels, and on his mighty promise to work all things together for our good. We'll be okay.

January 19

Notice the newbies

Pastor Mark Jeske

I hate first days. I hate being alone in a group where everybody else seems to know everybody else. I hate being ignorant of the group's rituals, behaviors, and expectations. It doesn't take much to embarrass me at times like that, and if the experience is too stressful, I won't be back if I can avoid it.

Do you suppose people who visit your church feel like that? Experienced church shoppers get turned off easily enough—what do you suppose goes through the mind of a brand-new Christian when she dares to visit you? Or one who was burned by bad experiences or bad leadership in the past and is gingerly trying out the church world one last time?

Our Lord Jesus has a huge heart for newbies and the de-churched. It is still his passion to kindle or rekindle the flame of faith in those hearts. **"A bruised reed he will not break, and a smoldering wick he will not snuff out"** (Matthew 12:20). His precious gospel message forgives the guilty, loves the broken, comforts the despairing, and values the outcasts.

The groups to which I came back a second time were ones where I was noticed and befriended, where it felt like the old-boy and old-girl networks would make room for me and make me feel welcome. Will you join me in church this Sunday and watch for the newbies?

A text for the ages

Jason Nelson

My children are irritated that I don't have a smartphone or GPS. I tell them I have a phone on the wall that seems pretty smart and there are maps in my head. I think they're afraid that I'm going to keel over somewhere and won't give off any signal. I tell them I may get one, but I am waiting for the technology to improve. They shake their heads and walk away.

I know sharing a message can be a breakthrough. Like Paul Revere's ride and Dr. Martin Luther King Jr.'s "I Have a Dream" speech, the world changed when the word got out. I pray device-savvy generations can lead us into an era of collaboration because they have instant communication with each other and access to the best information. It's their turn to change the world. I hope they have an app for that.

The Bible is a text that changed the world. It was so commonly known that cultures parlayed on its acceptance and united around its values. Art reflected its images, language its expressions, and society its substance. Chiseled in stone or ricocheting from a micro circuit, the Word of God is a text for the ages. Every generation holds a sacred trust to pass it on.

May our children and theirs love to receive this text and respond, **"It's news I'm most proud to proclaim, this extraordinary Message of God's powerful plan to rescue everyone who trusts him"** (Romans 1:16 MSG).

January 21

Internship

Pastor Mark Jeske

We're all so absorbed in the struggle to survive, caught up in the here and now, that we don't always pay attention to how God is describing our future life in heaven. Heaven won't be eight bazillion years of vacation. Work, growth, and significant service will continue, and our earthly life right now is only "spring training."

"Whoever can be trusted with very little can also be trusted with much, and whoever is dishonest with little will also be dishonest with much. So if you have not been trustworthy in handling worldly wealth, who will trust you with true riches? And if you have not been trustworthy with someone else's property, who will give you property of your own?" (Luke 16:10-12).

Jesus sees as a real spiritual sickness our tendency to hoard and spend for our own comforts and pleasures in the short term. We're in training right now—think of it as an internship. The Lord is always preparing you for bigger things.

That's why it is so important to cultivate integrity. *Integrity* means that you're all of one piece; that your principles are not for sale; that you treat high and low alike; that your word is good; that you are honest in public and in private, in big things and in little things; and that you don't show favoritism.

Every successful business depends on leadership development. Isn't it interesting that God also is intensely interested in leadership development? How are you coming along?

January 22

I am so broke

Pastor Mark Jeske

Billie Holiday got it cold: "Money, you've got lots of friends they're crowding around your door; but when you're gone and spending ends they don't come no more." Do you know the fear, the shame, the panic of being broke, or worse, of being over your head in debt? Have you ever encountered the repo man, a collection agency, bankruptcy, foreclosure, eviction?

God has a special place in his heart for the small and poor of the earth. Ironically, in this world, the poorer you are the less likely you will ever have access to a government leader. In God's world, wealth often makes people think they don't need God, and it is *the poor* who enjoy his smile. **"Do not let the oppressed retreat in disgrace; may the poor and needy praise your name"** (Psalm 74:21).

You will never be in a hole so deep that the eyes of the Lord can't see you, the reassuring voice of the Lord can't reach you, and the long arms of the Lord can't rescue you. You are never without resources if you are with the Lord. Call him up and tell him what you need.

And then pay attention to the people he sends. Social capital is capital too. God's solutions come sometimes in the form of cash but probably more often in the form of ideas, relationships, and opportunities.

When help comes, don't forget to say thank you.

The last Boomer standing

Jason Nelson

Those of us born between 1946 and 1964 face a daunting challenge. After dominating the landscape, it is our turn to step out of the way. Our legacy is uncertain. We can be associated with civil rights, voting rights, fair housing, gender equity, environmentalism, free love, the abortion holocaust, and the epidemic of drug abuse. We gave peace a chance and fought wars we couldn't win. Our religion and politics could be explosive. Private wealth and the national debt grew on our watch as the middle disappeared. The sing-along at the nursing home is going to change when we get there. Our music was hard, loud, and made a statement. *Kumbaya.*

We tried to keep the faith, baby. Did we? How will history judge our stewardship of life, liberty, and the pursuit of happiness? How will God judge our duty to bestow his values upon future generations? We are in our mellow years. If upon reflection there are things we regret, it's not too late. **"Even when I am old and gray, do not forsake me, O God, till I declare your power to the next generation, your might to all who are to come"** (Psalm 71:18).

And if there is such a thing as Boomer guilt, there is only one way to deal with it: **"Repent and be baptized, every one of you, in the name of Jesus Christ for the forgiveness of your sins"** (Acts 2:38).

____

____

____

____

____

Use power carefully

Pastor Mark Jeske

Don't you hate getting jerked around by small-minded government officials who seem to enjoy making you jump through hoops? Do you hate to wait? Don't you hate getting "put in your place" when people in power make you feel small and powerless?

Power corrupts, as Lord Acton said. But it's not only the super rich who can take advantage of the poor. Plenty of middle-class and even working-class people have opportunities to take advantage of those in society who are farther down the social and economic ladder than they.

Remember that the lowest in society have a special protector in God: **"He who oppresses the poor shows contempt for their Maker, but whoever is kind to the needy honors God"** (Proverbs 14:31). If you work in HR, if you do hiring and firing for your department or company, remember the human value of the worker as well as corporate interests. God gives some people surpluses not to fuel their materialism but to position them for mercy to those who are struggling to survive.

That doesn't mean that you have to fork over $5 to every panhandler who hustles you on the street. It does mean that God encourages you not to take advantage of people with less financial and social and political power. It does mean that everyone you meet was created, loved, and redeemed by God. Same as you.

___

___

___

___

January 25

Holy huddle

Pastor Mark Jeske

It is human nature to prefer the company of people just like you. Your tribe is a powerful organizing force. Much of the time this isn't a bad thing—professional associations, moms' playgroups, and sports activities thrive on people's similar needs and abilities.

It becomes a problem, however, when congregations are so homogeneous that outsiders can't break in and when the "club" members in the holy huddle don't know how to appeal to outsiders. Worse—maybe they don't even want to.

Social groups, churches included, don't want to change if they don't have to. It's an ancient problem, and only clear and determined leadership will change things. **"Now those who had been scattered by the persecution in connection with Stephen traveled as far as Phoenicia, Cyprus and Antioch, *telling the message only to Jews.* Some of them, however, men from Cyprus and Cyrene, went to Antioch and began to speak to Greeks also, telling them the good news about the Lord Jesus. The Lord's hand was with them, and a great number of people believed and turned to the Lord"** (Acts 11:19-21).

These unnamed men—from a Mediterranean island and from North Africa—helped build a racially and socially inclusive congregation in Antioch. May their tribe increase—the church today desperately needs congregations that know how to and want to reach out to people *not like them.*

___

___

___

___

God-devised mysteries

Linda Buxa

"God . . . devises ways so that a banished person may not remain estranged from him" (2 Samuel 14:14).

God works in mysterious ways. You hear that so often you might start to think it's an actual Bible passage, right? It's not. Though there is truth to it. God doesn't think the way we think. God doesn't do things the way we do things. The ways he has devised to end our banishment from him seem mysterious too.

To be clear, there is no doubt about the one way God used to end our eternal banishment. Only because Jesus has taken our sin away and given us his righteousness can we approach God.

That said, God devises plenty of ways to keep our wandering attention on him. For Jonah, who was literally running away, he provided a great fish to swallow him to bring him back. It took the prodigal son a long time and a lot of hunger to realize that being separated isn't all it's cracked up to be. For us it might be a car accident or a job loss or loneliness that brings us back to him.

God isn't interested in keeping you comfortable. He is interested in making sure you aren't banished. And he is not against using ways that seem mysterious to bring you back.

What in your life has been God-allowed or even God-sent that woke you up to your separation from him? Thank him for it today.

January 27

Hope I die before I get old

Pastor Mark Jeske

In a dog-eat-dog world, the older dogs get pushed around and shoved to the back of the line. Who wants to be old? One of my favorite TV channels plays a lot of old reruns, and almost all the commercials are geared to older people. There clearly is a market for their stuff. But honestly, who wants to be a person who needs those products? Who aspires to the world of step-in bathtubs, catheters, walkers, funeral insurance, and chair hoists built into your staircase?

It should not surprise you that the ways of God's kingdom are opposite to those of our culture. God invites us to see seniors as he does: repositories of great life wisdom. They are overcomers; they have been through fire and testing and emerged humbler, kinder, and wiser. They have lived long enough to see their prayers answered; they have lived long enough to notice with appreciation and serenity the handiwork of the Master Weaver in their long past.

Blessed is the family who looks up to and cherishes its grandparents and great-grandparents. Blessed is the congregation that cherishes the counsel and respects the legacy of its elders.

Ladies, when you decide to quit coloring your hair, do it with pride and self-confidence. Here's what God thinks of your silver mane: **"Gray hair is a crown of splendor; it is attained by a righteous life"** (Proverbs 16:31).

Everybody knows your name

Pastor Mark Jeske

Everybody feels a need to belong somewhere. That's what made the *Cheers* tavern so much fun. Remember the theme song? A place where everybody knows your name? As soon as you walked in you knew it was a warm and enjoyable place to be. "Hey—it's Norm!"

Wouldn't it be awesome if every church had that kind of people magnetism? A place to belong . . . a place where you were accepted unconditionally . . . a place where you could go to escape, to heal, to learn something, to find friends, to connect, to grow? God made people to need other people. We need to know somebody is interested in us, cares about how we're doing, knows and loves our children, and is always there for us. We need a place where we can get involved and serve and use our gifts and talents.

Here's what a happy church fellowship looks like: **"Selling their possessions and goods, they gave to anyone as he had need. Every day they continued to meet together in the temple courts. They broke bread in their homes and ate together with glad and sincere hearts, praising God and enjoying the favor of all the people"** (Acts 2:45-47).

Is your church a place like that, i.e., a place of sacrificial giving, genuine love, and a dominant spirit of celebration? How can you help your congregation to be as irresistible to wandering people as Cheers?

Jesus ain't no killjoy

Jason Nelson

The Bible doesn't report Jesus having fun. But he must have. He was true man. He was one of us. He had the full-on human experience. And he was true God. So he must have had some really good clean fun. He certainly enjoyed himself at that wedding before the wine ran out. He hung out with close friends at dinner parties. Fishing is always fun until a storm kicks up. I don't think he told jokes, but he must have chuckled at the antics of children who were first in his heart.

Following him doesn't mean we can't have fun. People are put off from Christianity by caricatures of somber folks devoting themselves to dull lives, as if you can't have a sense of humor and still take God seriously. The Bible does say, **"The boundary lines have fallen for me in pleasant places; surely I have a delightful inheritance"** (Psalm 16:6). The Bible's parameters for living are a foundation for a full life and leave lots of room for good times. God drew the lines broadly so that we can be delighted in his grace. There are lots of fun things to do that you won't regret the next day.

A clear conscience is the icing on the cake, or the celebration in the end zone, or the trophy mounted on the wall, or whatever you want to use as the measure of having fun. So go out and have some.

Generosity is joy

Pastor Mark Jeske

Do you love paying taxes? I didn't think so. Tax time is no fun for me either. I put it off as long as I can. I dread the tedious chore of filling out all the ever-changing forms. I dread not having had enough wages withheld and finding out that there will be no refund because I owe a lot more. I dread getting the official IRS letter informing me that my paperwork had mistakes and that I owe still more, plus interest, of course.

Does the passing of the basket in church remind you of tax time? Is it a "hafta" thing for you? Please don't ever think of giving money to God as a "hafta." It's a "wanna." St. Paul never got tired of proudly describing the inspirational attitude of the low-income congregation members in Macedonia: **"Out of the most severe trial, their** [the Macedonian Christians'] **overflowing joy and their extreme poverty welled up in rich generosity. . . . Entirely on their own, they urgently pleaded with us for the privilege of sharing in this service to the saints. . . . They gave themselves first to the Lord"** (2 Corinthians 8:2-5).

When you let go of money in church, it's not a tax. It's not a charge; it's not dues. It's a solemn moment of worship in which you acknowledge God as the Owner, God as the Giver, and God as the object of your worship.

Jesus brings me joy. Giving to Jesus brings me joy.

Let others help you

Linda Buxa

You know how the script is supposed to go:

How are you doing? Fine.
How was your day? Good.
What's up? Nothing.
Lie. Lie. Lie.

We all know the world is hard, so why do we spend so much time pretending it's not?

Part of God's plan was to place all sorts of people around us to help us get through all the sadness and pain that will inevitably hit. He then tells us, **"Carry each other's burdens, and in this way you will fulfill the law of Christ"** (Galatians 6:2). Yet don't we each think that while it's fine for someone else to need help, it's not as acceptable for us to need support—or even correction—too?

However, when we don't share our struggles, we suffer because our egos are too big to say, "I need help." We get lonely and start to believe that we are all alone. On top of that, we rob someone else of the joy that comes from serving, and we miss out on the blessings that come from being fully connected.

In Ecclesiastes chapter 4, God gently reminds us (because we all need reminding): **"If one falls down, his friend can help him up. But pity the man who falls and has no one to help him up!"** (verse 10).

Don't be pitiful. Let others help. Here's how to start:

How are you doing? I could use some prayers.
How was your day? Not so great.
What's up? Do you have a minute?

February

"GOD DID NOT GIVE US A SPIRIT OF TIMIDITY,
BUT A SPIRIT OF POWER, OF LOVE
AND OF SELF-DISCIPLINE."
2 TIMOTHY 1:7

February 1

A foretaste of heaven

Pastor Mark Jeske

The disciples' experience in the upper room the evening before Jesus' death was a lot like our lives as believers. Gloom hung heavy over the group—Jesus calmly predicted his betrayal by one of them and abandonment by all of them. He predicted his own suffering and death. He foresaw how hard their own ministries would be in the future.

And yet. And yet in the middle of those necessary but hard words came shining promises, outpourings of mercy, and pure gospel. He instituted a holy supper that would sustain their faith and strengthen it throughout their lives: **"Jesus took bread, gave thanks and broke it, and gave it to his disciples, saying, 'Take and eat; this is my body.' Then he took the cup, gave thanks and offered it to them, saying, 'Drink from it, all of you. This is my blood of the covenant, which is poured out for many for the forgiveness of sins'"** (Matthew 26:26-28).

That meal bound them to the blood of the Lamb, and that blood connected them forever to their forgiving God, to his power and guidance and protection and inspiration. That meal would sustain them until the Great Feast of heaven: **"I tell you, I will not drink of this fruit of the vine from now on until that day when I drink it anew with you in my Father's kingdom"** (Matthew 26:29).

Every time you go to Lord's Supper, you get a little experience of how good heaven will be.

Sometimes things end badly

Pastor Mark Jeske

I wish I could assure you that all human stories turn out great in the end. Alas, sometimes people we love reject the God we love. David, king of Israel from about 1040 to 1010 B.C., was off the charts in many ways—musician, poet, warrior, builder, and statesman. But he had several equally devastating weaknesses of character—he succumbed to the temptation to assemble a harem of wives and concubines, just like the heathen kings around him.

So strong in battle, he also seemed terribly weak in dealing with his treacherous and violent sons. Absalom, for instance, came to despise his father. He assembled a rebel army that succeeded in driving the vacillating David out of Jerusalem. He dared to raise his hand against the anointed of the Lord!

A bloody civil war ensued. At the climactic battle, however, Absalom was killed. There was no chance for reconciliation with either his father or his God. David's grief was inconsolable: **"The king was shaken. He went up to the room over the gateway and wept. As he went, he said: 'O my son Absalom! My son, my son Absalom! If only I had died instead of you—O Absalom, my son, my son!'"** (2 Samuel 18:33).

It's a sobering story with a sobering message: Time is short. Repentance matters. Faith matters. Obedience matters. The consequences are eternal.

Prayer is like that

Jason Nelson

Being a Christian writer has its challenges. Having nothing to say is one. So is getting tired of the sound of your own voice. So I stare at the screen hoping a good idea crawls out from among the pixels.

Prayer is like that. We don't know what to say anymore. We get weary of the routine of it and waiting for an answer. And then God tells us to do it without ceasing. Prayer is never one and done. It is to stream through every scene of our lives.

Fortunately, God is always listening. And he is very generous in what he accepts as a prayer. Be attentive to your subconscious rumblings and recognize a prayer in them. **"In the same way, the Spirit helps us in our weakness. We do not know what we ought to pray for, but the Spirit himself intercedes for us with groans that words cannot express"** (Romans 8:26).

Thank you, Holy Spirit, for seeing what we miss. Thank you for hearing a plea in our frustration and identifying its cause. Thank you for lifting us off our stiff knees so we can boldly approach God. Thank you for tracing our sighs to their source and proposing solutions to our heavenly Father. Thank you for not branding us weak because we don't know what to say. That is why we pray. Thank you for praying with us.

Amen.

Manage risk

Pastor Mark Jeske

The first decade of the 21st century certainly was a miserable financial experience for many people.

People who gambled too much money on new Internet stocks were scorched when the dot-com bubble burst. People who shouldn't have been able to buy a home were given no-document/no-money-down loans. People who had only hazy notions of home financing signed up for adjustable rate mortgages and then reacted in panic and dismay as the rates automatically adjusted upward (one escalator you don't want to be on).

The point: watch what you do; weigh what you do; keep your exposure to risk as low as possible. Never forget: **"The borrower is servant to the lender"** (Proverbs 22:7). The more debt you have, the more of a slave you are. Make friends with some financial planners and listen to them. They are probably smarter than you. Never get into a financial contract or investment that you don't fully understand.

Take your time. Think first. Look at the examples of others. Learn from the stories and mistakes of others. Think of the impact of your actions on your family. Find somebody smarter than you and get that person's advice on the loan you would like to take out. Explain to God what you are thinking about doing and listen to how your words sound in his presence.

February 5

Her Majesty, the queen of Sheba

Pastor Mark Jeske

The country of Yemen today is one of the poorest places in the Arab world, and its poverty glares all the more by comparison with its oil-rich neighbors. But Yemen was once a rich and prosperous trading center and oasis. Known as Sheba in the 900s B.C., it was governed by a formidable queen.

This remarkable woman is a hero to me because when she heard of King Solomon's wealth and achievements, she didn't just stew in envy or plot ways to try to dip into his river of cash. She packed up a camel train of servants and fabulous gifts and traveled to Jerusalem, *convinced that he was speaking for the Lord God.*

"She said to the king, 'The report I heard in my own country about your achievements and your wisdom is true. . . . Indeed, not even half was told me; in wisdom and wealth you have far exceeded the report I heard. How happy your men must be! . . . Praise be to the LORD your God, who has delighted in you and placed you on the throne of Israel'" (1 Kings 10:6-9).

The queen of Sheba was also a hero to Jesus himself. He cited her as a model of faith, in stark contrast to the hardhearted unbelief he saw all around him: **"The Queen of the South will rise at the judgment with this generation and condemn them; for she came from the ends of the earth to listen to Solomon's wisdom"** (Matthew 12:42).

Want to hang out?

Pastor Mark Jeske

Relationships are the people-glue that hold congregations together. In a happy, healthy church, the members open their lives and homes to amplify the church's message of welcome. The longer you've been connected to Christ and the more fully his Word, power, and Spirit flow through you, the better you get at it. You don't cling so tightly to your stuff but share it with a smile and **"offer hospitality to one another without grumbling"** (1 Peter 4:9).

The gospel message of a servant-Savior helps us become outwardly focused servants instead of self-absorbed customers. Visitors to our congregations will sense that in this place they will be helped, not hustled. As our world grows crueler and more selfish each year, genuine acts of kindness and friendship stand out and make our religious talk much more believable. Jesus loves it when we believe him that all our stuff is really his anyway. He loves it when people help people, and he loves to replenish the supplies of generous people so that they end up with more than where they started.

In spite of the popularity of social media, digital avatars, and virtual friends, there is no true substitute for a real, face-to-face friendship with someone who cares about your life. Do your neighbors know what the inside of your house looks like? Do you have the ability to be a people connector? Have you ever brought someone home from church?

February 7

W.A.I.T.

Linda Buxa

"Reckless words pierce like a sword, but the tongue of the wise brings healing" (Proverbs 12:18).

The other day I saw this reminder: W.A.I.T. It wasn't telling me to be patient, though. It was a reminder to ask: Why. Am. I. Talking?

As a chatty extrovert, I could use that acronym to save me from the painful question I all-too-often ask: Why. Did. I. Say. That? (No handy acronym for that, just embarrassment and regret.) I've left places knowing that I said too much, said the wrong thing, or hurt someone's feelings because of my quick tongue.

In the Old Testament, Job's friends did a great thing—they sat and grieved with him in silence for seven days. The trouble came when they did not WAIT. Instead, they opened their mouths—and they've had bad reputations ever since. I'm sure you have your own stories and failures too.

The good—no, great—news is that through faith we get credit for Jesus' perfect use of words all the time. We aren't punished or condemned for the times we've used our reckless words to pierce others. Instead, we are thankful for forgiveness and now get to use our words to bring healing.

We get to build others up when the world is beating them down. We get to encourage them to keep going when they want to stop. We get to tell them of the Savior who loves them so much that he spoke the three most healing words of all time: *It. Is. Finished.*

____

____

____

Live in the cloud

Jason Nelson

"Since we are surrounded by such a great cloud of witnesses, let us throw off everything that hinders and . . . fix our eyes on Jesus" (Hebrews 12:1,2).

Now there is cloud computing. Near as I can tell, it's a way to store data and share content all over the place. Sounds intriguing.

Jesus taught his disciples to log in to things above: "The kingdom of heaven is like. . ." Then he brought it down to earth so they could walk in his footsteps.

Spirituality is persistent mindfulness of our eternal connection to God through his Son, Jesus Christ, in communion with all who have believed in him. There is something holy and vibrant beyond us, and we are in the midst of it.

Living in the cloud elevates our perspective. Problems are temporary. Better days are coming. Hope is backed up by credible witnesses who were here and are now there because they fixed their eyes on Jesus.

There is joy in the cloud. Even now a little rains down on us. Appreciate every drop of it, and spread it around because there's lots of room in the cloud. Soon, **"the Lord himself will come down. . . . The dead in Christ will rise first. . . . We who are still alive and are left will be caught up together with them in the clouds. . . . We will be with the Lord forever"** (1 Thessalonians 4:16,17).

Love your church elders

Pastor Mark Jeske

A warm evangelism spirit is essential for a congregation to be healthy. New people need to feel important, noticed, embraced, and a part of the family. It is just as important that a congregation pay attention to people who were once spiritually active and no longer seem to demonstrate a pulse. The strayers are as important as the seekers.

Your congregation most likely has a group that is tasked with connecting with the straying. Perhaps they are called a care team or a board of elders. Their mission is people's spiritual well-being. They are chosen for their maturity, leadership ability, people skills, and knowledge of the Word. Here are the activities and attitudes that St. Paul wanted to see in a congregation's spiritual leaders: **"Warn those who are idle, encourage the timid, help the weak, be patient with everyone"** (1 Thessalonians 5:14).

Your elders can help you in your own efforts to reclaim a straying friend or family member. They will show you how to access your congregation's education and caring programs. They will pray for you and make sure you get a warm welcome and personal attention if you are able to bring someone back to church for a visit.

You can help build up the elders with prayer and words of encouragement. Spiritual mentoring and people management can often be exhausting and frustrating for these elders, and they need your help too. Love your elders.

Build your love muscles

Linda Buxa

You get out of it what you put into it. People who faithfully work out know this is true. Sitting at home on the couch makes you weaker. So does simply going through the motions. If you want to get stronger, you lift heavier weights. If you want to be faster, you have to do sprints.

When it comes to faith, thanks to what Jesus has done for you, you definitely do not get out of it what you put into it. You put in sin; Jesus gives you perfection. You put in guilt; he gives you peace. You put in death; God gives you life.

But when it comes to your faith community, you do get out of it what you put into it. Staying at home or only going through the motions makes you weaker and more vulnerable. God puts you in a group of believers to help you build your love muscles. He tells you how: **"Let us consider how we may spur one another on toward love and good deeds. Let us not give up meeting together, as some are in the habit of doing, but let us encourage one another—and all the more as you see the Day approaching"** (Hebrews 10:24,25).

Take the first step. Show up at church and introduce yourself. Get to know your spiritual workout partners.

One last thing, if you happen to be a regular at God's gym, remember how much courage it can take for a newcomer to walk in. Be welcoming. Be encouraging.

Issachar leadership

Pastor Mark Jeske

What qualities do you most want to see in your leaders? Honesty? Financial integrity? Marital faithfulness? Loyalty? Yes, all these and more.

The book of Chronicles in Scripture gives us unique insight into what constitutes great leadership. Consider the two hundred or so officers that the tribe of Issachar provided for King David's armed forces. The census for each of the other tribes' military presence lists tens of thousands of skilled fighters who came to David's side. But Issachar's contribution was in a class by itself—only the *officers* are mentioned: **"These are the numbers of the men armed for battle who came to David at Hebron . . . men of Issachar, who understood the times and knew what Israel should do—200 chiefs"** (1 Chronicles 12:23,32).

Of all the things I value in people I must follow, in both our social and spiritual world, I look for Issachar-type abilities: first, the sharpness of mind to *understand the times,* to know the people of today, to feel their pulse, learn their language, grasp their technology, understand their thought processes, know their needs, get their messages.

Second, great leaders also *know what to do*. They survey all the different tracks the train could run on and choose one. Great leaders articulate a plan and inspire the troops to volunteer, knowing that resources from God will follow whenever the mission is his.

February 12

Unshackled

Linda Buxa

In *Republic,* Plato, the philosopher who lived from about 427 to 347 B.C., described a group of chained prisoners facing the back wall of a cave. All they ever saw were shadows cast by people in the cave walking past a fire. Plato pictures a prisoner from that cave breaking free, seeing the light of the fire and the people casting the shadows, and then getting out of the cave to experience the sun's full light. Plato used that to describe people's progress from ignorance to a knowledge of what's real.

For people who believe in Jesus, that's another way we can describe our knowledge of God. Here on earth we are shackled by sin. Even though God has set us free from the eternal consequences, we still struggle with sin- and pain-clouded minds. We have a general idea, though, from the shadows we see on the wall, but we can't fully grasp how wide and high and deep God's love is for us.

Oh, but when Jesus comes, we will be fully free. We will turn and see him face-to-face. We will experience all of the Son's glory. We will finally, completely, get it. What a day that will be!

"Now we see but a poor reflection as in a mirror [or as in a shadow on a cave wall]**; then we shall see face to face. Now I know in part; then I shall know fully, even as I am fully known"** (1 Corinthians 13:12).

____

____

____

____

____

February 13

Husbands, lead

Pastor Mark Jeske

At first glance, the Bible's instructions for husbands sound right up our male fantasy alley. The husband is head of the wife? Cool. "Honey, go make dinner while I take a nap." But listen to how the Bible describes Christian headship: **"Husbands, love your wives, just as Christ loved the church and gave himself up for her"** (Ephesians 5:25). You might say that Christ loved us to death. His death.

This is Christ-love for husbands: loving her not for what I get out of it but loving to give, loving to make her life better, loving in terms that make sense to her. This is headship: not exhausting her with my expectations and demands but taking the lead in service and in giving myself up for her.

You have bigger muscles and a bigger frame, not to enforce your will but to provide her with a feeling of security. You have less emotional vulnerability so that you can be the rock in her life.

Let's review: What happens when you lead in your home the way Christ leads his people? She will love it. Christ will love it. You will love it.

February 14

God invented love

Pastor Mark Jeske

This day to express love through cards and gifts has a strange and murky beginning. The early Christian church honored the memory of a number of men named Valentinus and celebrated their feast day on February 14. Their legends describe them as heroic priests who were martyred in a time of persecution.

Over the centuries the observance acquired overtones of romance and pagan images like the boy-god Cupid shooting his little love arrows. None of that really matters. Thanks to this helpful observance, people have an annual reminder to nourish their relationships.

God himself invented the magnetism between male and female, and he gives his blessing to dating, love, marriage, and sexuality. Many Christians don't quite know what to make of the last of the Old Testament's books of poetry, the Song of Songs. It is exactly what it looks like—the libretto to a musical about the delight, beauty, passion, and ecstasy of being in love.

We all tend to take one another for granted, especially our loved ones. Not today! Go ahead—read the Song. Who needs to hear you say this today: **"How beautiful you are, my darling! Oh, how beautiful! Your eyes are doves"** (Song of Songs 1:15)?

Morning people

Jason Nelson

Some folks are just plain grumpy when they wake up. They roll out of bed with disheveled hair and a chip on their shoulder. A perky greeting from a morning person just makes it worse. It may be best to steer clear of them until their fog lifts. Kind of makes a person feel bad for looking forward to a new day.

Christians are morning people. Our faith is in God's faithfulness. Our experience with him prompts a positive outlook because he has never let us down. God delivers fresh mercy at dawn, and we are eager to load up. **"Because of the Lord's great love we are not consumed, for his compassions never fail. They are new every morning; great is your faithfulness. I say to myself, 'The Lord is my portion; therefore I will wait for him'"** (Lamentations 3:22-24).

We tend to get what we've been waiting for. If we wake expecting just another day of drudgery, we will probably get it. If we let the little pessimist in our head anticipate the worst and predict unhappy outcomes, our negativity sabotages our opportunities. Morning people have learned to watch for blessings and work at their best chances to reap them. We think, "God has been good to me in the past, and I've made it this far. Today is filled with potential. Tomorrow will be even better."

Living in the golden age

Pastor Mark Jeske

It's hard to imagine that George Washington and Abraham Lincoln were human beings. The stories and legends and the passage of many decades have made them seem superhuman. Their images are burned into our imaginations—Washington in his blue frock coat and buff breeches on his white horse, Lincoln looking sad-eyed into the camera as if anticipating his assassination.

And yet in their day they took plenty of abuse. People sneered at Washington for being a highborn aristocratic slaveholder, and Lincoln was hated not only in the South but by half the North as well. No one who lived in these eras ever thought he or she was living in a golden age.

King David led the people of Israel at a high point in the nation's history, and yet some hated him. **"As King David approached Bahurim, a man from the same clan as Saul's family came out from there. His name was Shimei son of Gera, and he cursed as he came out. He pelted David and all the king's officials with stones, though all the troops and the special guard were on David's right and left. As he cursed, Shimei said, 'Get out, get out, you man of blood, you scoundrel!'"** (2 Samuel 16:5-7).

It may seem today that we are governed by pygmies; we yearn for the giants of yesterday. Let's appreciate the people God has given us. It's just possible that our great-grandchildren will think we lived in a golden age.

____

____

____

____

Join the team; love the team

Pastor Mark Jeske

I think most of us underestimate our own selfishness. It's so much easier to see it in other people, and I know I'm not always paying attention when people (family included) send me hints about my own.

Teenagers especially struggle with this. They are naturally pushing away from their parents. They are trying on masks to figure out who they are. They are trying to be their own person and not just get sucked into their parents' identity. They crave independence. Their youthful energy makes their parents seem like old fools and their younger siblings like embarrassing baggage.

All of us are born with an attitude of "What's in it for me?" and "What are you going to do for me?" Cain's angry shout to God, "Am I my brother's keeper?" is still our native language. God has a better way: **"Serve one another in love. The entire law is summed up in a single command: 'Love your neighbor as yourself'"** (Galatians 5:13,14).

Our Servant-Savior, Jesus, provides both the healing forgiveness we all need as well as a role model to help those who feel themselves drifting away from their families. Realize that you are not quite as smart and slick as you think you are, nor are the other members of your family quite as dumb as you think they are. Your family is God's gift; it is your team. Love your team.

He doesn't despise us because we've sinned

Pastor Mark Jeske

Disobeying God sometimes brings a short-term thrill, but it always leaves smelly baggage behind. Sin breaks things; it never heals or fixes anything. Sin leaves you with *guilt,* which is part self-hatred, part fear, part feeling slimed and dirty.

Sin also leaves you with *shame*. Even in an age when it seems as though shame has been abolished, your soul feels as though God could never love you again. He is so holy, and you are so dirty. Shame makes you feel so unworthy and unclean that you can't lift your eyes up to heaven anymore. Shame keeps you from praying, from going to church, from Lord's Supper.

But Jesus doesn't despise you when you sin. He was speaking once with a Samaritan woman of pretty loose, ahem, morals, and he assessed her sinful lifestyle with painful clarity: **"You are right when you say that you have no husband. The fact is, you have had five husbands, and the man you now have is not your husband"** (John 4:17,18). Ouch! But—*he didn't despise her*. In fact, he spent the rest of the conversation assuring her that the water of life from him would bring her forgiveness and healing. He still wanted her in his heavenly family.

The Lord knows everything about you—your strengths, weaknesses, successes, failures, and the depressing secrets you have to drag around. He loves you still and invites you to throw your sins at the foot of the cross and cherish the forgiveness Jesus bought for them all.

Hide-and-seek

Linda Buxa

"You will seek me and find me when you seek me with all your heart" (Jeremiah 29:13).

Doesn't that passage make you feel like you're in some sort of religious hide-and-seek game with God? I wonder if he's in the basement. Nope. Maybe he's hiding under the bed. Not there either. I wonder if he's hiding behind the couch. No way.

I get a picture in my head that he runs from spot to spot, trying to make it impossible for me to find him. As if he's trying not to be found. That's not what God means.

In reality, I think it's more like the "I spy" game you play in the car. When someone says, "I spy something blue," all of a sudden you realize just how many blue things there are outside and inside your car. From the sky to the billboard to the jacket the person on the sidewalk is wearing to your work folder—there is blue everywhere.

If you think God can't be found, play "I spy." Start noticing all the ways he shows that he is real. Through his Word, through creation, through the people in your life, through Baptism and Communion, and through the Holy Spirit living inside of you. All of these are ways God shows you who he is to help you find him and love him with your whole heart.

___

___

___

___

___

In cash we trust

Pastor Mark Jeske

Becoming a good manager of God's stuff, especially his money, is difficult. It is learned behavior and it takes time. Our natural inclination is to *love money* and *use people* (for example: rapper 50 Cent's 2003 debut CD was entitled *Get Rich or Die Tryin'*). Jesus teaches us to love people and use money—see the difference? Jesus did the reverse—he embraced poverty so that we might become rich. Bob Dylan wrote a hit song in 1979 that contradicted the myth of pure personal autonomy. He called it "Gotta Serve Somebody."

He's agreeing with Jesus. **"No servant can serve two masters. Either he will hate the one and love the other, or he will be devoted to the one and despise the other. You cannot serve God and Money"** (Luke 16:13). Money makes a terrible master. Money is a terrible lover. Money can be an addiction as bad as heroin.

Stamped on U.S. currency is the legend *In God We Trust*. This is a sad joke for many Americans, who neither believe it nor follow it. But it is a great reminder for people who take Jesus' words seriously. We *can* love and serve God first and use money to honor him.

How do you measure your true wealth?

Where is your trust? Who is your God?

What is a pastor?

Pastor Mark Jeske

What do we pastors look like to you? Ivory tower or glass house residents? Holier-than-thous? Performance artists? Or maybe your wise spiritual guides? Steady friends? Compassionate counselors?

When you are trying to help somebody with big spiritual needs, your pastors can be your prayer partners, your strategic advisors, your question answerers, your Bible interpreters, and your encouragers. They can help you find books, pamphlets, people connections, and web resources. They can meet with both of you in a place that will seem nonthreatening (seriously—some of the best pastoring is done outside the sanctuary and church office).

Concern for people's souls is what drives pastors. It's why we jump out of bed in the morning and what keeps us up late at night. Our call from our congregation invests us with divine responsibility and pressure, and so God asks you, **"Obey your leaders and submit to their authority. They keep watch over you as men who must give an account"** (Hebrews 13:17). We can't lead if you are unwilling to follow.

Our very title, "pastor," is the Latin word for "shepherd." It is a beautiful reminder that our calling and work make us assistant shepherds to Jesus Christ, the Good Shepherd. Our calling also makes us *accountable* to him, one of many reasons why we will take your requests for spiritual help very, very seriously.

____

____

____

A lamb died for you then

Pastor Mark Jeske

Worship life in Old Testament times partially resembled ours today and partially looked very different. When people gathered in their *synagogues* on the Sabbath, they sang, prayed, gave offerings, and listened to Scripture read and explained just as we do.

But the personal worship at the *tabernacle* and later *temple* has no parallel today. What a vivid, unforgettable experience God designed for the animal sacrifices that he expected! Some were "whole" offerings or "burnt" offerings—these signified total dedication to the Lord. And some were "sin" offerings or "guilt" offerings, designed to show God's holy hatred for evil and to proclaim in graphic detail his mercy message that only the blood of an innocent victim was an acceptable substitute for that of the sinner.

"These are the regulations for the guilt offering, which is most holy: The guilt offering is to be slaughtered in the place where the burnt offering is slaughtered, and its blood is to be sprinkled against the altar on all sides" (Leviticus 7:1,2). The worshiper was right there as the animal was killed. How could you ever forget the sight of the priest's knife plunging into the animal's neck, blood pouring from its carotid artery, the basin filling, the animal slumping to the ground lifeless?

Its blood sprinkled on the great altar took away your sinful guilt before God. A substitute died so that you might live.

The Lamb of God died for you now

Pastor Mark Jeske

No Israelite who had participated in the giving of a sin offering or guilt offering could possibly mistake the message of the divine drama: *God's mercy is brokered through a substitute's death.*

Jesus Christ did many wonderful things during his 33 short years on this earth. He taught people the Word of God. He healed the sick and even raised the dead. He gathered and trained 12 disciples who would continue the work when he was gone. He obeyed all the laws of God, Israel, and Rome. But the greatest of all his works was to offer himself as a guilt offering for the world. His cross on Calvary was the greatest of all the altars. The lifeblood he lost is our gain, for it is attributed to us through faith in him.

Already at the very beginning of his ministry, his advance agent, John the Baptist, pointed people to Jesus and clarified the Savior's holy mission: **"The next day John saw Jesus coming toward him and said, 'Look, the Lamb of God, who takes away the sin of the world!'"** (John 1:29).

This is why we don't need to offer up slain animals anymore. Christ has been there, done that. The animals were temporary props, indicators pointing ahead. The Great Lamb is here. Say this to yourself: "Jesus Christ once and for all has taken away all of my sin."

____

____

____

____

February 24

God is in the small voice

Jason Nelson

Sometimes confrontation is our moral obligation. The difficult conversation can't be avoided anymore. We have a duty to one another. It is a duty to intervene at a critical moment and make a determined effort to prevent the self-destruction of a soul.

By the time we ramp up our courage to say something, the fuse has been lit. Emotions are pre-charged and ready to go off. Apprehension and defensiveness finally explode into an argument that makes matters worse. It doesn't go well. There is collateral damage.

So how do we express our deep concern to someone we care about? How do we make confrontation positive?

God is in the small voice. He is never in the storm. He is never in the fury. (See 1 Kings 19:12.) He is in a sincere expression of unconditional love. He is in the mature demeanor befitting a serious situation. He is in self-control.

God is in the soft tone. He is in a calm way of calling someone by name, not a name. He looks through our eyes into theirs when we speak his truth with respect.

God is in the gentle touch. He is never in a clenched fist. He reaches across a table to place one hand atop another to confirm affection.

God is in the small voice and the quiet that follows.

Cherish the child

Jason Nelson

It is unfathomable that a loving mother would take her seven-year-old daughter to a border crossing and tell her to head north because the child would be better off wandering alone in the U.S. than remaining in her violent town in Central America. How desperate a mother's love can be.

It is equally unfathomable that our divine Father would send his only Son from heaven to be enfleshed in misery on earth and then forsake him on a cross. How amazing the Father's love is for his adopted children. As a baby, the Son of God became a political refugee. He spent his life on earth as a displaced person. **"The Son of Man has no place to lay his head"** (Matthew 8:20).

The nativity of Jesus isn't a charming story of humble beginnings on a starlit night. It is a case in point of the harsh conditions and poverty so many children live in. It was the necessary beginning of Christ's humiliating journey to redeem us.

Much of the world is still unfit for children. Eighty percent of humanity lives on less than $10 a day. As a result, 22,000 children die quietly every 24 hours because they are meek, weak, and last in line (according to UNICEF). The meek and holy Child said of them, **"Their angels in heaven always see the face of my Father"** (Matthew 18:10). If we love him, we must show the world how to cherish them.

_____

_____

_____

_____

_____

February 26

Ladies' aid

Pastor Mark Jeske

It is one of the signs of the times we live in that ladies' aid church societies and the skill of home sewing is slowly disappearing. Women work outside the home now and don't have time to acquire homey skills like canning, darning, embroidery, and the making of clothes by hand. Fewer and fewer are able to teach the few who want to learn. Besides, machine-made clothing is so relatively cheap that sewing is at best a hobby, not an economic necessity.

Not so in New Testament times. All clothing was handmade. And every town had poor people who were clothed literally in rags. Though we know little about her, Dorcas seems to have been an older widow in Joppa on the coast who showed her Christian faith in making clothes and helping the poor.

"In Joppa there was a disciple named Tabitha (which, when translated, is Dorcas), who was always doing good and helping the poor. About that time she became sick and died. . . . All the widows stood around him [Peter]**, crying and showing him the robes and other clothing that Dorcas had made while she was still with them"** (Acts 9:36,37,39).

Dorcas' resurrection is a magnificent story. It is a demo version of what God is going to do for all believers when he returns. But I love Dorcas even more for her servant heart, a seamstress who put clothes on the poor.

___

___

___

___

___

February 27

Humble greatness

Pastor Mark Jeske

The stories that children probably come to love first about Jesus involve his power. What a miracle worker he is! Lord of the sea, master of storms, conqueror of disease, victor over demons, raiser of the dead—there is nothing he can't do. He is the ultimate superhero, cooler even than Batman or Superman.

As you get older, though, you come to appreciate Jesus even more in his acts of humble service. One of the most powerful stories in all of Scripture comes from Maundy Thursday evening. A few hours before his crucifixion, he taught his disciples a memorable lesson about how servant leadership looks.

Kneeling before each one, he took a basin of water and a towel and washed their feet. **"Do you understand what I have done for you? . . . Now that I, your Lord and Teacher, have washed your feet, you also should wash one another's feet"** (John 13:12,14).

It was by service and suffering that Jesus redeemed us. It is his example of humble service that informs and inspires our attitude each day. Would the people around you say that at least some of the time you look and sound stubborn, proud, or even arrogant? Do you gravitate automatically to an agenda that features *your* comfort, *your* wants, *your* pleasures?

What does foot-washing humility look like in your home? Make a list of three examples and do them today.

____

____

____

____

You need the Spirit

Linda Buxa

Between the messages the world tells you and the things you know about yourself, I bet you could come up with a whole list of the reasons you are a screwup. Over and over your conscience would whisper that you are quick-tempered, conniving, unlovable, judgmental, and weak. If you were left on your own, you might be tempted to truly believe the bad things you know about yourself.

That, right there, is the whole reason that when Jesus went back to heaven to get your room ready, he didn't leave you alone. Instead, he gave you the Holy Spirit: **"We have not received the spirit of the world but the Spirit who is from God, that we may understand what God has freely given us"** (1 Corinthians 2:12).

You need the Holy Spirit. Without him, you can't believe God's humanly incomprehensible message. When you were baptized, the Holy Spirit stamped God's name on your heart. When you read God's Word, the Holy Spirit helps you understand that Jesus willingly paid the exorbitant price of his life to buy you back from hell. The Spirit reminds you that God's mercy is new every morning, that he chooses to want you in his family. The Holy Spirit whispers over and over that you are forgiven, at peace, loved, valuable, and strong.

That's the message you need to hear. That's the message the Holy Spirit helps you believe.

March

"WE KNOW THAT IN ALL THINGS GOD WORKS FOR THE GOOD OF THOSE WHO LOVE HIM, WHO HAVE BEEN CALLED ACCORDING TO HIS PURPOSE."

ROMANS 8:28

Sex sells

Pastor Mark Jeske

The most disgusting thing about human slavery in America's past is that some people treated other people like things, like chattel, as objects—instead of as human beings. Sad to say, the entire sex-for-money world does the very same thing. It feeds on people's appetites, promises happiness, delivers only emptiness, and at the same time dehumanizes everyone.

Whether it's pornography, prostitution, or strip joints, whether it's men using women for gratification and women using men for money, these actions are sick parodies of true human love. The longer people live in that fantasy world the less able they are to form real relationships and healthy, lasting marriages. Men come to view women as just sperm receptacles, and women come to view men merely as ATM machines.

Here is wisdom from God—can you accept it? **"The prostitute reduces you to a loaf of bread, and the adulteress preys upon your very life"** (Proverbs 6:26). **"Her house is a highway to the grave"** (Proverbs 7:27). Though those two verses warn of the corrosive effects of prostitutes, the men who patronize them are just as guilty and at risk of rotting out their souls.

God's ways are so much better—choose either celibate singleness, enjoying your independence, or choose committed marriage, where you can express and live your sexuality without guilt. Respect the awesome power of the sex drive. Seeking a faithful Christian life partner is probably one of the most important things you will do with your life.

____

____

March 2

Right with God

Linda Buxa

Thanks to online banking, barely anybody actually *reconciles* a checking account anymore. You know, instead of just making sure you have enough in your account, you make sure your bank account is right, that your entries match the bank's entries.

Because of the diminishing use of the word, it might be tempting to overlook how often—five times in the following four verses—the apostle Paul uses some form of the word *reconcile.*

"Therefore, if anyone is in Christ, he is a new creation; the old has gone, the new has come! All this is from God, who reconciled us to himself through Christ and gave us the ministry of reconciliation: that God was reconciling the world to himself in Christ, not counting men's sins against them. And he has committed to us the message of reconciliation. We are therefore Christ's ambassadors, as though God were making his appeal through us. We implore you on Christ's behalf: Be reconciled to God" (2 Corinthians 5:17-20).

Maybe today you don't *feel* reconciled. You don't *feel* like your life is right. You don't *feel* like your life matches God's expectations.

Isn't it good news then that God isn't all that concerned about your feeling; he cares about fact. The fact is that by sending Jesus, God reunited us. When God looks at your account, he sees Jesus' numbers—and you are reconciled.

There's one more fact. We now get to tell others. Just like Paul, go out and implore people—beg people—to be reconciled too.

Find a Christian community

Pastor Mark Jeske

I have a few friends who homeschool their children. The vast majority of their fellow citizens, however, joyfully take advantage of the best schools that they can find.

Should parents homeschool their children in the Christian faith? In fact, raising your children in the training and instruction of the Lord is not optional for Christian parents. But even for strongly Christian families with regular home study and prayer, a Christian nurturing community is a valuable partnership in passing on the faith.

There is an extensive array of Christian elementary schools and Sunday schools available to you. They are fabulous gifts of God to parents who welcome help in transmitting the faith and in modeling Christian behaviors. Mary and Joseph brought their 12-year-old son to the temple in Jerusalem, not only to offer sacrifices but also to learn from the great teachers there. The young man apparently appreciated the instruction even more than they did—his parents left long before he was ready to leave. **"After three days they found him in the temple courts, sitting among the teachers, listening to them and asking them questions"** (Luke 2:46).

A congregation also provides parents with a friend network that can share child-raising wisdom and chores. Churches have worship and study materials for your home. And while it is good for Christian children to learn how to function in the "real world," it is important that they also have peers who love Jesus.

Pay your debts ASAP

Pastor Mark Jeske

Have you ever heard of the generational theory? The concept is that there are very different cultures, including money cultures, depending on how old you are. People from the Depression/World War II generation (the "Builders") hate debt, whereas people from the iPod generation (the "Millennials") tend not to worry about borrowing. Builders pay cash; Millennials just get another credit card.

When it comes to borrowing, the Builders are wiser. Every financial planner worth a dime will tell you to pay down debt as rapidly as possible. Interest payments just eat cash, and if you string out your payments too long, you will end up buying something twice. Out-of-control debt also destroys your credit rating and makes it harder to get a decent loan on really important things like a home.

If you struggle with debt, ask somebody you know who is a good money manager how to set up a plan. Don't get overwhelmed to the point where you just stop trying. Start the discipline of spending less than you take in, even if it's just a little at first. Cut up those cards.

Paying down debt ASAP also applies to personal loans from relatives or friends: **"Do not say to your neighbor, 'Come back later; I'll give it tomorrow'—when you now have it with you"** (Proverbs 3:28). That's not only good financial advice. It may also save a friendship.

Building God's reputation

Jason Nelson

People draw conclusions about God in lots of ways. The Bible tells us all people have a hunch about the divine from his law written in their hearts. That helps with civic order but is inadequate for salvation. Nature inspires awe for God. We love what he created and think of his attributes. I think God's favorite color is green. But these conclusions are incomplete at best. The most complete understanding of God comes from his Word and the Word made flesh. In Jesus we know God as our Savior.

What people think about God will also strongly be influenced by what they see in you and me. We have been baptized into his name. We claim to be his disciples. With his eyes wide open, God chose to align his reputation with ours. So I invite you to **"glorify the LORD with me; let us exalt his name together"** (Psalm 34:3).

What's the best way for us to do that? As we penetrate a dark world with the light of the gospel, what is the best way for us to build God's reputation? What will people see in our example and hear in our testimony that will cause them to admire God even more? How will their experience with us in congregations and communities cause them to admire God even more?

May the God we glorify enable them to observe, "Those are really great people. They must really have a great God."

____

____

____

____

____

Fearless leadership

Pastor Mark Jeske

You would think that every man, woman, and child among the Israelites who had experienced the stupendous display of God's power during their exodus from Egyptian slavery would be ready for anything. You would think that they would fear nothing, knowing the immense power of heaven that was behind them. Well, maybe for a bit, at first, but the passage of days and weeks of some hardships caused their courage to melt away.

Ten of Moses' twelve scouts brought back a fearful report of the land of Canaan that God had directed them to conquer. The people mostly believed those negative reports and complained bitterly about Moses' leadership, demanding that they be allowed to return to Egypt and beg to get their old slave jobs back.

Only Joshua and his friend Caleb still had enough confidence that the Lord of Israel could carry out the agenda he had commanded: **"Then Caleb silenced the people before Moses and said, 'We should go up and take possession of the land, for we can certainly do it'"**(Numbers 13:30).

The leaders who are my heroes are optimistic. They believe in a God of abundance, a God without limits. They believe in a God who does what he says he'll do. They are willing to go forward even when they don't have every future problem solved or every objection answered. They are leaders without fear.

Thank one another

Pastor Mark Jeske

We are born, all of us, with GDD—Gratitude Deficit Disorder. The notion that everything good in our lives was given by a gracious God has to be revealed to us. Without that critically important information from the Bible, we would live in the delusion that we made everything ourselves, or worse, that we were at the mercy of the gods of luck.

Learning to say thank you to other people is also learned behavior. We see ingratitude in our children and work hard to teach them how to show appreciation. We make them write thank-you notes to their grandparents for birthday gifts. But let's not assume that we grown-ups are totally healed. We can be terrible takers too.

St. Paul's letters are masterpieces and models of GDD therapy. The opening words of each are full of praises and thanks to God. But the final verses usually carry his heartfelt words of appreciation to the people whose sacrifices, hard work, and passion made possible a community of faith: **"Greet Priscilla and Aquila, my fellow workers in Christ Jesus. They risked their lives for me. Not only I but all the churches of the Gentiles are grateful to them"** (Romans 16:3,4).

How many people have you thanked this week? Does your church have a thanking culture? Does your spouse feel appreciated? Do the people you work with ever hear praise from you?

Remember whom you serve

Linda Buxa

It's been over 20 years since the *Lion King* was released. And for the past 20 years, parents and commencement speakers have passed along the wisdom that Mufasa shared with his son, Simba: "Remember who you are. You are my son."

It wasn't easy for that lion cub. And it's not easy for us as we're on the run from Satan, who prowls around like a roaring lion.

Satan tries to mess with your thinking. "You're a grown-up now, why do you need a Father? Look how many mistakes you've made. Look how often you've let him down. He can't possibly want you as his child."

Sometimes you believe him. You act like your own boss. You live as if you don't have a long-term purpose. You cover up your fears with bravado. You fill the aching emptiness with shopping and activity and food. You stop asking for his guidance because you know just what a mess you've made of your life.

God shares his wisdom: **"You did not receive a spirit that makes you a slave again to fear, but you received the Spirit of sonship. And by him we cry, '*Abba*, Father'"** (Romans 8:15).

Sometimes adults especially need childlike reminders: The God of the whole entire universe is your Father. You don't have to be afraid. You aren't on your own. You have a purpose. He sacrificed his Son so that roaring lion wouldn't be able to threaten you forever.

Even adults need to be told: Remember who you are. Remember whose you are.

Blood made the death angel pass over

Pastor Mark Jeske

God's judgment follows human sin. Always. Universally. Inescapably. That judgment came crashing down on the Egyptian enslavers of the Israelite people. The Israelites were sinners too, and they also were at risk of the angel of death.

God's mercy, however, always provides an escape from judgment, and his Word shows the way. Through Moses he told the believers among the Israelites: **"Go at once and select the animals for your families and slaughter the Passover lamb. Take a bunch of hyssop, dip it into the blood in the basin and put some of the blood on the top and on both sides of the doorframe. . . . When the LORD goes through the land to strike down the Egyptians, he will see the blood . . . and he will not permit the destroyer to enter your houses and strike you down"** (Exodus 12:21-23). That angel of death *passed over* Israel and set them free from slavery.

All Israel was to celebrate this "Pass-over" every year. There was to be no yeast (symbolically representing sin) in anyone's house for a week (thus giving rise to the alternate title "Feast of Unleavened Bread").

When you read about the Passover, ponder the terrible cost of sin and God's furious anger. But ponder also the tremendous redemptive love and power of a God determined to set his people free.

Christ is the ultimate Passover Lamb

Pastor Mark Jeske

The acts of God to set free the Israelite slaves were great indeed. The pharaohs had no limits on their power in northeastern Africa, but with ten mighty blows God broke their economic and military power.

A far greater rescue took place on Mount Calvary. Jesus' blood was spilled out with whips, nails, and a crown of thorns. This is why the annual Passover celebration is no longer necessary. **"Christ, our Passover lamb, *has been* sacrificed"** (1 Corinthians 5:7). Think of what this means for you: you are forgiven, set free from fear of your trial when you die, given immortality just like Christ's. Through faith in him you may spatter that blood on the doorway of your heart. That blood is the payment for all of your sins, and that means that the tyrant Satan has lost his grip on you.

Just as the Israelites symbolically got rid of all the yeast in their homes, we can renew our lives in service to our God. Powered by his Spirit we now delight in throwing off old sinful ways and finding new joy in God's ways. The last and greatest Passover took place on Good Friday and Easter.

Through your faith in Christ, his blood now marks your body and soul. The angel of death has passed over you. Calm down. You are safe.

Q&A

Jason Nelson

We want answers. We go to school to learn answers. We are tested to make sure we know the right ones. Some people have an answer for everything. But the right questions can have more impact than all the right answers.

Jesus was superb at asking the right question. One time he asked Peter, **"Who do people say the Son of Man is?"** (Matthew 16:13). It was a good question by a misunderstood Messiah. Then he followed with an even better question: **"Who do *you* say I am?"** (verse 15). He made the question unforgettable by making it personal. Peter gave the right answer, but I suspect he never stopped thinking about the question and spent the rest of his life discovering even more relevant ways to answer it.

That question is the drumbeat of our lives. Who do we say Jesus is? We are always in the process of answering it. In childhood we see Jesus in simple truth (cue: "I Am Jesus' Little Lamb"). He loves us and keeps the monsters under the bed. The battles of being working adults force us to elaborate on our answer as we try to manage overwhelming responsibilities (cue: "Fight the Good Fight"). And in old age we can strip it down for eternity because we are ready to focus on what matters most (cue: "What Is the World to Me?").

The final exam has one good question: Who do you say Jesus is?

___

___

___

___

March 12

No worries

Linda Buxa

Natural disasters. Rising grocery prices. Child molesters. Layoffs. Illness. Wars. Death. Everywhere you look you can find something to worry about. Even though you know there is a God in heaven who loves you, your heart wonders if he's real.

Then you read Matthew 6:25,27: **"Therefore I tell you, do not worry about your life, what you will eat or drink; or about your body, what you will wear. Who of you by worrying can add a single hour to his life?"**

If you thought I'd say, "See, look how easy it is. Just trust," you'd be wrong. Sometimes quoting a Bible passage might make you feel worse. You wonder why your faith is so weak that you can't put it all in God's hands. You completely relate to the father in the Bible who told Jesus, "I really do believe. Help me get over the part of me that still struggles to fully believe."

When your Father looks at you, he knew your first worry was being separated from him. So he sent Jesus who came to earth to not only pay for your sin but also to give you the credit for his perfect and free-from-worry life. Then, he knew this world would make you question if the plans he has for you really are meant to bring you closer to him, so he gave you the Spirit. He'll remind you of God's promises. He'll reassure you that it's not your job to worry less. It's his job to help you trust more.

The real gospel

Pastor Mark Jeske

It isn't very hard to work out a "spiritual" philosophy of life based roughly on how the business world works. People have invented variations on the same gig for many centuries. Start with a vague fear of the "Great Power" up there. Try to appease him/her/it with good deeds, prayers, and rituals. Take comfort in every little good thing you think you've done. Make yourself feel better by comparing yourself to people "worse" than you.

Alas, self-made religions only leave you hollow. Real peace comes only from the real gospel, which is based not on your performance but on Christ's. The real gospel is based on the absolutely outrageous concept that God forgives rotten and worthless sinners in advance: **"Now when a man works, his wages are not credited to him as a gift, but as an obligation. However, to the man who does not work but trusts God *who justifies the wicked*, his faith is credited as righteousness"** (Romans 4:4,5).

Astonishing! In the Christian faith you don't get what you paid for. You get what Christ paid for. He trusts you enough to front you his mercy, trusting that you will believe and appreciate his loving rescue, absorb the life philosophy of the Bible, accept a godly value system, and treat others as he has treated you.

Other religions' gods justify nice people. Only the Christians' God justifies the wicked.

What if I'm married to an unbeliever?

Pastor Mark Jeske

Some Christians acquire spouses who are not believers. Maybe they didn't care at the time. Maybe they assumed, or hoped, that the spouse would come to faith later. Maybe both were unbelievers at the time of marriage and then one came to faith. The question is the same: What do I do now that I'm yoked to an unbeliever?

It is not justification for divorce. It is both a high risk *and* a major opportunity. The risk is that the unbelieving partner becomes a deadening drag on the believer's faith. The splendid opportunity is that the believing spouse would be God's personal agent for the salvation of the nonbeliever.

It is an ancient dilemma. Here is St. Peter's counsel from the female point of view: **"Wives, in the same way be submissive to your husbands so that, if any of them do not believe the word, they may be won over without words by the behavior of their wives, when they see the purity and reverence of your lives"** (1 Peter 3:1,2).

None of us likes to be pushed around, and men are particularly testy about it if done to them by a woman. Guilt, pressure, nagging, bargaining, or begging won't work. What does? Showing that one's faith in Christ makes you an even better wife. Unconditional love demonstrated in a loveless world is irresistible over time. It is my privilege to know some marvelous men who once were brought to church by their marvelous wives.

The first thesis

Jason Nelson

When Martin Luther nailed the Ninety-five Theses to that old church door, he ignited a firestorm. The whole thing was a provocation to reconsider how people get saved. It was a call for change. The Reformation allowed Christians to see God through the clear lenses of grace, faith, and Scripture.

In the first thesis, Luther called out you and me: "When our Lord and Master Jesus Christ said, 'Repent' (Mt 4:17), he willed the entire life of believers to be one of repentance."

A life of repentance requires us to take stock of who we are. The standard is God's Word. The illusive element is honesty. Most Christians are comfortable with truth. We do truth nobly, even self-righteously. But few of us are comfortable with honesty. Honesty cuts like a knife. Honesty brings truth to bear in a very disagreeable way. Honesty makes us smite our own chests with the truth and leads us to the apostle Paul's conclusion, "I am a wretch."

But repentance doesn't resolve in self-deprecation. A new person steps up on a regular basis. We lean against the righteousness of God revealed in the gospel. We are inspired by the declaration that turned Luther around: **"The just shall live by faith"** (Romans 1:17 KJV). With good intentions bonded to faith, we can add daily to what we are. The first thesis of the Christian life is to take hold of Christ's righteousness and grow in it.

I'm afraid my family is coming apart

Pastor Mark Jeske

It is a thrill to have children. Their energy, laughter, craziness, and spirit bring joy to the often-tired grown-ups in their homes. They need us; we need to be needed. And yet parenting is exhausting—keeping helpless newborns alive, tending them through childhood illnesses, and teaching them how to act around other people. You will lose sleep and money helping them develop life skills.

But the worst aspect of parenting is our fear of what they might become as they get older. We parents can bear almost any strain when they are young. But if they grow up and reject our values, reject their families, and worst of all reject their Savior, our grief knows no limits.

What is your family history like? Are there young adults who are straying in the wrong direction? Does divorce stalk you? Are there children of unwed parents who have appeared? Are the generations estranged? Have your kids or grandkids been in jail?

Sometimes in spite of your best efforts and energy, in spite of making worship of God the highest and best home activity, children reject their spiritual inheritance. Samuel was a giant of a man, a courageous and hardworking prophet in terribly turbulent times. But his boys bitterly disappointed him: **"When Samuel grew old, he appointed his sons as judges for Israel. But his sons did not walk in his ways. They turned aside after dishonest gain and accepted bribes and perverted justice"** (1 Samuel 8:1,3).

We can't believe for our children. God's heart is breaking too.

God patiently loves even prodigals

Pastor Mark Jeske

When you are grieving over a "lost" child, check him or her for pulse and respiration. If they are alive, there is hope. God takes the long view, and he is patient, patient, patient. He waits and waits, watching for opportunity. Eventually even angry rebels burn out, because every force that is not from God sooner or later turns destructive. Every force that is not from God will cause brokenness and fear, not contentment.

Jesus told a timeless tale about a father with two sons—a "good" one and a "bad" one. The bad one took his inheritance early and squandered it. In friendless poverty he came to his senses and asked his father for mercy.

Here is hope for all prodigals, and it is true for the prodigals in your own family too. Jesus' forgiveness is big enough to cover every one of the sins of youthful rebels. While they live, there's time and there's hope: **"The Lord is compassionate and gracious, slow to anger, abounding in love. He does not treat us as our sins deserve or repay us according to our iniquities"** (Psalm 103:8,10).

Pray for the strays. Love them unconditionally, just as your Father loves you. Stop blaming yourself. Speak the truth in love. Never give up. Watch for opportunities. Some prodigals repent.

Parable redux: The sower

Jason Nelson

From Matthew 13—A farmer who was into organic growth went out to plant seed in a rugged land. He wasn't very careful about it. He never tested the soil to see if it was right for the seed. He just scattered it everywhere. For him it was about the abundance of the seed, not the worthiness of the soil. He thought if he could get lots of it around, it would grow the way it was supposed to.

Some places the seed never had a chance to germinate, and some places it grew quickly but then got some kind of blight. He was sad about that. Other places his seed grew, but so did noxious weeds. He didn't want to eradicate the weeds because that could also be toxic to his tender plants. He decided to let them grow together and sort it out at the end of the growing season. Other places his plants grew nicely, and there was a bumper crop.

Later, he taught an extension course for future sowers. His students asked why he planted the way he did. It seemed unconventional. He explained what he knew about soil types and the seed. He said in this land you can't always see where the good soil is or predict growing conditions. So it's best to scatter lots of seed.

The new sowers looked at each other knowingly and went out to scatter seed.

Bachelor farmer

Pastor Mark Jeske

Meet Boaz, a bachelor wheat farmer in the Judean breadbasket (that's what *Beth-lechem* means in Hebrew). A young widowed Moabite named Ruth was gleaning in his fields, picking up scraps to help support her widowed mother-in-law, Naomi. Though he may have thought that he was destined to be a bachelor all his life, God had a surprise for him later in life. Boaz was a relative of Naomi's late husband, Elimelech, and God led him to make an important decision.

"Boaz announced to the elders and all the people, 'Today you are witnesses that I have bought from Naomi all the property of Elimelech, [and his sons] **Kilion and Mahlon. I have also acquired Ruth the Moabitess, Mahlon's widow, as my wife, in order to maintain the name of the dead with his property'"** (Ruth 4:9,10).

This story is a big deal for two reasons: First, Boaz in this way was fulfilling the ancient sacrificial duty of the *kinsman-redeemer*. Families have to stick together, and this kind and gracious man took two vulnerable widows under his wing. Although we no longer have the custom of kinsman-redeemer, family cohesiveness is more important than ever, and Boaz is a hero to us today.

Second, God had chosen him for even greater things. He blessed Boaz and Ruth with a child, Obed, whom they were proud to lay on Naomi's lap. Their great-grandson turned out to be King David. That makes Boaz a personal ancestor of Jesus Christ.

I'm not leaving you

Pastor Mark Jeske

"Ruth replied, 'Don't urge me to leave you or to turn back from you. Where you go I will go, and where you stay I will stay. Your people will be my people and your God my God'" (Ruth 1:16). These words are heard often at Christian weddings. Indeed, the words Ruth spoke sound great coming from a Christian groom to a Christian bride and vice versa. They eloquently voice the commitment that any marriage must have to last.

They were spoken originally by a Gentile, Ruth the Moabite, to her Jewish mother-in-law, Naomi, a sad young widow to a sad older widow. Ruth's late husband, Mahlon the Israelite, had come to Moab during a famine in Israel and married her there. But he, his dad, and his brother all died, leaving three widows. Naomi, the older one, decided to go back to Israel to try to survive. Orpah stayed in Moab. When Ruth spoke the words above in a generous and sacrificial commitment to the older woman, she revealed her servant heart. She was willing to let go of her culture, relatives, ancestral religion, and property, all to provide support for a vulnerable older woman whom she loved.

When they got to Israel, Ruth appealed to Boaz as her kinsman-redeemer (see the previous devotion), and he accepted his responsibility. He acquired a tremendous wife and life partner.

I completely understand why so many Christian parents name their daughters Ruth.

___

___

___

Live distinguished lives

Linda Buxa

In the world, but not of the world. That's a phrase that Christians throw around so often you think it's an actual Bible passage. Really, it's more of a summary of Jesus' prayer for us in John 17:14,15: **"I have given them your word and the world has hated them, for they are not of the world any more than I am of the world. My prayer is not that you take them out of the world but that you protect them from the evil one."**

Because Jesus is our brother, we belong to the heavenly family. We need to stop blending in so much that people can't even tell we follow Jesus. Instead, we stay in the world enough so we can get to know the people around us. *We're influential,* sharing the hope that we have.

Daniel lived that way. As a teenager, he refused to eat the meat devoted to the Babylonians gods, yet he still served. In fact, as he worked for the Babylonians, he **"so distinguished himself among the administrators and the satraps by his exceptional qualities that the king planned to set him over the whole kingdom"** (Daniel 6:3).

Daniel's story is also why Jesus ended his prayer with the plea: protect them. When you find the balance of being in the world but not of it, you will offend people who can't stand the idea of God. Daniel's faithfulness got him thrown into a lions' den, where God's angel came to protect him. His angel is protecting you too. Count on it.

Wanna go to church?

Pastor Mark Jeske

God invented congregations for many vital purposes—public worship; teaching and learning the Word; fellowship; service training; spiritual care of the new ones, the old ones, and the straying; and enjoying the precious Sacraments of Baptism and Lord's Supper.

One of the most wonderful features of congregational life is the opportunity it gives for people to get involved in serving people. Jesus' foot washing was a demonstration of attitude, not so much a literal command. Today we don't wash other people's feet, but we can wash each other's dishes. We can continue Jesus' joyful spirit with acts of service great and small: cooking, accounting, snowplowing, painting, transporting, caring for children, organizing and planning, sending cards, mentoring, singing, managing IT, and landscaping.

Just like countries, no congregation is perfect. They are all conglomerations of sinners with many flaws, shortcomings, and only partially pure agendas. They have gaps in their ministries and sometimes hurt people instead of helping and healing. And yet you've got to love 'em because Jesus gets so many good things done through them.

Are you an active member of a congregation? **"Let us not give up meeting together, as some are in the habit of doing, but let us encourage one another—and all the more as you see the Day approaching"** (Hebrews 10:25). Time is short. Use God's resources so the Day won't catch you unprepared.

Pain memories

Pastor Mark Jeske

Movies that do well at the box office and sell a lot of DVDs portray characters with whom people want to identify. What are your top three? The biggest sellers tend to portray strong action heroes for the guys and tender love stories with meaningful dialogue for the women.

Jesus' stories pull you right in, just like great movies, because he understands the human situation so well. And even though we've all been pampered at one time or another, it's not with the rich man that we resonate in his Lazarus story. We head straight for the beggar because our own pain memories are so strong.

"There was a rich man who was dressed in purple and fine linen and lived in luxury every day. At his gate was laid a beggar named Lazarus, covered with sores and longing to eat what fell from the rich man's table. Even the dogs came and licked his sores" (Luke 16:19-21). Our ancestors' rebellion against God became a congenital birth defect. Through our human flesh and blood we are bonded with Adam and Eve not only physically but with their terrible sin as well. Every time we sin we affirm their horrible choice.

Curses fell upon the human race when they (and we) sinned. The most immediate is *pain*. No one escapes. Everybody hurts—Lazarus hurt; we hurt. We long for God's soothing touch now, and we yearn for our ultimate escape into heaven.

Both are ours through Christ. Now and in eternity.

Don't tell me, show me

Pastor Mark Jeske

Christian missionaries in Third World countries will tell you that a teaching ministry is much more effective if accompanied by a mercy ministry (clinic, agricultural training, disaster relief, water well drilling, etc.).

In post-Christian America we have come full circle. Christians and Christian churches would probably do well to envision themselves as missionaries and mission outposts once again. Their words can have an impact, but their words plus kind and authentic acts of joyful service make their overall witness much more powerful.

Jesus commissioned his disciples to be talkers. After all, language is needed to communicate the gospel of God's mighty acts in history. But he commissioned them to be lovers of people as well, and that servant attitude is not optional: **"A new *command* I give you: Love one another. As I have loved you, so you must love one another. By this people will know that you are my disciples, if you love one another"** (John 13:34,35).

The history of the growth of the Christian church provides many examples of "show me" community service that we do as well as or better than anybody: child care, education, care for the elderly, teen mentoring, food and clothing distribution, and compassion for people with disabilities. Our world is starving for authentic love. The way we treat each other and the way we show love for our community show what we really think of Jesus.

Why the church?

Jason Nelson

If God grants me an exit interview, I have one question: Why the church? Why did he make people responsible for something where the stakes are so high? Surely the almighty God had other options. When Jesus ascended to heaven, he commissioned his followers to be his church. They didn't get it, and he left anyway.

We're talking about the church of cathedrals and revival tents, of controversies and Holy Communion. This is the church of reformations and counter-reformations. It is shaped by geography, history, ethnicity, and strong personalities. It goes through expansion, decline, and soul-searching. This is the human face of the body of Christ.

The church is a work in progress, and it won't be complete without you. **"You are Christ's body—that's who you are! You must never forget this. Only as you accept your part of that body does your 'part' mean anything"** (1 Corinthians 12:27 MSG). When we share the gospel with others, we become more convinced ourselves. As we invest our ability and money in ministries, we become more committed to its cause. When God gave us faith, he gave us a vested interest in the church because he made us an integral part of it. **"So here's what I want you to do, God helping you: Take your everyday, ordinary life—your sleeping, eating, going-to-work, and walking-around life—and place it before God as an offering"** (Romans 12:1 MSG). Be the church.

Baptism clothes

Pastor Mark Jeske

One of the most adorable features of family baptisms is when the baby wears a long white handmade baptismal "dress" that has been handed down for generations. They are beautiful—eyelet lace, tiny satin ribbons, billows of linen. A proud grandmother may say shyly that that dress was used for her baptism many decades earlier, and those dresses are stored carefully and shared with each new little Christian in the family.

The Bible teaches us that there are baptismal clothes even more valuable than that antique linen: **"You are all sons of God through faith in Christ Jesus, for all of you who were baptized into Christ have been clothed with Christ"** (Galatians 3:26,27). The painful truth is that we are all born outsiders, outside of God's family. We are also born sinful, our spiritual appearance to God as though our clothes were filthy.

Our baptism changes both of those conditions. The gospel of Christ that rides along with the splash of water pronounces us to be God's children—heirs of eternal life. We are also clothed with the shining garments of Jesus Christ himself. Baptism is pure gospel—its power doesn't depend on a thing we have done for God—it is all his gift to us.

Neither does it depend on the purity of the baptizer. We just get to celebrate our new identity and revel in how good our new clothes make us look to God our Father. We shine like Christ himself!

March 27

What if he/she wants to leave?

Pastor Mark Jeske

Even with a "till death us do part" promise at one time, a marriage, in order to survive, needs two willing participants. St. Paul lists a situation in which a believing spouse may seek a divorce without sinning: **"If the unbeliever leaves, let him do so. A believing man or woman is not bound in such circumstances"** (1 Corinthians 7:15).

Note the two conditions: 1) one partner wants out and the other is innocent; 2) the one who has given up on the marriage and his or her promise is an *unbeliever*. The point: if a person is a believer, there is still hope. Believers never give up. Believers listen to the Word, listen to their pastor and counselors, and listen to their families. Believers repent of their own sins and forgive those of their partners. An unbeliever feels no such obligations.

When you are abandoned in such circumstances, you are no longer bound to your marital vows. But before the injured spouse claims desertion and calls an attorney, it is proper to make sure that he or she has exhausted every option. Just because the law allows no-fault divorce doesn't mean that God approves.

Above all, it is God's view that matters most to a believer's heart. It is his approval that we should crave more than any other. When we do things right, we can live without guilt and go forward without lies and excuses.

Your status update

Linda Buxa

Social media is reprogramming our brains. Typical users are logging in 15 times a day, hoping for the rush of adrenaline that comes from a notification. College students—and some older honest people too—confess that they spend a lot of their brainpower thinking about what they will tweet, post, or update.

Wouldn't it be awesome if we were as connected with our God as we think we are with our online friends? If we, like King David, could honestly say, **"Oh, how I love your law! I meditate on it all day long"** (Psalm 119:97)?

When you meditate on his words all day—or check in with him 15 times a day—you get a rush of peace. You realize that his words are about how he planned and worked to update your status—all because of Jesus. You were dead; now you're alive. You were God's enemy; now you're his friend. You were a slave to sin; now you're a slave to righteousness.

Check in with God's words over and over so **"the peace of God, which transcends all understanding, will guard your hearts and your minds in Christ Jesus"** (Philippians 4:7).

Take that comfort and peace and share it with the one-third of people who say they feel lonelier because of the connections they've made on social media. Take the time to share that because Jesus took on human flesh, he connected himself to us forever. Because he gave us the Holy Spirit when he went back to heaven, we are never alone.

The many become one

Pastor Mark Jeske

Every culture on earth has bonding rituals—you know, traditions and activities that draw many individuals together to become one in a significant way. Like 50,000 sports fans in a stadium screaming for their team. Like an intensely partisan political rally getting juiced for a candidate. Or like a civil rights march to right a wrong and remedy an injustice.

Holy Communion is a communal event—you read your Bible at home, you pray in solitude, but Jesus did not design the Communion experience for you to self-administer all by yourself. In Communion the many become one, joined together by a common faith in Christ and a common understanding of the Sacrament's significance.

St. Paul used the analogy of one loaf of bread to describe the beautiful human bonding that occurs: **"Because there is one loaf, we, who are many, are one body, for we all partake of the one loaf"** (1 Corinthians 10:17). Life is hard, and one of God's gifts for the journey is people, fellow pilgrims, to walk with us. Satan does his best work when we are isolated, lonely, and confused. Communion sends a message to our hearts that we are not alone—that we are bonded to Christ and bonded to some great people for the duration.

Next time you are kneeling at the altar, sneak a look to your right and left—these dear people are your spiritual posse.

I feel left out

Pastor Mark Jeske

Being an outcast is an unfortunately common experience. I can still remember being the last one chosen for playground softball, and the only reason I was chosen at all is that the teacher made the captains involve everybody. I still remember my sophomore basketball season on the bench as a third-stringer. Most women can remember the experience of being left out of the desirable girls' group. Every high school cafeteria has kids sitting at tables who feel like they don't fit in anywhere.

It is one of God's supremely urgent priorities for his congregations that no one is marginalized or made to feel like an outsider. People may enter as loners, but God's goal *always* is to draw them into meaningful relationships: **"I appeal to you, brothers, in the name of our Lord Jesus Christ, that all of you agree with one another so that there may be no divisions among you and that you may be perfectly united in mind and thought"** (1 Corinthians 1:10).

Is it hard for you to take the risk of being accepted by strangers? Do your fears keep you away from congregational life (and thus also away from the Word, Lord's Supper, and fellowship)? The reverse question: are you a long-time member of your Christian organization? On a scale of 1 to 10, how well do you think your group connects with and assimilates seekers, outriders, and loners?

____

____

____

____

____

Spending money God's way

Pastor Mark Jeske

Do you tend to be a Scrooge or a spendaholic? Here is another example of when it's best to steer the middle course in life. God gives no special honor to misers and skinflints, but there is also terrible danger in out-of-control spending.

Be intentional about the money flowing from you. Do you go shopping when you are feeling bad about yourself? Do you need new clothes to feel important? When you find something on sale, do you then buy three (that you didn't really need)? Do you just love spoiling yourself? Do you have trouble saying no to your urges? Do you just love to party? Are these hard words to hear: **"He who loves pleasure will become poor"** (Proverbs 21:17)?

Far too many people live in misery and fear because they have maxed out four credit cards and now can't even make the minimum payments. They bought way too much house, their adjustable-rate mortgage just went up again, and foreclosure looms.

Our Savior Jesus' personal life is an inspiration to us. He lived simply and humbly. People are more important than stuff; in the same way, your value and worth are not calculated from the flash of your possessions. If you are married, make all financial decisions together. If you can't control your spending, admit it to someone you trust and ask for help.

April

"HE WAS PIERCED FOR OUR TRANSGRESSIONS,
HE WAS CRUSHED FOR OUR INIQUITIES; THE
PUNISHMENT THAT BROUGHT US PEACE WAS
UPON HIM, AND BY HIS WOUNDS WE ARE HEALED."
ISAIAH 53:5

April Fool's Day

Pastor Mark Jeske

We love stories about outrageous and successful pranks, but only when they are sprung on other people. I hate being made to look like an idiot, and I bet you do too.

April 1 can be a nightmare for friends and coworkers of pranksters. Fake e-mails, rubber vomit on your desk, salt shakers rigged to dump their entire contents on your plate—you better be vigilant all day. People have been observing an annual trick day at least since Chaucer's *The Nun's Priest's Tale* in 1392 and probably long before that. There is a streak of cruelty in most people that enjoys other people's fear and embarrassment.

You may be pranked on April Fool's Day, but there is a far worse kind of folly to avoid—the folly of atheism. Satan is the father of lies, according to Jesus, and he loves to mislead people. **"The fool says in his heart, 'There is no God'"** (Psalm 14:1). If the guy in the office next to me thinks he made a fool out of me, well, it will wear off and life will go on. If God thinks I'm a fool, I'm in serious trouble. **"The fear of the LORD is the beginning of wisdom"** (Proverbs 9:10).

Hell will be full of people who thought that there is no such thing as hell.

God, where are you?

Pastor Mark Jeske

Our lives as Christians are not one long and endless string of happy moments, everything always working out well, all problems quickly melting away like ice cream on the sidewalk in July, plenty of everything, lucrative jobs, happy homes, great health, and perfect children.

Not only do we have problems just like everybody else on the planet, those problems linger. Sometimes things get worse. **"Why, O Lord, do you stand far off? Why do you hide yourself in times of trouble?"** (Psalm 10:1). One of the really compelling features of the book of Psalms in the Bible is its honesty. The psalms were provided by God for individual believers to read in their devotional lives—they are written in the first person.

And they are real. There is not always quick and easy resolution to the griefs and troubles of the writer, just as your struggles sometimes drag on for many years. The psalm writers bring their pain and complaints directly to God, like the writer of Psalm 10 who accuses God of disappearing when he was needed most.

God hears everything his people say. He hasn't left us to flounder and fail. He wants us to know that our struggles do not mean that he has stopped loving us or lost his superpowers or is stumped. His season of waiting will teach us to respect our frailties and limitations, adjust our agenda to his, and watch for his time of deliverance. It will come.

Oh, there you are

Pastor Mark Jeske

Can there be a greater relief than realizing that all your fears about a God who is weak, heartless, or clueless turned out to be not true? Waiting produced patience; hardship made you tougher; having little kept you humble; and your struggles made you more compassionate to other strugglers. When God decided to move into action, it embarrassed you that you ever doubted him.

Here's how God looks when he's moving: **"The Mighty One, God, the LORD, speaks and summons the earth. . . . Our God comes and will not be silent; a fire devours before him, and around him a tempest rages. He summons the heavens above, and the earth, that he may judge"** (Psalm 50:1-4). It only seems as though evildoers are getting away with their selfish and destructive deeds. God sees; he remembers; he speaks; he acts. He chooses the time.

All of our lives fit into his beautiful tapestry. None of our suffering is wasted; none of our good deeds is ever ignored. Nothing that happened was ever purely accidental; everything is useful to his grand scheme. Over years, over decades, he slowly shapes us to be more useful to him.

His throne is not empty; his angels haven't all retired; his mastery of nature, weather, illness, beast and fowl, heavenly bodies, and the very elements of the earth has not slipped one millimeter. At just the right time he speaks. Evil is restrained; his people prosper and flourish.

Passover

Pastor Mark Jeske

Have you ever attended a Passover celebration? You may have Jewish friends who go to temple and observe the special meal.

A few Christians do choose to celebrate Passover, since those stories belong to Christians too. The heroes of the exodus are also our heroes. What Christians should not do, however, is get so deep into the ritual that the original meaning is lost. The original Passover was a matter of life and death, and the meal should recall God's acts of severe judgment and of tender mercy.

God instructed Moses how to observe the first Passover: **"On that same night I will pass through Egypt and strike down every firstborn . . . and I will bring judgment on all the gods of Egypt. I am the Lord. The blood will be a sign for you on the houses where you are; and when I see the blood, I will pass over you. No destructive plague will touch you when I strike Egypt"** (Exodus 12:12,13). If you attend a seder, remember how the angel of death "passed over" the blood on the doorposts of believers' homes and spared them.

As beautiful as a seder meal can be, the Easter celebration is even better, for it commemorates our exodus from sin's curse, the grave, condemnation, and hell. Paul writes, **"Christ, our Passover lamb, has been sacrificed"** (1 Corinthians 5:7). The Lamb of God has taken away the sin of the world. That includes yours.

Eternity in my heart

Pastor Mark Jeske

Blaise Pascal was a 17th-century French mathematician, physicist, and Christian philosopher. He said once, "There is a God-shaped vacuum in the heart of every man which cannot be filled by any created thing, but only by God, the Creator, made known through Jesus."

Pascal was right. There is no meaning in the universe if you deny the Creator, no love in the universe if you deny Christ the Savior, and no wisdom in the universe if you deny the Spirit. King Solomon, speaking as "the Preacher" (i.e., "Ecclesiastes") wrote brilliant lines on the emptiness of life without God: **"I have seen the burden God has laid on men. He has made everything beautiful in its time. He has also set eternity in the hearts of men; yet they cannot fathom what God has done from beginning to end"** (Ecclesiastes 3:10,11).

Even unbelievers believe in the afterlife and want to go to heaven, because that yearning to be reunited with the divine has been put in their hearts whether they realize it or not. Alas, they cannot fathom what God has done and with reckless bravura design their own roads to heaven, every last one of which is a dead end.

Don't live your life with a vacuum inside you. Let the Word of Christ fill your soul and spirit so that you may enjoy your eternity.

April 6

The real thing

Pastor Mark Jeske

Most of us have absolutely no idea when we are going to die. At best, even as the day approaches, we have only hazy guesses. Jesus Christ, however, knew exactly how much time he had left on earth, for he knew in terrible detail how and when he would be slain. That means that he chose the content of his last teachings to his disciples with great care and that he designed carefully some important actions for their learning and encouragement in the upper room on that fateful Thursday evening. He gave them a demonstration of servant-leadership by humbly washing their feet.

And then he gave himself to them through the first ever sacramental meal we now call the Lord's Supper: **"Then he took the cup, gave thanks and offered it to them, saying 'Drink from it, all of you. *This is my blood of the covenant,* which is poured out for many for the forgiveness of sins'"** (Matthew 26:27,28).

He knew that his time on earth was mostly over and he would soon be returning to heaven. But he gave unspeakably great comfort and encouragement to his disciples by giving *himself* to them, the *very blood* that would soon be poured out for the forgiveness of their sins and guarantee of his continuing presence in their lives. Through the mystery and marvel of his powerful words, all believers from that day forward would absorb into themselves the very price of their salvation.

Every time you go to Lord's Supper, it's the real thing.

____

____

____

____

A little peace goes a long way

Jason Nelson

Please pray every day for people trying to make peace. They are heroes we can't live without. They rise above the conflict *du jour* to pursue the harmony tomorrow might bring. Peace is very hard to come by, and most days everything is a struggle. We are battle hardened and ready for the next fight, but deep down we want even a little peace, because a little peace goes a long way.

Peacemaking isn't an exclusive activity. Anyone may participate. **"You're blessed when you can show people how to cooperate instead of compete or fight. That's when you discover who you really are, and your place in God's family"** (Matthew 5:9 MSG).

Blessed are the peacemakers who lean over a backyard fence to end a dispute between neighbors. Blessed are the peacemakers who calm a troubled marriage so a husband and wife can fall in love again. Blessed are the peacemakers who organize a prayer vigil on a blood-stained street. Blessed are the peacemakers who persuade irrational combatants to call a cease fire. Blessed are the peacemakers who unite opinionated people around one agenda. Blessed are messengers of the gospel who proclaim peace with God through the forgiveness of sins. Blessed are all peacemakers who give us a taste of heaven. Maybe we would have more peace on earth if we had a few more peacemakers.

Still useful

Pastor Mark Jeske

The longer you live, the more years you've had to make mistakes. The longer you live, the more dumb things you've said, enemies made, promises broken, sins committed, and spiritual breakdowns and mutinies carried out. And still God loves you.

God deals with his believers primarily in mercy, not the law. His great delight is not in punishing foolish sinners with the severity they so richly deserve, but in restoring fools and failures like you and me to be useful to him again. In golf these are called mulligans. In Christianity this is called forgiveness and restoration.

In spite of careful preparation and multiple warnings, Jesus' disciple Peter failed his big test miserably. He was being trained as an evangelist for Christ, i.e., one whose job would be proclaiming Jesus' identity and work. But during Jesus' trial, Peter was intimidated by a servant girl into swearing three times that he had never heard of Christ.

The risen Christ called his fallen and broken disciple back into service: **"When they had finished eating, Jesus said to Simon Peter, 'Simon son of John, do you truly love me more than these?' 'Yes, Lord,' he said, 'you know that I love you.' Jesus said, 'Feed my lambs'"** (John 21:15). Peter must have thought, "Seriously? You still have a use for me?"

You and I can take great comfort in that same desire in Christ's heart. He is truly a God of second chances. It's not too late to answer his call.

___

___

___

___

A model of obedience

Diana Kerr

Growing up, my mother was always good at nudging me out of my comfort zone. I remember one specific instance as a kid when she sent me up to the counter at McDonald's so I could sheepishly inform them, "Um, my Happy Meal didn't have a toy in it. Could I please still have a toy?" I dreaded those moments, but when Mom pushed, you obeyed.

Have you ever noticed that Jesus' first miracle resulted from his mother's urging? While at a wedding where the wine had run out, Mary approached Jesus with a classic motherly nudge. **"When the wine was gone, Jesus' mother said to him, 'They have no more wine.' 'Dear woman, why do you involve me?' Jesus replied, 'My time has not yet come.' His mother said to the servants, 'Do whatever he tells you'"** (John 2:3-5).

It's almost humorous how Mary dismissed Jesus' resistance. And we know what happened next. God in human form set aside his own desire to obey his mother. In Jesus' mind, the timing wasn't ideal, yet even he was not above obedience to his mother. The Son of God did not forget that he's also the son of Mary.

You may not always agree with your parents or those whom God has placed in authority over you. You may not always be up to the task they ask you to do. But God calls you to obey them and honor them nonetheless. Often, they're blessed with a vision and understanding greater than your own.

Divine patience

Pastor Mark Jeske

I can't remember how many times I have had a difficult conversation with a parent or aunt or grandparent about a wayward family member. Sometimes the only thing I can think to do is pray with them that the Lord will keep the wanderer alive long enough for a change of mind and heart to take hold.

How wise is our God! How merciful is his patience! Jesus once told a story about a landowner who was ready to turn an unproductive fig tree into firewood. **"'For three years now I've been coming to look for fruit on this fig tree and haven't found any. Cut it down!' . . . 'Sir,' the man replied, 'leave it alone for one more year, and I'll dig around it and fertilize it'"** (Luke 13:7,8).

Perhaps the Lord can melt a hard heart by sending treasures and blessings in the hope that the drifter will recognize a divine miracle and realize how much he or she is loved. More likely God will realize that he needs to use a two-by-four to get the person's attention.

God's patience means that he and we have a little more time to love and encourage people we care about whose lives seem disconnected from God. You and I are God's gardeners, digging, weeding, fertilizing, and watering his trees to bear fruit for him. You and I are God's evangelists, loving, inviting, praying for, warning, and encouraging people he still loves. The stakes are high: fruit or firewood.

____

____

____

____

Whose stuff is it anyway?

Diana Kerr

What are you going to do with your money when you die? Unless you're an Egyptian pharaoh, you probably aren't planning to take it with you. So who's going to get that money?

"Who cares?" people think. "It's no good to me anymore." We value money and possessions *so* highly until we're gone and they can no longer personally benefit us.

Perhaps Christians should put a bit more thought into the matter. Establishing a will can ensure that the money God has entrusted to us will go to good use even after our death. The Bible has a lot to say about wealth and material blessings, and it's clear that God thinks they are his, not ours. **"The earth is the Lord's, and everything in it, the world, and all who live in it"** (Psalm 24:1). When we examine our hearts and refocus our mind-set so that we view ourselves as stewards rather than owners, it's easy to see the responsibility and opportunity in the blessings God provides.

What to do now? Pray that God transforms your heart and mind so you truly embody what it means to be a steward. Think about setting up a will. Find Christian friends you can mutually encourage to live generously. And think outside the box—God doesn't just want your money. He's entrusted you with all sorts of other blessings—your brain, your home, your time, your possessions, your health.

And he expects you'll use them to his glory.

Hell is for real

Pastor Mark Jeske

Adam and Eve brought three curses on their descendants: physical suffering, death, and hell. Hell is an eternal condition, first in soul and then soul and body. People today don't appear to take it seriously; after all, no one has ever seen the real thing and come back to tell about it. The word *hell* is either an adult spice word for emphasis or else the scene of the *Far Side* cartoons where a red-suited devil with a pitchfork and horns bosses unhappy people around. It seems that most Americans, and sadly many Christians, don't believe in a literal hell.

Jesus did. He helped design it—a place of endless desolation, torment, hatred, and despair. Jesus did—he experienced it on the cross so that he could release us from its threat. Jesus did—and he described its misery in this parable:

"In hell, where he was in torment, [the rich man] **looked up and saw Abraham far away, with Lazarus by his side. So he called to him, 'Father Abraham, have pity on me and send Lazarus to dip the tip of his finger in water and cool my tongue, because I am in agony in this fire'"** (Luke 16:23,24).

Do you get it? Even the small relief brought by a drink of water will be denied the people who have rejected their Savior. Please—you must listen to the utterly earnest voice of Jesus.

Freedom in forgiveness

Diana Kerr

Genesis 32 sounds like the lead up to an epic battle scene in a dramatic war movie. Jacob's fear is obvious as he prepares to reunite with his brother Esau for the first time in decades. I imagine his stomach had been churning for days.

Family reunions aren't *that* bad, are they? This one was. The last time these brothers had seen each other, Jacob had covertly stolen the blessing his father, Isaac, had reserved for the firstborn son, Esau. Genesis 27 tells us that **"Esau held a grudge against Jacob because of the blessing his father had given him. He said to himself, 'The days of mourning for my father are near; then I will kill my brother Jacob'"** (verse 41).

No wonder Jacob was terrified, and no wonder he expected the worst. Grudges ran long and deep in Bible times just like they do today.

Esau's response is shocking, refreshing, and inspiring. **"Esau ran to meet Jacob and embraced him; he threw his arms around his neck and kissed him"** (Genesis 33:4). By human standards, he had every right to treat Jacob harshly, sustaining a tension between the two that would never end. But his reaction was a game changer.

When Esau chose forgiveness over grudge holding and revenge, it didn't just benefit Jacob. Esau had a weight lifted off his shoulders, and he had his brother back. I dare you to release some resentment you're hanging onto and opt for forgiveness.

You'll free the other person and yourself as well.

Lead us not into temptation

Pastor Mark Jeske

"When tempted, no one should say, 'God is tempting me.' For God cannot be tempted by evil, nor does he tempt anyone; but each one is tempted when, by his own evil desire, he is dragged away and enticed. Then, after desire has conceived, it gives birth to sin; and sin, when it is full-grown, gives birth to death" (James 1:13-15).

Temptations are evil suggestions to a believer's heart and mind to rebel against God's will. While God indeed allows, and sometimes even may send, hardships upon his children, his purpose in that is always good: to test out their faith as genuine and to draw them closer to him, away from this sick and dying planet. God never, ever wants his children to choose evil. Our temptation problem is not from God but really comes from within. Cooking away in each person's heart is a sinful self that will never be converted. It restlessly seeks to dominate our thinking and values. It will never submit to God.

James reminds us of these things so that we will not be fooled into thinking that the growth of our *Christian* self will mean that our *evil* self will just automatically wither away and disappear. We need, honestly and humbly, to recognize the enemy within our own hearts, an enemy that can and will conceive and give birth to evil thoughts, evil words, and evil deeds. We will humbly accept James' warning, daily repent of our sins, and trust Jesus' forgiveness.

An unrepentant attitude causes spiritual death. You know that, right?

____

____

____

God is a pattern maker

Jason Nelson

God is a pattern maker. Like every skilled craftsman, he uses the good patterns repeatedly. There is the two-eye pattern. Every critter I can think of has two eyes spaced evenly on its head. Yes, there's the flounder. Its eyes migrate to the top of its head, which is convenient for a fish spending its life on the bottom of the ocean. There's the fur-on-the-surface pattern. Hairy things of all kinds wear their coats on the outside where they can do some good. The most genius of all is the vine-branches pattern. It is the order of dynamic systems. We see it in a river and its tributaries, in our spinal cords and peripheral nerves, in a mighty oak and its limbs.

We see it in our relationship with God. We aren't distant satellites. There's no daylight between him and us. We are attached directly to God through Jesus. **"I am the vine; you are the branches. If a man remains in me and I in him, he will bear much fruit; apart from me you can do nothing"** (John 15:5).

Everything good is rooted in God. God's goodness surfaced in Jesus Christ. We are branches that remain in God's love because Christ the vine kept God's commands. Branches with a strong attachment can take some pruning and survive blustery times. Branches with a strong attachment produce heavy fruit. Because we are attached to the vine, we can absorb his Word and pattern our lives after his.

April 16

That's not what I wanted

Pastor Mark Jeske

Young children are known for honesty, sometimes painful honesty. The things they blurt out without thinking to their relatives at Christmastime can make parents flinch with embarrassment. Unable to conceal their childish disappointment as the wrapping paper comes off, their faces scrunch up: "That's *not* what I wanted."

A paralyzed man two thousand years ago had legs that didn't work any longer, but his heart worked plenty well. It was pounding furiously as his friends brought him near Jesus, the famous healer. Imagine his excitement when his friends managed to penetrate the crowd and get Jesus to notice their disabled friend. Jesus did indeed give him a gift, but perhaps not the gift he was hoping for. **"Some men brought to him a paralytic, lying on a mat. When Jesus saw their faith, he said to the paralytic, 'Take heart, son; your sins are forgiven'"** (Matthew 9:2).

The man wanted new legs. But the gift he was given first was actually far more valuable. Even healthy people, even champion athletes, eventually sicken and die. But if your sins are forgiven, you become one with Christ. His Easter resurrection victory becomes yours, and you become immortal like him. Maybe you have seen miraculous healings and recoveries of those you prayed for; maybe some people you love will have health struggles their whole lives. Jesus loved the paralyzed man enough to address his spiritual needs *first* and strengthened his faith.

And then Jesus gave him his new legs.

____

____

____

Armed for battle

Diana Kerr

Have you ever witnessed the sport of paintball? In paintball, players try to eliminate opponents by shooting dye-filled capsules at each other with special paintball guns. Although paintball is supposed to be fun, I've heard that getting hit stings pretty badly.

Most people who paintball wear a layer of clothing to protect themselves. They know they're entering a "war zone" and attack is imminent. They'd be foolish to show up without ample clothing to shield them from some of the paintballs' sting.

Do you actively, consciously protect yourself from the devil's attacks? Or do you venture into life's war zone each day without considering how you'll handle his flaming arrows? You *know* his attacks are coming, so there's no reason not to be prepared. Ephesians urges us to **"take up the shield of faith, with which you can extinguish all the flaming arrows of the evil one. Take the helmet of salvation and the sword of the Spirit, which is the word of God"** (6:16,17).

What exactly is that protection which softens the blow of the devil's arrows? God's Word, a strong prayer life, and supportive Christian friends, to name a few.

Just like a day spent on a paintball battlefield, you're sure to face attack throughout your life. You will never be able to avoid Satan altogether, but you can prevent or at least minimize the impact of his attacks.

Don't forget who and what will protect you.

If egos went missing

Jason Nelson

Imagine a day when our egos run away. They don't get what they want, so they take their ball and go home. They refuse to participate and vow never to return. Imagine a day when they decide to punish everyone by pulling out. What would a day without egos be like? Well, meetings would be shorter. Productivity would increase. The future would unfold seamlessly. And everyone would sleep better.

God instructs us to send our egos packing and follow our Savior Jesus' example. **"Do nothing out of selfish ambition or vain conceit, but in humility consider others better than yourselves. Each of you should look not only to your own interests, but also to the interests of others"** (Philippians 2:3,4).

To get beyond ourselves, the Bible points us to Jesus and urges us to have an attitude that is **"the same as that of Christ Jesus"** (verse 5). By nature, we aspire to be minor deities and claw our way up the pedestal. We sweet-talk others to convince them they would be better off with us on top. Forgive us, Lord, for outsized egos.

If anyone could flaunt his status, it is Jesus. He is God, but he didn't play that card. He took on the nature of a servant and was humble through and through. He disregarded his own well-being and went to the cross for the benefit of others. In last-shall-be-first fulfillment, **"God exalted him to the highest place and gave him the name that is above every name"** (verse 9).

He provides for me

Pastor Mark Jeske

Without a doubt the 23rd is the most famous of all the psalms. Many Christians know it by heart. It is often heard at funerals and murmured to people in their hospital beds. It has provided comfort and hope to millions of stressed believers over the centuries. Its author, King David, wrote it from his own personal experience as a teenager, when he was put in charge of tending his father's flocks. He knew sheep. He knew their needs, their value, their vulnerabilities, and their foibles. It is just possible that he pastured and watered his flocks in the same Bethlehem hills that heard the Christmas angels.

Though David was a king and the head of a mighty army, he had vivid memories of his days as a lonely fugitive, running to stay alive, one jump ahead of his enemy Saul. David drew great comfort from knowing that his God provided the same value for him that David himself had once provided for the sheep he tended: **"The Lord is my Shepherd, I shall not be in want"** (Psalm 23:1). David knew fatigue, hunger, fear, harsh living conditions, and intense disappointment. But he found that *God always got him what he really needed,* one day at a time.

You are not alone as you make your way through your life. Your hardships and fears are known to the One who has committed himself to you as your Shepherd. He will see to it that you get *what you really need,* one day at a time.

___

___

___

___

April 20

He restores me

Pastor Mark Jeske

One of the hazards of reading extended metaphors in the Bible is the difficulty of knowing exactly how the ideas in the word pictures actually apply to your own life. The Shepherd Psalm is couched almost entirely in images, and you can muse dreamily on the happy pictures of sheep and their shepherd in a meadow and not get the point for your life *right now*.

Right now you might be underwater financially, in danger of losing your job, struggling with poor health, afraid of being left alone, your thoughts miserable and depressed. Your recent efforts at making things better may have failed, and you feel surrounded by dream crushers who make you feel small and insignificant. You are also sadly aware of how you have disappointed God with sinful words and actions.

That's why we are glad to have Jesus in our lives. He brings refreshment to the weary: **"He makes me lie down in green pastures, he leads me beside quiet waters, he restores my soul"** (Psalm 23:2,3). After David's hardships, God gave him relief. After you have struggled, your Shepherd will send you kind words, a new friend, helpful medication, a financial boost, or new insights into the significance of your accomplishments. When you are dragging because of your guilty knowledge of your own sins, his words of unconditional love and forgiveness will refresh your soul. You still matter to him!

Watch for these moments! They are not coincidences; they are your loving Shepherd's acts of restoration.

He guides me

Pastor Mark Jeske

The farther south you go in the land of Israel, the less rainfall there is. As farming gets more difficult, people's lives depend on the raising of smaller livestock—sheep and goats. One of a shepherd's main tasks is to find edible grass and a water supply for his animals. It is part of the job to stay on the move, always searching out the next day's food and water. Sheep are not naturally good at foraging—they depend on guidance from their shepherd.

I don't think you need any help from God to find a path to your nearest supermarket. But you know how many times you've lost your way morally and spiritually. Satan is an absolute wizard at weaving a spell of deceit and confusion and self-delusion so that you get all turned around. Wrong turns into right, white to black and black to white, and suddenly other people hear you arguing that 2+2=5.

We need our Good Shepherd and his solid and changeless Word: **"He guides me in paths of righteousness for his name's sake"** (Psalm 23:3). How should I conduct myself in the business world? Are there different rules for church and marketplace? How is marriage supposed to work?

To walk "righteously" means to be right with God, both in your spiritual status before him and in the way you talk and act. The Bible is your map and your headlamp so that you will know how to walk in God's ways, i.e., live in such a way as to please him.

He protects me

Pastor Mark Jeske

The physical world that your eyes can see and the infrared, UV, and atomic world that scientific instruments can "see," are not all there is. The Bible reveals what is going on behind the scenes in the very real *spiritual* world. God and Satan, angels and demons, are in constant conflict, warring for control of earth and its people, including control of you.

Nervous sheep like you and me are worried about physical breakdowns like illness, injury, and death, but far worse is the danger of *evil,* of falling into Satan's clutches, of selling our heavenly inheritance for some cheap and temporary advantage in the here and now. Our Shepherd Jesus is mightier than Satan, and his angels are mightier than the demons. We don't have to be afraid: **"Even though I walk through the valley of the shadow of death, I will fear no evil, for you are with me"** (Psalm 23:4).

Because Jesus has already gone through death into the grave and back out again, alive and glorious, we know that we will too. Death for us is nothing more than a doorway that we will pass through on our way into heaven, and whether it comes sooner or later doesn't really matter.

Our Shepherd's protection also keeps us safe from the dark lord and his corruption. When you pray for Christ's help in the Lord's Prayer, "Deliver us from evil," you can have absolute confidence that he is up to the task.

He corrects me

Pastor Mark Jeske

People like to see pictures of their country's military technology—it gives them a feeling of security to see those sleek jet fighters and aircraft carriers and know how they are being protected. In the same way, sheep are comforted by their shepherd's rod. The rod is his weapon, a club chosen and shaped carefully for balance and power. It can be swung or thrown, and though used mostly as a defensive weapon, shepherds will use it on the ribs of balky sheep who are disrupting the march.

The staff is a long, slender walking stick, often with a crook at the top end. The staff is helpful for lifting newborn lambs to present to the ewes; this avoids getting human scent on the lambs and risking rejection. As he stands in the middle of the flock, that long staff is an extension of the shepherd's touch, nudging, steering, getting attention. The crook end is also most helpful in disengaging a sheep's wool from brambles or thistles.

"Your rod and your staff, they comfort me" (Psalm 23:4), says David. Repentant Christians are glad not only for divine protection from satanic wolves but glad also for correcting pokes, nudges, or even whacks. Sheep stray, get tipped over helplessly, and eat potentially poisonous plants; we "human sheep" have our own ways of drifting off, living carelessly, and committing spiritual suicide.

What a great comfort it is to know that our Good Shepherd is watching over us and will reach into our lives to warn and avert!

April 24

He welcomes me

Pastor Mark Jeske

Most of the 23rd psalm is about the journey; the last two verses are about the arrival. Christ is portrayed no longer as Shepherd—now he is Host, throwing open the doors of the mansion, welcoming his weary travelers home: **"You prepare a table before me in the presence of my enemies. You anoint my head with oil; my cup overflows. Surely goodness and love will follow me all the days of my life, and I will dwell in the house of the LORD forever"** (Psalm 23:5,6).

In heaven there will be no enemies. We will eat in peace; Satan, who will be permanently gnashing his teeth in hell, will not be able to molest us anymore. We will be given princely welcomes, just as lotions used to be provided for honored guests' dry skin. After a life journey marked by hardship and deprivation, our new life will be abundant, symbolized by an overflowing cup.

Our earthly lives are always marked and driven by our fearful realization that time is short. We feel the pressure to get it now, get it fast before the game is over. When we enter Paradise, we can exhale once and for all and relax, since we will be in the Lord's presence forever. The Lord's goodness and mercy that we have sensed and tasted on earth will surround us completely in heaven. Sin, guilt, fear, and death will trouble us no more.

Hang on, fellow sheep! We're almost there!

April 25

Just because we can

Jason Nelson

The Internet gives us absolute freedom of expression. It is pure democracy. Anyone can publish unchecked thoughts and images on popular social media platforms. More are being developed. You could become famous if your stuff goes viral. But the pitfalls are historic. Henry David Thoreau nailed it in 1854: "We are in great haste to construct a magnetic telegraph from Maine to Texas; but Maine and Texas, it may be, have nothing important to communicate" (*Walden*).

Everyone has a megaphone, **"but no man can tame the tongue. It is a restless evil, full of deadly poison"** (James 3:8). The tongue and its digital extensions still spew venom. Democracy is all about having robust and civil dialogue about competing views. But trashing another's reputation, belittling someone's appearance, or lashing out in anonymity are sins. So, **"keep your tongue from evil and your lips from telling lies"** (Psalm 34:13). There is no cause that is furthered through slander. There is no grievance that justifies defaming someone's good name.

Be careful what you post. It will be out there a very long time. Someone will find it and believe it. You will have a follower. Speech is not regulated in a free society under the assumption that people can control it themselves. The guiding principles are rooted in God's Word. Sure, we can say anything we want. But just because we can, doesn't mean we should.

Denominational humility

Pastor Mark Jeske

There are many Christian organizations and denominations. Mostly that's a good thing. Monopolies breed tyranny, and some degree of competition is healthy for any business or nonprofit. It's good for people to have choices. If they are abused or underserved in one, they can move to another.

It's good for religious denominations to be proud of their heritage and confident of their theological convictions. What is not good is when pride leads church leaders to glorify themselves or empower themselves or look down on other Christians. **"'Master,' said John, 'we saw a man driving out demons in your name and we tried to stop him, because he is not one of us.' 'Do not stop him,' Jesus said, 'for whoever is not against you is for you'"** (Luke 9:49,50).

It's good to work very hard at grounding your belief system in the Bible, to sift and probe and test every idea and make it subject to God's inspired Word. It's bad, though, to think of a Christian not in your organization as the enemy. People are loyal to the denomination into which they were born, or where they have a lot of relatives and friends, or to the one that gave them a chance to serve.

The line we all should want to walk is to take great care with our doctrinal statements and message but to show kindness and respect to others who confess Christ as Savior but "are not one of us."

True and lasting strength

Diana Kerr

I feel sorry for anyone whom others view as weak. Weak people get teased, overlooked for job promotions, and kicked off of reality TV shows. Weakness is hardly something we boast of; in fact, we often do everything we can to minimize our weaknesses. The world eagerly points us to all sorts of solutions—energy drinks, big muscles, powerful jobs, a fat bank account, or innovative medication. Yet we can't truly rely on any of them. Your caffeinated beverage doesn't care if it makes you "crash" with three hours of the workday still remaining.

This may be old news to you, but it bears repeating because we forget so easily: **"God is our refuge and strength, an ever-present help in trouble"** (Psalm 46:1). Did you notice that? *God.* You are not your source of strength. Your significant other is not your source of strength. Not even that irresistible home gym system you bought from TV is your source of strength (although I imagine you *would* get physically stronger if you actually used it). None of these things are inherently bad—in fact, they can indeed be helpful—but they trick us into relying on a false sense of security.

We fall into the trap of relying on worldly fixes so easily. How many times do we need to hear that God is our strength before we start living as if we truly believe that is true?

Lean on the reliable strength of your God, who is there for you in any circumstance and available around the clock.

April 28

A really narrow gate

Pastor Mark Jeske

The deceased are always heroes at their own funeral.

Have you ever heard a minister tell the mourners of what a bad person their late relative and friend was? That he most likely had already begun his torments in hell? No matter how a person lived her life, the last words at her wake will always apply a coat of saint paint. She may not have set foot in a church in 40 years, but the bereaved will comfort themselves with happy images of their late friend experiencing a grand heavenly reunion with all the old gang.

Perhaps we should ask Jesus if that's true. Does everybody eventually slide into heaven by and by? **"Someone asked him, 'Lord, are only a few people going to be saved?' He said to them, 'Make every effort to enter through the *narrow* door, because many, I tell you, will try to enter and will not be able to'"** (Luke 13:23,24). God's grace is *inclusive*—the Father created all; Jesus died for the sins of all; the price of forgiveness for all was paid in full on Calvary.

But all those wonderful benefits flow to you only if you believe the gospel. Faith is *exclusive*—only believers are saved, receive the precious "not guilty" verdict on judgment day, and pass through the gates of pearl. Those gates really are narrow—all your own plans and philosophies and remedies and self-justification will avail you nothing on that day. All you need is Jesus.

____

____

____

____

____

Call the doctor

Pastor Mark Jeske

The Lord God took great pains to prepare the world for the gift of Jesus Christ the Savior. Humanity had to wait thousands of years until God was ready. An entire nation was built from one couple, Abraham and Sarah, and that nation would one day give birth to the Messiah. Religious leadership was set up through priests and teachers to prepare that nation, Israel, for God's supreme gift.

It is one of the appalling ironies of all time that so many in Israel, and so many of Israel's religious leaders, were not interested in the Christ when he finally did come. Some felt self-sufficient because they trusted in their good works. Some felt safe because they were of the right families or chosen bloodline. Some felt confident because they trusted in the efficacy of the religious rituals they performed.

An even greater irony is that it was among the outcasts of society that Jesus found people who were aware that they were sick with sin and needed healing. **"On hearing this, Jesus said, 'It is not the healthy who need a doctor, but the sick. . . . I have not come to call the righteous, but sinners'"** (Matthew 9:12,13).

Call the doctor! You have the disease too, the disease of sin. It's congenital, it's contagious, and it is always fatal. Only the soothing medicine of the gospel of Jesus can make you well again.

Paging Dr. Jesus!

____

____

____

____

Beauty is soul deep

Jason Nelson

It is estimated that people around the world spend $160 billion annually trying to look beautiful, or at least not quite so homely (*The Economist*). Good looks are universally admired and are a blessing from God if you happen to get them. There is nothing wrong with making the most of one's appearance. But we all have met nice-looking people who were not so attractive once we got to know them.

Western art usually depicts Jesus as a handsome chap who looks like he came from somewhere in Minnesota. But Isaiah said, **"He had no beauty or majesty to attract us to him, nothing in his appearance that we should desire him"** (Isaiah 53:2). Jesus was an ordinary-looking Jewish guy of his time. In his suffering, he looked **"like one from whom men hide their faces"** (verse 3). Intense pain disfigures a person's appearance. Had we been there, we would have looked away. But we are drawn to him because his suffering was for us.

Mother Teresa wasn't cute by cover girl standards. The plight of the poor, sick, and dying of Calcutta moved her to adorn herself with "the poverty of the cross" so she could minister to them. She didn't turn away from the contagiously ill who lived like animals. She lived among them and worked to ease their suffering. The beauty of Christ isn't superficial. It is soul deep in his followers.

May

"I CAN DO EVERYTHING THROUGH HIM
WHO GIVES ME STRENGTH."
PHILIPPIANS 4:13

Kiss those trophies good-bye

Diana Kerr

Do you consider yourself a nostalgic person? Do you hang on to old photos and mementos? Over the years I've kept an almost embarrassing amount of awards that I've received. I've got a bin full of trophies and plaques, a tub of medals, a box of ribbons, and multiple copies of newspapers with my name in them. I could go on, but I think I've shamed myself enough.

My collection of accolades isn't wrong, but maybe my reasoning behind it all is faulty. As I consider why I hold on to the past, I tell myself it's because I don't want to forget—I don't want to lose the memories. The little truth woven into that is that I want to remember how great I was. I worked so hard to achieve those accomplishments, and tossing a trophy makes me feel like that accomplishment is gone.

Whether I get rid of the trophies someday or never at all, eventually they'll be gone. All of them will—all of our literal and metaphorical trophies—our homes, our clothes, our sports memorabilia, our great bodies, our fame or success . . . God tells us in Isaiah 65:17, **"Behold, I will create new heavens and a new earth. The former things will not be remembered, nor will they come to mind."**

Our earthly trophies will not only be gone; they won't be memories anymore. Does that realization change the way you play the game of life?

____

____

____

____

____

Grace really is amazing

Pastor Mark Jeske

John Newton had a hard life—born in 1725, his mother died when he was 6, a sailor at age 11, press-ganged into the British Navy at 18, and flogged with 96 lashes when he was caught trying to desert.

He sailed on a slave ship, and then became a captain who led three voyages that brought kidnapped Africans to the New World for sale. Even after he quit sailing, he continued to invest in slave enterprises. His slowly growing Christian faith led him to become a pastor and then a vocal advocate for abolition. He became an advisor to William Wilberforce, a member of Parliament whose antislavery work resulted in the Slave Trade Act of 1807 that banned the trade in human beings in the British Empire.

St. Paul deeply appreciated the God who could have mercy on a wicked man like him: **"To the man who does not work but trusts God who justifies the wicked, his faith is credited as righteousness"** (Romans 4:5). To the end of his life, John Newton remained grateful to God for grace, grace that saved his wretched life and transformed him into something useful to God. One of his greatest legacies was the autobiographical hymn that he wrote for himself and every other wretched sinner on earth: "Amazing Grace."

May I say that I am grateful that God saved a wretch like me as well?

Walk with the wise

Diana Kerr

You've probably heard the saying that goes something like this: "You are the sum total of the five people you spend the most time with." It's basically a modern version of Proverbs 13:20: **"He who walks with the wise grows wise, but a companion of fools suffers harm."**

You will become like the people you hang out with, for better or worse. Yeah, you can blame your friends for your screwups, but maybe you need to blame yourself for hanging around those friends in the first place.

Remember when you were a kid and your parents had strong opinions about the friends who were "bad news"? Well, now you're an adult—you get to choose your friends on your own, no parental opinions involved. Just remember that there are consequences to those choices. Do you want friends who will cause you to compromise your values or friends who will strengthen your values? Do you want friends who will make you timid about bringing faith into a conversation or friends who challenge your faith and its presence in your life? Do you want friends who will make it easy for you to stray from God or friends who won't allow you to stray?

Don't be shy in asking God for help in surrounding yourself with friends who will make you wise in his ways. And a little hint about the five people you spend the majority of your time with. Make Jesus one of those five people.

____

____

____

____

Who are you, Jesus?

Pastor Mark Jeske

A ten-year-old boy said once, "I believe in Jesus, but sometimes I wonder if he is real. Sometimes he seems like a character from a book."

Jesus is indeed a character in a holy book, but he is most certainly also real. Today he comes to us through Word and Baptism and Lord's Supper, and the subtlety of his presence eludes unbelievers and sometimes stresses believers. People want visuals and action and proof.

On the other hand, Jesus did once walk the streets of earth. He did speak directly with people, heal the sick, and raise the dead; and people still found reasons not to believe in him then either. It isn't sight that saves you. It's faith. Jesus once asked his disciples, **"'Who do people say the Son of Man is?' They replied, 'Some say John the Baptist; others say Elijah; and still others, Jeremiah or one of the prophets.' 'But what about you?' he asked. 'Who do you say I am?'"** (Matthew 16:13-15). Even the angels hushed for a moment waiting for the answer. **"You are the Christ, the Son of the living God,"** Peter answered (verse 16). He was able to see through his Lord's humble disguise, Jesus' outward appearance as a poor traveling rabbi.

Keep reading Bible stories to your kids and grandkids. It's how God chooses to reveal the Savior to people today. The Scriptures are still able to make people wise for salvation.

Kids too.

Bring 'em back alive

Jason Nelson

I like being a dad. I've taken the job quite seriously. I really love being a grandfather. I have discovered I don't have to take that job seriously at all. My children are good parents. They are loving and responsible. They talk about how they were raised and want to repeat the process. They express appreciation for what their mother and I taught them. That takes me off the hook so I can be a fun, loving grandfather.

Having grandchildren is the culmination of life for family women and men. **"Children's children are a crown to the aged, and parents are the pride of their children"** (Proverbs 17:6). I offer this encouragement to young parents. Raise your children the way you want your grandchildren raised. Love them with all your heart and build their consciences with the Bible's teachings. Set the example. Be thoughtful and persistent to discipline them appropriately. Look forward to the day they make you proud because they are raising their children the same way.

I see a little fear in my children's eyes when they bring their kids for a day with me. They sense something is different. They can see I have changed my approach with children. They know theirs could end up dirty, sticky, spoiled, and tired. But I promise to bring them back alive, because that is now my only rule for child care.

Pray for workers

Pastor Mark Jeske

Perhaps it seems as though the world has plenty of pastors. After all, every church seems to have one (or more), right?

Jesus didn't think so two thousand years ago, and I doubt if he thinks so today. **"When he saw the crowds, he had compassion on them, because they were harassed and helpless, like sheep without a shepherd. Then he said to his disciples, 'The harvest is plentiful but the workers are few. Ask the Lord of the harvest, therefore, to send out workers into his harvest field'"** (Matthew 9:36-38).

Every significant human endeavor needs to have leadership, and so does the church. When people are not fed well with Word and the Lord's Supper, when their path is not lit by the Light, the evil one pounces and they are harassed and helpless. God's prophets Jeremiah and Ezekiel bitterly criticized the terrible leadership that the people of Israel were saddled with in their day, which resulted in suffering, defeat, and captivity.

Jesus thought then, and he certainly thinks now, that there is a great harvest of souls ready to be called to faith and built up in their faith. Where will that leadership come from? Good leaders are God's gifts, and we invite those gifts through our prayers. We appreciate the good leaders we have and need to recruit the next generation. Please pray for your pastor today.

And then pray that there will be someone to replace him in the future.

___

___

___

Help us, Lord!

Pastor Mark Jeske

Does the concept of a national day of prayer resonate with you? I could understand if it didn't. You may say that it's not the government's job to call people to prayer—it's the church's job. And in a sense you'd be right.

But any government has a lot to gain from inviting its citizens to pray for the country's well-being. Since Christians (me included) are so often lazy and forgetful, we can stand the reminder. Besides, God himself encourages believers to intercede with him on behalf of their fellow citizens: **"Seek the peace and prosperity of the city to which I have carried you into exile. Pray to the Lord for it, because if it prospers, you too will prosper"** (Jeremiah 29:7).

If God had blessings in reserve that he would dump out upon the corrupt and violent Babylonian Empire at Jeremiah's time, how much more could he be holding in reserve above the skies of our country today? What if he's just waiting for his children to ask? Imagine if all the Christians in our country would ask for less violence, less injustice, more prosperity, and more peace?

This is not to say that our country deserves God's blessings because it is a Christian country. In many ways it is not. But God answers prayer not on the basis of the merits of the petitioner. He answers prayer on the basis of the pure grace purchased for us by his Son, Jesus. Help us, Lord!

Time is short—what to do?

Pastor Mark Jeske

Are you an impulsive spender, or are you very intentional, a planner, in your money use? Do you have a budget? Could you produce an annual income/expense summary for your household? Jesus once told an admiring story about a dishonest business executive who was about to be fired.

"'I know what I'll do so that, when I lose my job here, people will welcome me into their houses.' So he called in each of his master's debtors. He asked the first, 'How much do you owe my master?' 'Eight hundred gallons of olive oil,' he replied. The manager told him, 'Take your bill, sit down quickly, and make it four hundred.' Then he asked the second, 'And how much do you owe?' 'A thousand bushels of wheat,' he replied. He told him, 'Take your bill and make it eight hundred'" (Luke 16:4-7).

Can you say, "embezzlement"? This manager was brilliant. Crooked, but brilliant. Knowing that he had but hours left with control over the business, he deliberately falsified the accounts receivable ledger in order to give some very handsome gifts to his boss' customers. Do you grasp the concept? These customers would feel a sense of obligation to him and would help him out after he was cut loose.

Do I need to mention that Jesus doesn't want you to falsify your company's records? So then what was Jesus' point? Read tomorrow's devotion to find out.

Make friends with God's resources

Pastor Mark Jeske

Jesus' audience now expected to hear in the story that the manager was arrested and thrown into prison. They expected to hear words of condemnation from their storyteller. But Jesus slipped in a plot twist. The boss had to laugh ruefully at his own error and admire the resourcefulness of his former manager.

"The master commended the dishonest manager because he had acted shrewdly. For the people of this world are more shrewd in dealing with their own kind than are the people of the light. I tell you, use worldly wealth to gain friends for yourselves, so that when it is gone, you will be welcomed into eternal dwellings" (Luke 16:8,9).

The manager was commended not for his embezzlement (a crime back then as it is now) but for his foresight, speed, and willingness to invest resources in people, not himself. Note that the manager didn't just try to loot the business and run off with cash. He invested in people.

Jesus observed (sadly) that believers ("people of the light") are much more naïve about money matters than unbelievers. He who never owned much of anything during his 33 years now urges you to believe his powerful principle: you lose what you spend on yourself. When you invest in human need or in the mission of communicating the gospel, you will have everlasting satisfaction in heaven. Plus—the people you helped on earth will be organizing your welcome party there!

Global sizzling

Pastor Mark Jeske

"Some say the world will end in fire, some say in ice. From what I've tasted of desire I hold with those who favor fire." Robert Frost wrote one of his most brilliant little poems musing on how the curtain will fall on the universe as we know it. However, the world's end won't come because of man-made fire, the fire of wars and weapons, or the fire of technology run rampant. The fire will fall from God, punitive and purging.

"Long ago by God's word the heavens existed and the earth was formed out of water and by water. By these waters also the world of that time was deluged and destroyed. By the same word the present heavens and earth are reserved for fire, being kept for the day of judgment and destruction of ungodly men" (2 Peter 3:5-7).

If you are connected to Christ in faith, you don't have to fear the fire. It will destroy all evil as fire destroys vermin, lice, fatal viruses, and bacteria. Don't grieve for material possessions lost. God can and will replace them all a hundred times over.

We aren't going to end the world. God is.

We aren't going to create a new world. God is.

Believers in Christ get to live there. Forever.

____

____

____

____

____

Self-sacrifice

Jason Nelson

Christianity is centered in self-sacrifice. The most solemn day of the Christian year is Good Friday, when we worship God for sacrificing himself. That's how he showed us what love is. **"This is love: not that we loved God, but that he loved us and sent his Son as an atoning sacrifice for our sins"** (1 John 4:10).

When Jesus' self-sacrifice was enough, he moaned, **"It is finished."** His resurrection three days later was a stunning reversal of life over death and guaranteed the same victory for us. That set us on a path to show his love to others through self-sacrifice. **"Dear friends, since God so loved us, we also ought to love one another. No one has ever seen God; but if we love one another, God lives in us and his love is made complete in us"** (1 John 4:11,12).

If we could choose how to complete God's love, we would opt to dabble in harmless demonstrations of courtesy. Making nice to others is a religious thing, right? None of us minds doing that. It is self-sacrifice when we take a loss and feel the pain for the glory of God and good of others. Jesus didn't want to drink from that cup either. But there was no other way. We'll know self-sacrifice when we see it because we would rather not go through with it. But Christ's love compels us to.

____

____

____

____

____

Isn't he the Prince of Peace?

Pastor Mark Jeske

Just when you think you're starting to understand the Bible's basic messages, you trip over something that upsets your whole mental equilibrium. For instance, is not Jesus the ultimate peace bringer? In the messianic age, will not the wolf live with the lamb (Isaiah 11:6)? Is not one of Jesus' official titles the "Prince of Peace" (Isaiah 9:6)? Did not Jesus come to reconcile us with God and with each other? Didn't the Christmas angels proclaim "peace on earth" because of Christ's birth?

Yes indeed to all of the above. But we must listen to all of God's Word, not just the happy parts. It is a paradox that Jesus *came also to do the opposite*. He once told his disciples, **"Do not suppose that I have come to bring peace to the earth. I did not come to bring peace, but a sword"** (Matthew 10:34). Jesus could see ahead into human history, and he was honest enough to predict to his disciples that one of the sad results of their gospel proclamation would be a dividing of people.

Believers will suffer persecution, not only from hostile government forces but sometimes at the hands of family members or their own synagogues and churches. The great evangelist John Wesley famously remarked once that when the gospel is proclaimed clearly, it will either convert you or enrage you.

You can expect both outcomes when you speak the Word to those around you.

____

____

____

____

May 13

A little taste of heaven

Pastor Mark Jeske

Holy Communion always has a *backward* focus to it, doesn't it? We do this in *remembrance* of Jesus, remembering his institution of the Holy Supper in the upper room just hours before his arrest and condemnation; remembering his suffering for our sake, his violent, terrible death and burial, and his triumphant resurrection for us.

Communion has a *present* significance. We receive forgiveness and mercy and hope *right now,* the very moment we receive the sacred meal. As we kneel at the altar, we are bonded together with our fellow communicants, re-welded into God's church right then and there. Right then and there we become one with Christ, physically and spiritually.

Communion also has a powerful *future* significance. Jesus said, **"I tell you, I will not drink of this fruit of the vine from now on until that day when I drink it anew with you in my Father's kingdom"** (Matthew 26:29). The wonderful environment that Jesus created for his disciples around the table that evening is only a foretaste, only the first installment, of wonderful feasting and love to come at heaven's grand banquet. The taste of bread and swallow of wine whisper Jesus' words of hope in a believer's ear that the best is yet to come.

Let your Communion experience pull you forward with confidence, optimism, and the certainty that the Father's kingdom has a place for you at the table.

Run away

Pastor Mark Jeske

In the classic comedy movie *Monty Python and the Holy Grail,* King Arthur and his motley knights aren't exactly paragons of courage and stamina. When confronted with a threat, they flee. "Run away!" they shout to each other.

Does it look like Jesus "ran away" from a messy world full of pain and problems? Not at all. His ascension capped off everything that he had accomplished. It wasn't a retreat, but rather the royal procession to his heavenly coronation as King of kings and Lord of lords. From his throne above he now rules over all things to bless and benefit the believers.

His ascension guarantees that our prayers will be favorably received: **"Since we have a great high priest who has gone through the heavens, Jesus the Son of God, let us hold firmly to the faith we profess. For we do not have a high priest who is unable to sympathize with our weaknesses, but we have one who has been tempted in every way, just as we are—yet was without sin. Let us approach the throne of grace with confidence, so that we may receive mercy and find grace to help us in our time of need"** (Hebrews 4:14-16).

Though temporarily absent in body, he is always present in spirit. He will return to earth the same way he left. In the meantime, he wants us to know he's in charge. He's here. He cares. He helps.

May 15

How is it with your soul?

Jason Nelson

The English clergyman John Wesley asked people he met, "How is it with your soul?" He didn't ask, "How's it going?" The answer would have been superficial. Our love for each other must run deep, because people are like icebergs. There is much more beneath the surface.

Helpers to King Saul inquired about his soul. They noticed when he wasn't right **(see 1 Samuel 16:15,16)**. They noticed that a spirit of sadness was terrifying him and that he was tormented by an awful depression. They sent in David to calm Saul's troubled soul.

Concern for someone's soul includes concern for their mental health. People we love are inwardly terrified by depression and other mood disorders. The symptoms don't show up on X-rays but can be observed by those close to them. These are serious illnesses that befall people in an imperfect world. And like other illnesses, they are treatable. Unfortunately, there is stigma attached to getting help. David's music calmed Saul's troubled soul. Today we have other therapies.

Mental illnesses are not a curse from God but crosses to bear. Our loved ones need our patience, understanding, and assistance in bearing them. If you know someone who is unusually sad or volatile, please inquire about their soul. Please direct them to treatment. And if a spirit of sadness is terrifying you, please get help so that it may be well with your soul.

____

____

____

____

I'd start with John

Jason Nelson

An acquaintance recently asked me, "If I want to start reading the Bible, where should I begin?" The question made me think. The obvious answer would be to start at the beginning. Maybe do a "through the Bible in 365 days" program. Then I thought the psalms make for good Bible reading. But instead I said, "If it was me, I'd start with John."

I'd start with John's gospel, where we learn that God and his Word are synonymous. I'd underline the nutshell message: **"God so loved the world that he gave his one and only Son, that whoever believes in him shall not perish but have eternal life"** (John 3:16).

I would move on to John's epistles to see the light and feel the love. God is light. In him there is no darkness at all. We walk in the light through the blood of Jesus Christ. And God is love. **"Whoever lives in love lives in God, and God in him"** (1 John 4:16). We can love others because he loved us first.

I would take a peek into John's Revelation to get a feel for everlasting life with God. **"He will wipe every tear from their eyes. There will be no more death or mourning or crying or pain, for the old order of things has passed away"** (Revelation 21:4).

And then I said, "I'd read everything else in the Bible, with John in mind."

____

____

____

____

Personal humility

Pastor Mark Jeske

The third Beatitude gets no respect. "Blessed are the meek? Yeah, right."

The meek are roadkill in high school hallways, district attorneys' offices, and Hollywood. If you want to sell books, build a career, get famous, win tournaments, or get wealthy, you've got to put yourself forward, destroy your competition, go on the attack, take no prisoners, take no ____ from anybody, right?

Well, hold on a minute. Does anybody care what Jesus thinks? **"An argument started among the disciples as to which of them would be the greatest. Jesus, knowing their thoughts, took a little child and had him stand beside him. . . . 'He who is least among you all—he is the greatest'"** (Luke 9:46-48). Jesus not only talked about humble service; he lived it. He exemplified it. He found greater joy in bringing benefit to others than in bringing comfort and attention to himself.

What is it about a small child that Jesus found so compelling? Maybe it's that small children let others go first or know that they are supposed to be quiet and listen or that they need help to succeed. The more people are full of themselves, the emptier they are of God's Spirit. The more people obsess about their agendas, the less interest they have in God's. Tell me something—whose approval do you most crave? Your peers'? The media's?

Or God's?

____

____

____

____

May 18

Chosen

Diana Kerr

Were your parents excited about your birth? Maybe your answer to that is an obvious "yes." Maybe you found out at some point growing up that you were unwanted. Maybe you don't honestly know. Maybe you've never met your father or you don't remember your biological parents.

No matter your circumstance at birth and throughout your life since then, you've no doubt experienced the pain of not being chosen or wanted. Maybe one of your siblings was clearly the favorite child, maybe you watched someone else get the final spot on the varsity team or be awarded a job you wanted, or maybe you feel invisible to your own spouse sometimes. It hurts to feel unwanted. Despite those pains, and whether you were born into loving arms that were anxious to hold you or into a situation of regret or disinterest, you were and are wanted by God. Isaiah's confidence in the Lord's longing for him is a confidence you can adopt too: **"Before I was born the Lord called me; from my birth he has made mention of my name"** (Isaiah 49:1).

Whoa. What a cool thought! Before your parents ever laid eyes on you, before they fought over whether to name you John Jr. or Steven, God knew your name and he wanted you as his. In fact, it goes back further than you think. *Before God even created the very first parents,* he knew *you* were coming someday and he chose you, specifically *you,* for his team.

____

____

____

____

____

Husbands, pay attention

Pastor Mark Jeske

Men and women certainly have different styles of communication. Millions of arguments and hard feelings have arisen when spouses misunderstood each other or missed important messages completely.

Women thrive on communication and use a wide variety of ways to send messages and behavior cues. Men miss about half of them because they generally aren't looking, aren't listening, and might not detect anything if they were.

The apostle Peter was a married man and knew exactly what he was writing about: **"Husbands, in the same way be considerate as you live with your wives, and treat them with respect as the weaker partner and as heirs with you of the gracious gift of life, so that nothing will hinder your prayers"** (1 Peter 3:7). *Considerate* means "Pay attention!" Literally the original Greek says, "Live with her *according to knowledge*."

Good leaders adapt to their surroundings. Husbands, don't insist that your wife adapt her communication style to you. Study her. Learn her language, verbal and nonverbal. There is a marvelous benefit in letting your wife train you in female communication. You will understand the other 50 percent of the human race a lot better. Pay attention!

There's more—if she feels that you are listening and responding to her messages, you will find that your needs and wishes and wants have a much greater likelihood of being attended to.

I am only a servant

Pastor Mark Jeske

Letter writers in the ancient world preferred to sign their letters at the beginning. This is not so strange—today we look to the end of a letter or to the return address to know the writer's identity. What is surprising, though, is how James identifies himself. Although he is the (half) brother of Jesus Christ himself, he prefers humbly to call himself Jesus' *servant* (or even *slave*): **"James, a servant of God and of the Lord Jesus Christ, to the twelve tribes scattered among the nations: Greetings"** (James 1:1). Perhaps he was painfully aware of his early disbelief in Jesus' true identity and the rejection of his messianic claims.

James provides no other information on his identity. He probably thought this unnecessary, since by the mid-40s A.D. he would have been very famous as one of the leaders of the mother church in Jerusalem.

James mentions his Savior's name only twice, here and in chapter 2, verse 1. But that mighty, glorious name throws a long shadow over the entire letter. James is going to assume that his readers know the great works of their salvation—in chapter 2 he calls Jesus "our glorious Lord." Everything he writes really concerns the believer's faith response to God's forgiving love in Christ. And so his word "Greetings" in verse 1, which literally means "Rejoice!" sets the context for all that follows. This was also Jesus' first word to Salome, Johanna, and Mary on Easter morning (Matthew 28:9).

And it's his word to you too.

___

___

___

The long runway

Jason Nelson

The albatross runs along the surface of the ocean to take flight. Once airborne, it can soar gracefully, but getting there is a long, noisy, awkward procession. Some birds can explode upward in a heartbeat. Not the poor albatross.

In the Sermon on the Mount (Matthew 5–7), Jesus covered a lot of ground, including going the extra mile. **"If someone forces you to go one mile, go with him two miles"**(Matthew 5:41). He was addressing situations where we are pressed into service longer than we would like. That can happen to parents who had a target date for kicking their kids out of the nest. More young people need a longer runway to take off. The mile markers for growing up come and go: 16, 18, 21, . . . 26! There is still no wind beneath their wings; just Mom and Dad pushing them toward independence and covering their expenses.

We set deadlines for them to finish school, get a job, and be responsible. Each time we really mean it, but something happens and we reluctantly grant an extension. We never expected faith, hope, and charity to be tested so close to home. It is a dilemma to parent young adults who have legal autonomy but still can't take care of themselves. It's hard to accept that they see a more distant horizon. But as long as they stay out of the ditches and on the runway, we need to hang in there with them.

____

____

____

____

____

Dancing for Baal

Diana Kerr

The story in 1 Kings 18 almost makes me feel bad for the prophets of Baal. In this epic showdown of Elijah versus Baal worshipers, a bunch of hopeless men strive *desperately* to elicit a response from their fake god.

In an attempt to call on Baal to prove his existence and light an altar on fire, these prophets make total fools of themselves. They dance around the altar, shout loudly, and even cut their bodies to get what they want from Baal.

They get nothing in return. **"But there was no response, no one answered, no one paid attention"** (1 Kings 18:29). It's hard to read this account and not think, "Duh. What a joke. I could have predicted that. That's what they get."

And yet a glance in the mirror shows me dancing and shouting like a lunatic for my own "Baals." I may be "smart" enough not to bow down to a chunk of stone or wood, but I bow down to other things. I dance for my own Baals—praise, success, perfection, reputation, and love. When my striving isn't enough, I strive harder, craving validation and fulfillment through them. But none of those gods give me what only God can give.

I like Elijah's approach a lot better: a simple word and God answers. A single sentence and God provides. The dancing and shouting for Baals will tire you out and get you nowhere. The real God doesn't require a song and dance.

____

____

____

____

____

What are your most valuable assets?

Pastor Mark Jeske

Business owners know the importance of conducting regular inventories of their products and equipment. Financial officers know the value of conducting regular audits to verify their company's true financial position. Have you ever done a personal inventory? What are your most valuable personal assets?

What is dearest to your heart? Your new car? Your financial portfolio? Your home? Your position at the company? Your reputation in the community? Here is another of Jesus' paradoxes: **"Whoever finds his life will lose it, and whoever loses his life for my sake will find it"** (Matthew 10:39). Every tangible thing in your life will be taken from you sooner or later. Your money, clothes, home, and ride will not pass the grave or judgment day. If that's where your heart is, you will lose all.

On the other hand, certain intangible things are truly eternal and you can take them with you. These things include your relationship with your Savior Jesus and your fellow believers. The Bible promises you that if you seek God's kingdom and God's righteousness, all the other things will be added in as a bonus. But without faith in Christ, you will end up with nothing.

Losing your life for Jesus' sake doesn't mean being recklessly dangerous or suicidal. It does mean that we see our heavenly home as ultimately more valuable than our temporary camping places in this life. It also means that the Christian martyrs who lost their lives because of their faith did not lose everything. In fact, they gained everything.

Spirit gusher

Pastor Mark Jeske

It's not as though the Son of God made his first appearance on earth when he was born in Bethlehem. The Old Testament tells us of various appearances of the "angel of the LORD" who spoke and acted like the second person of the Trinity. And it's not as though the Holy Spirit had to wait until Pentecost to make his grand entrance. The Old Testament is full of references to the "Spirit of the Lord."

But here's what changed 50 days (in Greek *pentekostos* means "50th") after Easter: Jesus more than compensated his apostles for his absence by not only sending but *outpouring* a gusher of the Spirit upon the believers. Jesus told his nervous disciples a few hours before his arrest: **"I will ask the Father, and he will give you another Counselor to be with you forever—the Spirit of truth. The world cannot accept him, because it neither sees him nor knows him. But you know him, for he lives with you and will be in you"** (John 14:16,17).

You may think that on Sundays you *go* to church. What a concept that in fact you *are* the church! Yes! Seriously! The Holy Spirit, the third person of the Trinity, actually lives within you, creating and nourishing the faith you need through the Word, changing your life to be more Christ-like, maturing your understanding, and tuning you up to be all that he has created you to be.

The gospel's parallel

Pastor Mark Jeske

If Satan cannot keep you from becoming a believer, his next line of attack will be to get you to become enamored of the rules and laws of God. With some flattery and lies he will try to make a good Pharisee out of you, careful about rituals, superficial in Bible knowledge, presenting a facade of religiosity to the world, and contemptuous of others farther down the spiritual ladder.

The gospel message of God's love for you has a parallel, a twin teaching. Here is God's plan for you—that you would treat other people with the same kindness, mercy, patience, and love that he has for you. You were loved to be a lover of people. You were forgiven so that you would become a forgiver of others. He was generous with you so that you would find the joy of being generous. **"Above all, love each other deeply, because love covers over a multitude of sins"** (1 Peter 4:8).

Law-driven Christians find a sad satisfaction in using the Bible to play "Gotcha!" with one another. It's not hard to find fault with people, to criticize and beat them down either for their inadequate doctrinal formulations or moral mistakes. God knows what dopes we can all be.

It takes someone who has internalized the gospel deep down to find joy in helping to make people look and feel good, to let their broken past history stay under the cover of charity and instead build them up to be useful to God today.

Know your enemy

Pastor Mark Jeske

There are many differences between the warfare our troops engage in today and the battles fought by our grandparents. For instance, WWII combatants wore uniforms. You knew who the enemy was. Today warfare in the Middle East and Afghanistan is asymmetrical; that is, the enemy is in civilian clothes and blends in with the civilian population.

You have an enemy from hell who is far more dangerous than any guerrilla fighter planting IEDs by the side of the road. Whether you like it or not, you are going up against Satan. St. John was allowed to see how ugly and dangerous Satan really is: **"Then another sign appeared in heaven: an enormous red dragon with seven heads and ten horns and seven crowns on his heads. His tail swept a third of the stars out of the sky and flung them to the earth"** (Revelation 12:3,4).

The point of that dreadful vision: the horns represent Satan's immense power, the crowns his claim to be king and lord of the earth, and the tail the cunning he exhibited in seducing one-third of the angels of heaven to follow him into his rebellion against God. Those angels are no longer the kindly servants and protectors God created; they are now demons who enjoy tormenting you.

Satan is a dragon who hates you, belching malevolent blasts of rage against God and threats toward you. Now you know.

Study your enemy

Pastor Mark Jeske

Pro football teams take their week of practice very seriously. Their scouts and analysts always work ahead in order to provide up-to-date information on their next opponent. They scour statistics to develop their strategy; they watch game film so that they will know how their opponent operates; they have the reserves run their opponent's plays all week.

You need to study your enemy as well. Satan masquerades as an angel of light. In some ways it would be a lot easier to detect him if he and his demons still possessed people on the scale they did at Jesus' time. Everyone then could see that the devil was a monster. But he's back to his sly and subtle ways, talking with the same friendly, silky inner voice that first seduced Eve to commit spiritual suicide.

Study your enemy! Take him seriously! **"Be self-controlled and alert. Your enemy the devil prowls around like a roaring lion looking for someone to devour. Resist him, standing firm in the faith"** (1 Peter 5:8,9). If you know your Bible, you will know his lies when you hear them. If God's Word is a light for your path, you will know when you are on the wrong road. If you know your Bible, you will be able to tell who are your real friends and who are the destroyers.

If you know your Bible, you will recognize the voice of Jesus, your Good Shepherd, whose protection will keep you safe from Satan.

____

____

____

____

Respect your enemy

Pastor Mark Jeske

People so badly want heaven on earth. In the decades before the Civil War, idealist dreamers who wanted to perfect humanity established dozens of "utopian" communities all over the American Midwest. Robert Owen, for example, founded New Harmony, Indiana, to build "a New Moral World of happiness, enlightenment, and prosperity through education, science, technology, and communal living." His utopia lasted only a couple of years. New Harmony and the others all broke down for the same reason—you can't perfect sinners. Satan keeps coming after us.

Respect your enemy. He is relentless. He is also mortally wounded and enraged by Christ's victory on Calvary. St. John heard the voice of an angelic messenger with grim news for us all: **"Woe to the earth and the sea, because the devil has gone down to you! He is filled with fury, because he knows that his time is short"** (Revelation 12:12).

Satan could not defeat God and was thrown out of heaven. Satan could not defeat Christ and could not prevent the resurrection and triumphant ascension of the Savior. All that is left to him is to attack God's children, hoping to drag as many of us into hell with him as he can.

Respect your enemy. He cannot overpower you by force, but he can try to persuade you to commit spiritual suicide. He cannot rip you out of Jesus' arms, but he will try to persuade you to jump. Soon Jesus will come for us. In the meantime, hang on!

Overcome your enemy

Pastor Mark Jeske

On the face of it, there could hardly be a more absurd concept than you and I taking on the devil and overcoming him. He is ageless and knows all the tricks. He is formidable, able to counterfeit the very miracles of God. He is invisible and flies everywhere around the world. He has access to our minds and can whisper his lies to us all. How could you have a chance against this foe?

By yourself, zero chance. With Christ, 100 percent success. Your faith in Christ makes you one with your Savior. **"They overcame him by the blood of the Lamb and by the word of their testimony"** (Revelation 12:11). You were there being tried with Christ. You were crucified with him. You were buried and then rose again with him. Christ's victory over Satan is yours too! You overcome Satan by the blood of the Lamb of God who takes away the sin of the world.

You overcome him also by the word of your testimony. Satan's schemes collapse when confronted with the gospel. As Luther wrote in his hymn "A Mighty Fortress Is Our God," "One little word can fell him." St. James tells us that we can indeed resist the devil and he will flee from us. Never believe the devil's trash—you are God's beautiful design. You are loved from all eternity. You are forgiven fully through Christ. Satan is going to be shackled in hell forever, and you are on your way to Paradise.

Take that, Satan! You lose!

Outwardly dying, inwardly renewed

Diana Kerr

Here's a cheery thought for you: you're dying.

Whether you like to admit it or not, whether you think about it or not, whether you're 23 or 93, you're aging and therefore dying. Every tick of the clock brings you closer to the end of life.

Some of you are probably hyperaware of this reality. You have wrinkles and aches and pains that remind you of this truth all too often. You watch your strength, energy, and eyesight fade; and it's worrisome. Often, it's downright frustrating. If you're not quite elderly but struggle with some sort of illness, you're probably wise to this feeling as well.

If your imminent death wasn't a passing thought for you previously, maybe I've got you thinking about it now. Maybe you're suddenly reminded that you *have* slowed down a bit lately. Don't lose heart. Don't freak out. There's hope for all of us, whether your concerns are those subtly emerging crow's-feet or perhaps something more serious like your pesky dependence on a walker. *You don't need a vibrant body to have a vibrant soul.* **"Therefore we do not lose heart. Though outwardly we are wasting away, yet inwardly we are being renewed day by day"** (2 Corinthians 4:16).

God may not miraculously restore your health, but he's not going to let you flounder. He knows a secret, and he wants you to know it too: a strong spirit—a strong faith and a strong prayer life—is the ticket to the best life.

Really good excuses

Pastor Mark Jeske

There is a popular stereotype of Jesus as a first-century Mr. Rogers—always walking slowly, always talking softly with a pleasant smile, always asking questions about how certain topics make you feel. If you do any reading in the four gospels, i.e., his authorized biographies, you will notice right away that Jesus had a tart tongue. He did not hesitate to smack his disciples when they disappointed him with their small faith or lack of understanding, and he was merciless in skewering hypocritical "church people" of his era.

On one occasion he invited various people to follow him. He got one excuse after another, and here's the thing—the excuses all sounded reasonably plausible. Like: **"Another disciple said to him, 'Lord, first let me go and bury my father.' But Jesus told him, 'Follow me, and let the dead bury their dead'"** (Matthew 8:21,22). Does Jesus sound just a little crabby to you? Would he pull you away from your own father's funeral? Did he not himself show great compassion for the bereaved?

Here's the point: That funeral and all the lengthy estate legal problems and arrangements would effectively keep the man busy for weeks and months. He would never experience the incredible adventure of accompanying the Son of God for personal teaching and mentoring.

Do you have really good excuses that keep you from significant leadership or service to God's kingdom? from leading that Bible study? going on that marriage retreat? filling that board of directors' seat?

June

"GO AND MAKE DISCIPLES OF ALL NATIONS, BAPTIZING THEM IN THE NAME OF THE FATHER AND OF THE SON AND OF THE HOLY SPIRIT."
MATTHEW 28:19

June 1

The thrill is gone

Pastor Mark Jeske

Taste is fickle. You love a certain musical group, but then their appeal fades and you never listen to another one of their songs again. You love a certain restaurant but then lose interest. You go crazy with paintballing or snowboarding or salsa dancing but then drift away.

People drift away from God too. When you are caught up in a spiritual love affair, at first God's words and ways seem exciting and compelling. You love going to church, love reading your Bible, love praying, and love serving with other Christians. But life happens. You get distracted. You find other passions. You feel disappointed and unfulfilled. The thrill is gone.

It suddenly dawns on you that you are playing Russian roulette with your eternity. Whoa—I could be flirting with hell! What happened to me? Where did my original love go? At times like that, let a repentant sinner named David give you words: **"Restore to me the *joy* of your salvation and grant me a *willing* spirit, to sustain me"** (Psalm 51:12).

How do you get the joy back? Joy comes from worship. Take inventory of the blessings in your life and give glory to God. Joy comes from serving others. Find pleasure in being part of a service project bigger than you. Joy comes from generosity. Whose life have you made better today? How can you be a broker of God's mercy to somebody who really needs it?

____

____

____

____

Supply chain

Jason Nelson

In 1949 Aldo Leopold wrote, "There are two spiritual dangers in not owning a farm. One is the danger of supposing that breakfast comes from the grocery, and the other that heat comes from the furnace" (*A Sand County Almanac*). A third would be that cash comes from the ATM. Taking the necessities of life for granted is dangerous. To mitigate the danger, Leopold urged people to plant a garden and split a little wood.

The ache of hard work points us up the supply chain. Solomon asked, **"What does the worker gain from his toil?"** (Ecclesiastes 3:9). Along with everything else, we derive an ethic that **"every good and perfect gift is from above, coming down from the Father of the heavenly lights"** (James 1:17). It is a sacred paradox. Self-sufficiency exposes the intricacies of our dependence on God.

Every productive person knows how quickly it all can go bad. Nothing worthwhile comes easy. There are many disruptions we can't see coming. Geopolitical crises, a malicious hacker, droughts, fires, storms, and worn-out equipment threaten to wipe us out. How will we eat and stay warm then? The weak links are tempted to cash it in. Problem solvers stay at it. They roll up their sleeves and go to work. They know all equity is sweat equity. Innovation and effort will be rewarded from above. It is a heritage, a habit, and a theology. Hardworking people give God credit for what they have.

Great expectations

Diana Kerr

It's almost comical how perceptive women are to their husband's flaws. "You really shouldn't eat that. You're getting a beer belly, and you haven't worked out in weeks." A patient husband might accept the nagging, while another might not be afraid to point out that his wife isn't exactly the same size she was on their wedding day either.

It's too bad we're so good at holding others to higher standards than our own. We expect better behavior from spouses, children, siblings, coworkers, friends, and pastors than we expect of ourselves. When they don't live up to our expectations, we sometimes even call them out.

We're not the only ones suffering from this hypocrisy disease. After King David killed off his mistress' husband, the prophet Nathan visited him and told him a story. The fictional story was of a wealthy man who killed another man's only lamb. David failed to see that the story referred to him, and his response was all too familiar to our own in this type of situation: **"David burned with anger against the man and said to Nathan, 'As surely as the LORD lives, the man who did this deserves to die! He must pay for that lamb four times over, because he did such a thing and had no pity'"** (2 Samuel 12:5,6). Ouch. Wrong answer, David.

Thanks to Nathan, David eventually learned his lesson, and it's a lesson for us too: don't set the bar so high for others when you can't even make it over the bar yourself.

But he's a nice boy!

Pastor Mark Jeske

One of the most curious ironies of Jesus' ministry is that the "nice people," the "church people," the "respectable people" mostly had no use for him. Jesus' teachings resonated much more deeply with the outcasts and fringe dwellers and pariahs, the tax collectors and prostitutes. Here's the reason: the good news of the coming of the Savior is nothing special if you don't think you need one.

Ever heard this in your home? "Mom, Alex is such a nice boy, but he doesn't believe in Jesus. Why can't he go to heaven?" The fact that some people can set up a veneer of respectability does not negate the rottenness within every human heart. The Holy Spirit gave St. Paul this painful but helpful insight: **"There is no one righteous, not even one; there is no one who understands, no one who seeks God. All have turned away"** (Romans 3:10-12).

The tax collectors and lowlifes at Jesus' time knew that. They were astounded to hear of a merciful God who cared even for them.

Alex and the other Pharisees, past and present, feel that they are good enough. On the Last Day, they will have their facade peeled away and will join the rest of the sinners under God's condemnation. In the meantime, until that dreadful day arrives, it's not too late for them to repent and claim Jesus' forgiveness.

Remember: Paul was once a Pharisee too.

She's only sleeping

Pastor Mark Jeske

Parents are not supposed to outlive their children. Parents know that they are supposed to be the defenders and protectors of their kids, and when a child is seriously ill and then dies on their watch, it is a crushing blow.

Jairus was the president of his local synagogue, and his sixth-grade daughter became seriously ill and died. By the time he was able to get Jesus to come to visit, the house was full of people trying to distract the grieving family. **"When Jesus entered the ruler's house and saw the flute players and the noisy crowd, he said, 'Go away. The girl is not dead but asleep.' But they laughed at him"** (Matthew 9:23,24).

Music and musicians and lively parties are wonderful, but this was the wrong time, and a room with a 12-year-old corpse was the wrong place. Jesus pronounced the only words that could give comfort at a time such as this. He told the family not to worry because their daughter was only taking a nap.

These are words for you to use when you need them. The most powerful message to share with any bereaved family is the gospel promise of resurrection to eternal life through Jesus. When Jesus took the dead girl's hand and lifted her back into life, he gave a demonstration of what he will do for all believers on the Great Day. Our cemetery is only a dormitory.

Follow your "please" with a "thank-you"

Diana Kerr

Those silly lepers. We read Luke's account of Jesus healing ten men with leprosy and think, "I'd never be like that. *I'd* be the one who came back to thank him."

I thought this myself until God brought *me* major healing from a crippling chronic illness. For years I prayed for relief and promised God I wouldn't forget him if he spared me from the pain. When the day arrived that I was officially free from medication, I praised and praised God. I vowed I'd never stop. I'm sorry to say my gratitude for that incident has since become a little lackluster.

It's natural to quickly shift our energy from gratitude back to asking. God gives us something wonderful, but we focus instead on the *long* list of other things we still want from him.

Luke 17:17,18 might make us cringe: **"Jesus asked, 'Were not all ten cleansed? Where are the other nine? Was no one found to return and give praise to God except this foreigner?'"**

God loves to shower you with blessings, but he's not immune from the pain your lack of gratitude brings him. It's like a father completing a tree house for his son, who never stops to thank his dad and climbs right up to play, ignoring dad until he realizes he needs him to build a tree swing too.

When God answers your prayers and blesses you, don't immediately move on to the next want on your wish list. Don't let your "pleases" outweigh your "thanks."

What does "prodigal" mean?

Pastor Mark Jeske

"The younger son got together all he had, set off for a distant country and there squandered his wealth in wild living" (Luke 15:13).

Hey, if you think a father giving his son his inheritance in cash while still alive is unbelievable, this verse about the prodigal sounds totally real. In fact, it sounds like a reality TV show. If the kid actually did manage to get his hands on the cash, of course he'd live like a pig. Hardly anybody respects unearned money. In today's world the money would disappear up his nose or at blackjack tables, or he'd be fleeced by professional female entertainers. Money always seems to attract a crowd.

"After he had spent everything, there was a severe famine in that whole country, and he began to be in need. So he went and hired himself out to a citizen of that country, who sent him to his fields to feed pigs. He longed to fill his stomach with the pods that the pigs were eating, but no one gave him anything" (Luke 15:14-16).

Sin always ends badly. The devil does indeed own the short term, and he can provide a blast of excitement up front. But it's all hollow; soon the brokenness and depression roll in. And isn't it amazing how fast your "friends" evaporate when your cash is gone?

Do you know anybody whose life sounds like this? Have you had "prodigal" stretches in your life?

____

____

____

____

Restoration

Pastor Mark Jeske

The prodigal was hoping for a meal and maybe a shower. He got an embrace and tears from his father. But wait—it gets even better. He gets full restoration to his former place in the family.

"The father said to his servants, 'Quick! Bring the best robe and put it on him. Put a ring on his finger and sandals on his feet. Bring the fattened calf and kill it. Let's have a feast and celebrate. For this son of mine was dead and is alive again; he was lost and is found.' So they began to celebrate" (Luke 15:22-24).

The father takes the same risks as before. He risks that his generosity will be abused and squandered again. He chooses to trust his repentant son and prays that he will grow up spiritually.

The reason this sounds so outrageously wonderful is that it's not how we would act. When we forgive each other, there's some begrudging. We read the riot act first. There are conditions. There is hesitation. There is hedging. We hold back. We give warnings.

Let's dedicate ourselves as individuals and in Christian groups to representing the Father as Jesus wishes: a heart aching for repentance in his wayward children, a heart leaping with joy when they turn, a heart brimming with generosity when they're back.

Which animal are you?

Pastor Mark Jeske

It's a popular online game to quiz people, If your life were this or that TV show, which character would you be? And to Harry Potter fans, which house in Hogwarts would you be assigned to and why? Or, if you were an animal, which would you be?

Jesus actually played that game in a way. He offered two animal models to aspire to—and once again, infuriatingly enough, they are opposites. More paradox from the Teacher: **"Be as shrewd as snakes and as innocent as doves"** (Matthew 10:16). What could he possibly have meant by that?

Jesus' point: At different times you will need to present two different faces to your world. When you are threatened financially or legally or physically, be sharp and shrewd. Evaluate risks and work out emergency plans. Watch carefully what's going on and be very cautious whom you choose to trust. Expect hustlers and chiselers to be lying in wait for you. Expect manipulation and betrayal, not because Jesus wants gloomy pessimists on his team, but because he needs realists.

At other times present a trusting, soft, and open persona. When wounded people are looking for sympathy and healing, when guilty fools are hoping for a second chance, when the broken ones are looking for hugs and acceptance, it's time for your dove behaviors. You can be Jesus' welcoming arms to the victims of the evil one.

Okay, snakes *and* doves. Now, Lord—help us to know which animal to be when.

Don't go easy on me

Diana Kerr

My grade school basketball coach had a tendency to make girls cry, but he was my favorite. I admired him because he never spared me from truth or pain.

Countless times when he brought me out of a game, he sat me on the bench right next to him and yelled at me. If we played a sloppy game, he'd make us run extra drills in practice. Some of my teammates preferred the kind of coach who'd go easy on you, but I knew my coach's actions showed that he cared deeply about his athletes. He molded me into a far better player as a result.

I forget this lesson sometimes when it comes to receiving discipline from the ultimate Coach, the Good Shepherd. I want the Good Shepherd to use his staff to rescue and encourage me, but I don't always want a whack from the rod to show me I'm out of line. King David reminds me that the staff and rod are both a blessing: **"Your rod and your staff, they comfort me"** (Psalm 23:4). If anyone understood the value of being reined in by God's rod, it was David. He longed for both the rod and staff to keep him safe. Without them, David knew he'd stray from God.

The next time the Good Shepherd uses a situation to give you a whack, thank him for keeping you in line and close to him. Your heavenly Coach loves you too much to go easy on you.

____

____

____

____

____

Reach for a psalm

Jason Nelson

When you're in the mood to praise the Lord and would like to be poetic about it, reach for a psalm. **"My heart is stirred by a noble theme as I recite my verses for the king; my tongue is the pen of a skillful writer"** (Psalm 45:1).

When you're at a table full of food and know it's all a gift from him, reach for a psalm. **"Give thanks to the LORD, for he is good. His love endures forever"** (136:1).

When the diagnosis is serious but the prognosis is good, reach for a psalm. **"Therefore my heart is glad and my tongue rejoices; my body also will rest secure"** (16:9).

When a hard week ends and you will worship with friends, reach for a psalm. **"I rejoiced with those who said to me, 'Let us go to the house of the LORD'"** (122:1).

When you want to raise a holy ruckus, reach for a psalm. **"Praise him with the sounding of the trumpet . . . praise him with resounding cymbals"** (150:3-5).

When only some flash and boom will do, reach for a psalm. **"Your thunder was heard in the whirlwind, your lightning lit up the world; the earth trembled and quaked"** (77:18).

When you need a little quiet time with him, reach for a psalm. **"Be still, and know that I am God"** (46:10).

When you're in the mood to praise the Lord your God, reach for a psalm.

I'm different

Pastor Mark Jeske

King Saul was at war with the Philistines. It went badly, and he and three of his sons were killed in battle. His grandson's nanny prepared to flee in terror with the little boy, expecting to be overrun at any moment. In her haste, she changed his life forever: **"Jonathan son of Saul had a son who was lame in both feet. He was five years old when the news about Saul and Jonathan came from Jezreel. His nurse picked him up and fled, but as she hurried to leave, he fell and became crippled. His name was Mephibosheth"** (2 Samuel 4:4).

They got away, but the little princeling was disabled for the rest of his life. Now he was different from everyone else, and because of his reduced mobility he was dependent on other people to survive. How frustrating it is to stick out like that, not to be able to do all the things that other people do.

Are there people in your family who feel significantly different from other people? Do you feel that way? Our Christian faith brings unique power to help people cope with disability. First, we share Christ's message of unconditional love, that all people, not only the beautiful and athletic and perfect, have great worth before God. Second, all people have unique and important gifts to bring to God's kingdom. Third and best of all, the Great Resurrection will not only bring all believers to eternal life but will bring complete restoration of our mortal bodies.

All God's children matter!

Good for business: Tell the truth

Pastor Mark Jeske

Just as some people believe there should be a separation of church and state, others believe that church and business are equally incompatible. I would like to take the contrarian view. I think our Christian faith is good for business. I think Christians make the best bosses, Christians make the best workers, and Christian values make the best company philosophy.

One reason: because we know that the devil is a liar and the father of lies. God wants us to tell the truth at home, at school, and at work: **"Keep your tongue from evil and your lips from speaking lies"** (Psalm 34:13). Lying to the IRS or SEC or OSHA will catch up with you eventually. Your company's brand is a priceless asset—it represents the promises that you say you will keep.

Salespeople will build better relationships with customers when they won't lie about their products and services to make a quick sale. Telling the truth consistently will build a reputation that people come to trust. There's an old sales slogan that it is better to have one customer one hundred times than one hundred customers once. I think God would agree.

Executives need their reports to tell them the truth about how the business is really doing, not hide inconvenient bad news. Shareholders depend on financial information that is accurate, not doctored. Companies that don't punish whistle-blowers will be healthier than those where employees are afraid of reprisals if they speak up.

Good for business: Serve your customers

Pastor Mark Jeske

It is one of the paradoxes of the Christian faith that our Savior Jesus, divine and all-powerful from eternity, came to this earth as a humble human being. He came not to be served but to serve and to give his life as a ransom for us all. He demonstrated true leadership to his disciples on the night before he died by kneeling and washing their feet. He invited them to find satisfaction in that posture as they in turn served others. They discovered that he was right—joy comes from acting like Jesus.

A serving mentality is good for business. Customers will come back to a company that makes them feel important, listens to them carefully, takes their needs seriously, keeps its promises, admits and fixes its mistakes, and works hard to earn their trust and confidence. Among all his other daily activities, God watches business transactions carefully to see how we treat other people. **"Shall I acquit a man with dishonest scales, with a bag of false weights?"** (Micah 6:11).

If our Christian faith informs our sales practices, we would no more rip off a customer than our own mothers. Our company won't try to sell people things they don't need, won't take advantage of unsophisticated buyers, won't push damaged or flawed goods, and won't bait and switch. Our company's goal will be to make our customers' lives better.

We succeed when they succeed.

Good for business: Work hard

Pastor Mark Jeske

My grandparents had a sign on their kitchen wall for years. It read, "I like work. It fascinates me. I could sit and look at it for hours." The sign was a joke—they both came from immigrant stock and were hard workers all their lives. But it expresses the inner longing of the lazy sinner in each of us.

God made us to work. He himself labored mightily to create our beautiful world, and he works every minute of every day sustaining the working of stars and planets, rainfall and evaporation, seeds and fertility, gravity and friction. His first words to his first man, Adam, were instructions to carry out an inventory of the Garden of Eden.

The Christian faith is good for business because it teaches a powerful work ethic: **"We hear that some among you are idle. They are not busy; they are busybodies. Such people we command and urge in the Lord Jesus Christ to settle down and earn the bread they eat"** (2 Thessalonians 3:11,12). A company that has a culture where work is disrespected and avoided wherever possible will not last long.

A successful company has leaders who are not afraid of long hours and intense effort, who work hard to improve their products and services, stay lean and efficient, recruit and promote the best possible talent, and inspire their workers to produce the best possible quality.

Am I describing your company?

____

____

____

____

____

Good for business: Care about employees

Pastor Mark Jeske

Think back to some of the places where you have worked in your career. Isn't it true that the jobs you liked the best had management that treated you fairly? How are you being treated in the job you have now? The Christian faith is good for business because it encourages bosses to care for their employees, not tyrannize them, manipulate them, take advantage of them, cheat them, put their health at risk, or lie to them.

God watches how employers treat their employees, and he rewards or withholds blessings depending on what he sees: **"Now listen, you rich people, weep and wail because of the misery that is coming upon you. . . . You have hoarded wealth in the last days. Look! The wages you failed to pay the workmen who mowed your fields are crying out against you. The cries of the harvesters have reached the ears of the Lord Almighty"** (James 5:1-4).

Throughout human history the wealthy and powerful have often expanded their wealth and power at the expense of others lower in the food chain. Healthy companies have bosses who listen to what their employees tell them, show appreciation for hard work and improved skills, make employees feel valued and human, show flexibility in times of personal need or emergency, and do not chisel their workers out of their agreed-upon wages and benefits.

The last thing a business needs is to have the anger of the Lord God resting upon it.

Good for business: Respect your boss

Pastor Mark Jeske

Do you like your current boss? Do you respect him or her?

The Christian faith is good for business because it values order and authority. God is a God of order and hates chaos. He has built divine authority into family and government to provide a valuable structure for everyday living that provides safety and security.

He also values order in economic enterprises: **"Teach slaves to be subject to their masters in everything, to try to please them, not to talk back to them, and not to steal from them, but to show that they can be fully trusted, so that in every way they will make the teaching about God our Savior attractive"** (Titus 2:9,10). Slavery in the Americas was brutal and repulsive. Slavery in the Roman world in biblical times was much milder and was practiced everywhere. Many, many early Christians were slaves. This passage does not endorse slavery; it merely recognized an immense reality and gave practical advice on how to navigate a world where people are subject to the will of others.

What Paul wrote about servants back then applies to all *employees* today. Our Christian faith inspires us as employees to let our bosses dictate our daily agenda. They get to tell us what to do, and we try to please them, show them respect, show them honesty and integrity, and win their trust.

An added bonus from God—not only will those values improve the company, but they also make God look good too.

All the instruction we need

Diana Kerr

Raise your hand if you've ever wished the Bible offered you more specific instruction or advice. (My hand is raised.) Wouldn't it be nice to have a burning bush in your front yard from which God would speak to you with a booming voice whenever you had a difficult decision to make? "Don't take the new job offer." "Let your sister's family move in with you." "Stay away from that overly friendly woman at work—you're married and she wants to be more than friends."

The truth is that God gives us plenty of instruction, but we often fail to follow it. Right after Moses gave the people of Israel the Ten Commandments in the Old Testament, he gave them this crowning piece of advice: follow these commands if you know what's best for you. **"Be careful to do what the LORD your God has commanded you; do not turn aside to the right or to the left. Walk in all the way that the LORD your God has commanded you, so that you may live and prosper and prolong your days in the land that you will possess"** (Deuteronomy 5:32,33).

We long for more pointed recommendations from God, but so rarely do we heed the instructions he *does* give us. A lot of our problems or decisions would be nonissues if we simply did what God commanded and walked in obedience.

The best part? His commands are not to punish you. He gives them to you **"so that you may live and prosper."**

June 19

Suffering is joy. What!?

Pastor Mark Jeske

During his public ministry, Jesus often seized people's attention with provocative, seemingly contradictory statements: "The last shall be first," he said. "Blessed are those who weep." James begins his letter in the same way by inviting believers to think of the painful trials and testing in their lives as *positive* experiences: **"Consider it pure joy, my brothers, whenever you face trials of many kinds, because you know that the testing of your faith develops perseverance. Perseverance must finish its work so that you may be mature and complete, not lacking anything"** (James 1:2-4).

How is a thought so outrageous even possible? Well, in two ways. First, experiencing suffering and trials matures us. Our faith grows up when we have to sweat, be frustrated, wait, and persevere, just as our muscles need regular workouts to grow strong. Unused muscles stay weak and atrophy. Everyone knows this saying: no pain, no gain. Our faith gets tougher when it feels resistance *and overcomes.*

Second, trouble can be good when it drives us to our knees to ask God for help. Our faith grows when we learn that God gives generously to all. It is arrogant to think that we are completely self-sufficient. As Paul said, "When I am weak, then I am strong, for his strength is made perfect in my weakness." Suffering can be joy when we see God working great things around us.

Praying isn't begging. It is accepting God's invitation to be more of a partner in your life.

___

___

___

Whose poor are they?

Jason Nelson

My town has one homeless man named Gene. You would recognize him if you saw him. The entire town is keeping him alive. He kills time by walking the street, and no one hassles him. He uses the bathroom in the bank. He has survived bitter cold by spending nights in the post office lobby. Good Samaritans have taken him for breakfast. People give him a buck or two because he still drinks his lunch out of a brown paper bag. Gene may have brought this on himself, but there isn't a lot of judging going on. The people of this town know we usually bring it on ourselves.

Jesus once said, **"The poor you will always have with you"** (Matthew 26:11). He wasn't being dismissive. He was stating a fact. A review of his other comments reveals he assumed his disciples were already helping the poor.

No one is debating that poverty is a problem. More people are falling into it. But whose poor are they? Should public policy provide a safety net? Will the private sector let wealth trickle down to them? Can charitable organizations meet their needs until they get on their feet?

It's a tough call. Jesus made it tougher when he said, **"If you want to be perfect, go, sell your possessions and give to the poor, and you will have treasure in heaven. Then come, follow me"** (Matthew 19:21).

Whose poor are they? They are ours.

My brother needs to know

Pastor Mark Jeske

Evangelism, i.e., telling other people the story of God's rescue plan for the human race, is not just a church program or something that happens through Christian mass media. In its commonest and perhaps most powerful form, it is one family member telling another.

A Galilean fisherman named Andrew had a deep spiritual side and had been listening to John the Baptist speaking. When he met Jesus, the object and focus of John's messages, he knew immediately that there was someone in his life who needed to know these things: **"Andrew, Simon Peter's brother, was one of the two who heard what John had said and who had followed Jesus. The first thing Andrew did was to find his brother Simon and tell him, 'We have found the Messiah' (that is, the Christ). And he brought him to Jesus"** (John 1:40-42).

In their extended families, individual believers today have many, many "Simons," people who just need to meet Jesus to fall in love with him. Think right now—are there people in your family whom you suspect might not be saved if judgment day were today? Who is your Simon? Write the name down. Look at it often. Pray for him or her. Figure out a way how you might invite that person to meet the One who loves us unconditionally, died and rose for us, and will intercede for us on the Last Day.

You can't believe for them. But you can tell them.

____

____

____

____

June 22

Fusion

Pastor Mark Jeske

There are many unions in Communion.

There is a breathtaking mystical union between you and Christ as you receive him in the Sacrament. There is a wonderful bond between you and your fellow communicants. The Bible says that all together we are "one loaf of bread," as it were. And then there is the union between the bits of bread and Christ's own body, between the wine and the blood of our Savior.

"Is not the cup of thanksgiving for which we give thanks a *participation* in the blood of Christ? And is not the bread that we break a *participation* in the body of Christ?" (1 Corinthians 10:16). The original Greek word translated as "participation" in this passage has the idea of "fellowship" or "communion," that is, there is a fusion or welding of these two things together.

So every time you eat the bread of Communion, you are indeed eating bread, but you are *also* receiving the very body of Christ—yes, the same body whose hands and feet were pierced with Calvary's nails. Every time you drink the cup of Communion, you are drinking some wine, but you are *also* receiving the very lifeblood of Christ, the sacrificial payment for your many sins. A court physician named Samuel Kinner put that divine mystery this way in 1638: *"I leave to you how this can be; Your Word alone suffices me."*

Me too, Jesus.

____

____

____

____

The politics of waving

Jason Nelson

I walk a lot on a country road, so I do a lot of waving at passersby. Everyone waves back, but not in the same way. Some nonchalantly lift their hands. Others wave enthusiastically. A few folks are hesitant, like they aren't sure I am waving at them, but no one else is on the road. And there is the rural salute—an index finger lifted smartly off the steering wheel of a pickup. I should try to wave at people the way they like to wave at me.

There are over seven billion of us on the planet. God equipped us to interact with each other in many ways, and it's a delicate dance. It is necessary to respect other's mannerisms to build a relationship with them and introduce them to Jesus, who is everyone's friend. Paul of Tarsus was an educated Jew and Roman citizen. He traveled Europe and Asia, bringing the gospel to people different from him. He adapted. **"I have become all things to all men so that by all possible means I might save some"** (1 Corinthians 9:22). For the sake of the gospel, he became what people needed him to be.

The nations are migrating to our neighborhoods. Our missionary journey is a short stroll down the street. There are newcomers in cities and the countryside. If we want to become all things to all people for the sake of the gospel, something about us will have to give.

Problems are an altar

Jason Nelson

Even in a perfect world, there was a problem.

prob·lem (prŏb′ləm) n. 1. A question to be considered, solved, or answered (thefreedictionary.com).

"The LORD God commanded the man, 'You are free to eat from any tree in the garden; but you must not eat from the tree of the knowledge of good and evil, for when you eat from it you will surely die'" (Genesis 2:16,17).

Adam and Eve were brand-new people in paradise, and God gave them a perfect opportunity.

It wasn't a trick. It was an invitation to worship him by obeying him, and he equipped them to do it. He gave them freedom to choose because that makes people happy. But we know how that ended. A lot changed after the deceiver slithered in, the blaming stopped, and the door to paradise was sealed for a time.

One thing hasn't changed. God allows problems in our lives for the same reason. They are personalized altars that invite us to submit to his will and bless his name. Veterans of faith confront problems by overriding the nagging questions: "Why?" "Why is this happening to me?" They have learned to ask: "What now?" "What does God see that I am missing?" "What does he have in mind this time?" They pause and pray. They pursue alternatives and find less resistance. They look up and thank God that he didn't give them what they wanted.

The gospel is not irresistible

Pastor Mark Jeske

Do you ever fantasize that it would have been much easier to believe in Jesus if you could have seen him? heard him? eaten his miracle food and watched one of his healings? Well, not so fast. You may have been put off by his humble appearance or his sharp-edged teachings or his claims to be divine or his claims on your life.

Still, when you saw him go toe-to-toe with Satan, the prince of darkness, and throw him back to hell, the only conclusion you could possibly have drawn is that you have just seen God himself in action. You have to work at it to stay an unbeliever, and you would need some sort of rationalization for his dazzling feats.

The Pharisees came up with an interesting theory for Jesus' miracles: **"A man who was demon-possessed and could not talk was brought to Jesus. And when the demon was driven out, the man who had been mute spoke. . . . But the Pharisees said, 'It is by the prince of demons that he drives out demons'"** (Matthew 9:32-34).

Absurd, right? Of course. But it shows that Jesus' powerful messages and miracles were not irresistible. People who are determined not to believe the truth or be moved by displays of clearly divine power will always find an excuse, *any* excuse, not to worship Jesus as Lord. On judgment day, the most horrible verdicts will be handed down to those who did not want Jesus as their Savior. They will be granted their wish. Forever.

Evangelism works

Pastor Mark Jeske

Nobody is born a believer. Nobody is born a child of God. Nobody is born saved. All of us, every last one in human history, need to be *converted* to faith.

How does that happen? While I would concede the possibility that someone would carefully research major world religions, read the Bible on her own, and come to faith by herself, it is a thousand times more likely that a caring Christian would bring the gospel testimony that turns on the lights and then help the new believer process a new worldview.

The Samaritan woman who found her Savior at the well wasted no time in sharing what she had learned: **"Many of the Samaritans from that town believed in him *because of the woman's testimony*"** (John 4:39). You know what? Evangelism works. God has given us everything we need—his Word in language we can understand, gifts and power from the Spirit, and an open-ended commissioning to make disciples of the world. All that's left to us is to do it.

You don't have to be a brilliant orator, charismatic organizer, clever writer, or mesmerizing salesperson. You can just be you, telling the hopeless that there's hope, telling the dying that there's life in Christ, telling the lonely that their Father misses them and would like to hear from them.

The Holy Spirit will do the rest.

It shouldn't make sense

Diana Kerr

"Something is wrong when our lives make sense to unbelievers." I read that sentence and it struck me hard. Why are we surprised when people don't understand our actions as Christians? If we want to glorify God and not ourselves or the world, shouldn't we honor him no matter how others react?

I have one major regret from college: I lived a safe, watered-down version of my faith. I went to church and never turned away from God, but I lowered my standards so I was just unchristian enough to fit in. Through my words and actions—or lack thereof—I tiptoed around situations I knew were wrong so I didn't stir things up.

First Peter 2:11,12 has a different idea: **"Dear friends, I urge you, as aliens and strangers in the world, to abstain from sinful desires, which war against your soul. Live such good lives among the pagans that, though they accuse you of doing wrong, they may see your good deeds and glorify God on the day he visits us."**

Don't live your life just to fit in or avoid causing waves. Stand up for what you believe in a loving way, even if it's not popular. People will notice. Your God deserves obedience and glory, and there's a world of people all around you who need to come face-to-face with salvation and the truth more than they need your participation in their Christless living.

Here's to living a life that *doesn't* make sense to unbelievers, in the very best way.

____

____

____

Look to the stars

Pastor Mark Jeske

One huge advantage country people have over city dwellers is their ability to see the full night sky, sparkling with uncountable twinkling lights. Like Abraham, look up when you are struggling: **"Don't be deceived, my dear brothers. Every good and perfect gift is from above, coming down from the Father of the heavenly lights, who does not change like shifting shadows. He chose to give us birth through the word of truth, that we might be a kind of firstfruits of all that he created"**(James 1:16-18).

The apostle James wants troubled and wounded Christians to see that God has no desire to hurt his children. Everything in our lives that is truly good comes from God the Father who dwells above the heavenly lights (the stars). He doesn't change, loving us one minute and then turning on us. He is Yahweh, the Lord, the God of steadfast covenant love, who does not change like shifting shadows. He gave us our physical lives, and then he gave us rebirth through his mighty Word into spiritual life so that we might be a kind of "firstfruits," that is, the prime, prize part of all creation, the part that he is proudest of.

Isn't that amazing? God is proud of you. He sees everything right and good that you do, remembers it all, and will praise you for it. Let him replace your shame with quiet satisfaction and contentment in his gracious love and care.

Look to the stars!

Busted!

Pastor Mark Jeske

These are marks of a child: procrastination, living in dreams instead of reality, excuses, and the fantasy that the day of accountability will never come. Jesus told a powerful story about an employee who betrayed his boss' trust and hid company assets off books.

"His master replied, 'You wicked, lazy servant! So you knew that I harvest where I have not sown and gather where I have not scattered seed? Well then, you should have put my money on deposit with the bankers, so that when I returned I would have received it back with interest'" (Matthew 25:26,27).

The master saw through the excuses and judged correctly that Mr. One Talent had betrayed his trust. Money that is not invested loses its value to inflation, and so even giving back the original amount on the day of reckoning involved theft.

The certainty of the coming final day of reckoning should bring about three impulses in our hearts. First, shame and embarrassment for all the times we have thought and acted like the wicked employee. Second, heartfelt gratitude for the forgiveness that Jesus brings so that we will be spared that type of condemnation. Third, sober awareness of the shortness of time and a determination to make our lives count for something.

You have been entrusted with serious resources from God. How have you decided to invest them? Don't put it off. The audit might be today.

____

____

____

____

June 30

If only . . .

Pastor Mark Jeske

"Take the talent from him and give it to the one who has the ten talents. For everyone who has will be given more, and he will have an abundance. Whoever does not have, even what he has will be taken from him. And throw that worthless servant outside, into the darkness, where there will be weeping and gnashing of teeth" (Matthew 25:28-30).

Whew! Jesus' story certainly ends on a harsh note, doesn't it? Why do you suppose he talked to people that way? Clearly because he thinks it's imperative that people take the wrath of God seriously. People who refuse to worship him usually end up worshiping themselves.

You've probably heard any number of jokes about hell. Hell isn't funny. Jesus says that there will be weeping and teeth gnashing—bitter regrets, self-recrimination, self-loathing, everlasting resentments against all whose "fault" it is to end up there, and hating God and oneself most of all. The worst will be for those who knew better and threw their salvation away. Imagine an eternity of "If only . . ."

Satan himself will not be the dark lord of hell. The Bible says that he will be prisoner #0001, cast into the lowest part, for all the evil he has done.

Somebody in your life needs to know these things. Tell the story.

July

"IT IS BY GRACE YOU HAVE BEEN SAVED, THROUGH FAITH--AND THIS NOT FROM YOURSELVES, IT IS THE GIFT OF GOD."

EPHESIANS 2:8

Miscarriage of justice

Pastor Mark Jeske

Everybody knows the first principle of the justice system: convict and punish the guilty and set the innocent free. That idea comes from God's sense of justice that he built into ancient Israelite law: **"Acquitting the guilty and condemning the innocent—the Lord detests them both"** (Proverbs 17:15).

And yet. How ironic that God saved the world, saved you, by contradicting his own law. In the court of the Jewish Sanhedrin and in the praetorium of Pontius Pilate, the innocent Jesus Christ was convicted of capital crimes and sentenced to a brutal and shameful public execution. He willingly submitted to that miscarriage of justice so that in God's court guilty fools like you and me could be acquitted.

Imagine that! On Calvary, God had it both ways—he both condemned and punished all human sinfulness (in Christ) and forgave a world full of sinners (in Christ). What looked like a horrible miscarriage of justice became the sweetest legal proceeding ever. *Ever.* The Bible has a word for this seeming miscarriage of justice—it's called *grace.*

God's grace toward you means that he made the first move to reconcile you with him, your lost Father. God's grace means that your sinful debts have been paid for. God's grace means that, as Isaiah said, he laid upon Christ the iniquity of us all. Fair? No. Wonderful? Yes.

Believe it. Live it. Share it.

I hope her marriage is as good as mine

Jason Nelson

My wife and I got married as very young people by today's standards. My approach wasn't too sophisticated. I saw her one day in college. She looked good to me, so I got to know her. She still looked good to me, so I asked her to marry me. At some level I must have looked good to her because she said yes. We made a commitment to God and each other to stop looking and make a marriage.

Solomon said, **"He who finds a wife finds what is good and receives favor from the LORD"** (Proverbs 18:22). I'm not aware of any passage stating the converse is true, so I ought not to pretend I know what marriage is like for a woman. But I found what is good, and I hope it's good for my wife too. I know it would be better for her if I really understood my God-given responsibility. **"Husbands, go all out in your love for your wives, exactly as Christ did for the church—a love marked by giving, not getting"** (Ephesians 5:25 MSG). I confess that early on I tried to make sure she understood her responsibilities. I had no right because I had no clue. I know I have some catching up to do.

I want her marriage to be as good as mine is because after all these years, she still looks good to me.

July 3

God loved us first

Linda Buxa

Why do we love God? We love God because he first loved us. Well, that's the answer we are supposed to give, isn't it?

Honestly though, sometimes I *act* as if I love God, but really I'm just going through the motions. Sometimes I act as if I love God because that is what you expect. I act as if I love God because I want my life to go well. I act as if I love God because I want to look good.

If I hadn't confessed it, you might never know that because I hide it well—and rationalize it even better. I bet you do too.

Proverbs 16:2 strips away our pretenses: **"All a man's ways seem innocent to him, but motives are weighed by the Lord."**

This proverb would leave me feeling really—*really*—guilty if it weren't for Jesus. He took the punishment for all the times my motives were more about me and less about God. He suffered God's anger for the times I put my comfort in front of him. He bore the brunt of the punishment for when I talked about God's love but failed to show it.

He lived his entire life loving his Father with a pure heart. We get the credit for that. Then his love fills us with the peace that passes all understanding.

We really do love God because he loved us first—from before we were even born with a love that never ends. His love never fails.

____

____

____

____

July 4

The eyes of the Lord

Pastor Mark Jeske

I hope you get a chance to see some fireworks around this U.S. national holiday. They are not only stunningly beautiful in the summer night sky, but they remind those of us living here that we are at peace. Some people right now in other parts of the world hear the thump of real artillery and see the fiery strings of real machine gun tracer rounds. Independence Day fireworks in the U.S. are also subtle reminders of the cost in lives and treasure of the great wars that formed this country, ended slavery, and kept the Union together.

But our true security is not in the size and sophistication of our military strength. **"Blessed is the nation whose God is the LORD. . . . From heaven the LORD looks down and sees all mankind. . . . He who forms the hearts of all, who considers everything they do. No king is saved by the size of his army; no warrior escapes by his great strength. . . . But the eyes of the LORD are on those who fear him, on those whose hope is in his unfailing love"** (Psalm 33:12-18).

We enjoy the blessings of God upon us to the degree that we are attuned to his agenda. It's never too late to go through your own personal repentance and renewal. It's never too late to invest your energy, talents, and time into your congregation's ministries. It's never too late for a nationwide Christian revival of Word and Spirit.

____

____

____

____

____

Are your children employable?

Pastor Mark Jeske

It's probably the hardest part of parenting—getting your children to the point where day after day they will actually simply do what you tell them to do. When they're small, they might not understand; kindergarteners forget; when they're grade-schoolers, they might be distracted; when they're teens, they have attitude. Excuses abound. But I don't think I've done my job as a parent if I haven't taught my children simple obedience to my instructions.

We are born sinners, and in each little heart is a beast that cares only for its own agenda. Keeping the beast under control and learning a serving mind-set is difficult, but it is absolutely vital for our society and for the child. **"The wise in heart accept commands, but a chattering fool comes to ruin"** (Proverbs 10:8). You can assume that your children will say no to you, sometimes with defiance. The real question is what you do next.

If you cannot allow other people to tell you what to do, you are unemployable. "Going to work" and "having a job" means that you are there to please your boss. He assigns the roles and tasks; she defines them; he sets the bar of expectations; she then pays you money; and the cycle starts all over again.

Children who have not learned to obey their earthly father will probably refuse to obey their heavenly Father as well.

July 6

I know your afflictions and poverty

Pastor Mark Jeske

We all like to hear the happy stories of triumphs in the lives of Christians. When people with a microphone are giving a testimony, their speeches always seem to end up in victory. There's always a market for "I'm a winner" presentations. Who wants to hear a personal testimony from a Christian who is tormented with afflictions and can't pay her bills?

God does. He wants to hear from us not only when everything is working well for us, when we have plenty of money, feel good, have a job, and our family is intact. He knows us and he loves us also when we suffer from leukemia, MS, cerebral palsy, or Down syndrome. He loves us when we are sitting in an attorney's office to declare bankruptcy or receive a divorce petition. He loves us though we may be in a jail cell or in rehab or psychiatric counseling.

He knows we're broken. That's why he knew he needed to send a Savior—because we couldn't save ourselves. To the Christians in Smyrna God said, **"I know your afflictions and your poverty—yet you are rich!"** (Revelation 2:9). Their, and our, riches are based not on money or real estate or shares in a business. They are based on his covenant love expressed to us in the holy life and work of Jesus Christ. Their, and our, riches are based on our membership in God's family, on our ability to call God *Father.*

____

____

____

____

____

I won't have enough

Pastor Mark Jeske

If you lived through the Great Depression or if you are a child of a couple that did, your consumer behaviors will probably fall into one of two categories: either you will live high ("I am never eating oleo or shopping at a thrift store again!") or you will almost make a fetish out of living small. "Use it up; wear it out; make it do or do without" is a great slogan if your income is limited. Thrift is good! Great even. But it can become fear, an irrational anxiety that you will never have enough.

If you have thoughts like that or feel those impulses in your spirit, it's time to reconnect with our God, whom the Scriptures depict repeatedly as a God of abundance: **"Now he who supplies seed to the sower and bread for food will also supply and increase your store of seed and will enlarge the harvest of your righteousness. You will be made rich in every way so that you can be generous on every occasion"** (2 Corinthians 9:10,11).

God always provides. But when we have a self-written script of scarcity, we don't see his gifts; and when we do see them, we don't draw the right conclusions and don't celebrate them or take comfort from them. God always provides, and he does it not only to keep you alive, warm, and dry but also so that you can be generous too.

Leaders give first

Pastor Mark Jeske

There is nothing, *nothing*, that can kill an organization faster than poor leadership. Similarly there is nothing more important to the health and growth of an organization and its mission than good leadership.

Leaders imagine a different future, and they live in that new mental space. They articulate a vision of something bigger and better. Leaders lead. They go first. They do not stand in the back and wait for others to sacrifice and take risks. This is equally true of Christian congregations as it is of community service nonprofits. In a capital campaign, for instance, good leaders will not only work to craft a great plan; they will step up and make their own financial commitments first.

King David's pre-construction planning and organization for the building of the first temple in Jerusalem was a great success. You know why? He went first, with lavish contributions of his personal wealth. And: **"Then the leaders of families, the officers of the tribes of Israel, the commanders of thousands and commanders of hundreds, and the officials in charge of the king's work gave willingly. The people rejoiced at the willing response of their leaders, for they had given freely and wholeheartedly to the Lord"** (1 Chronicles 29:6,9).

Good leaders release energy for service among those who follow. Good leaders release generosity in those who follow by their own personal commitments.

First.

____

____

____

Encourage one another

Jason Nelson

The human relations principle of the New Testament is encouragement. **"Therefore encourage one another and build each other up, just as in fact you are doing"** (1 Thessalonians 5:11). The *modus operandi* is to focus on the positives you see in others, regularly affirm the daylights out of what you like, and say very little about what you don't. That is how we build each other up. That is how we bring out the best in our brothers and sisters.

Opposing schools of thought have adherents. In our belittling natures we want to catch people doing something wrong and then criticize it. Some managers just believe in being tough on people. But if your favorite tool is a hammer, everybody looks like a nail. Some of us live or work where the prevailing culture is very discouraging. The only feedback is negative. That is unmerciful and contaminates the well for everyone. It betrays the fact somebody needs building up, big time.

Trying to be an encourager can be exhausting. It is laboring against our own downside. There is a lot of tongue biting involved. Bless you if people have come to expect affirmation from you. Bless you if you have encouraged them in godliness and given them self-confidence. They appreciate what you say and look forward to living up to your positive expectations. And they also get the message when you say nothing at all.

July 10

I can't

Pastor Mark Jeske

"I know I should, but I can't." Ever heard those words? Ever heard yourself saying those words? Even St. Paul heard them coming out of his own mouth. In Romans 7, he admitted sadly that he had the desire to do what is good, but he could not carry it out. The evil that he didn't want to do—that he kept on doing.

But he didn't quit there, sitting by the side of the road in defeat, surrendering the battlefield to Satan. **"Who will rescue me from this body of death? Thanks be to God—through Jesus Christ our Lord!"** (Romans 7:24,25). Those are hope-filled words for anybody who feels trapped in "can't." Who want to stop drinking but can't . . . who want to stop their emotional outbursts but can't . . . who want to break off an affair but can't . . . who want to finish school and get that degree but can't . . . who know we should get married but can't stop cohabiting. . . .

Through Christ we are forgiven of all sins and failures. Through Christ we are restored to God's family, assured of our love and value, and enabled to let go of the bag of rocks we were dragging. Through Christ the Holy Spirit's wisdom and power are reignited in us all over again to continue the struggle. Through Christ we believe that our tomorrows will be better than our yesterdays.

"I can do everything through him who gives me strength" (Philippians 4:13).

The law is the law

Linda Buxa

My son and I were heading into town when an oncoming sheriff turned on her lights and made a U-turn. Assuming she had been called to an emergency, I pulled over to let her pass. Instead, she pulled up behind me. Oh.

My mind was racing, trying to figure out why. I wasn't speeding because I had just turned left; I couldn't have accelerated that quickly. (Okay, I *could* have. But I knew I didn't.)

Then she informed me that I had treated the stop sign like a yield sign. (Okay, I believe that.) Fortunately, she simply gave me a friendly reminder to make a complete stop at that intersection.

As my son tells that story to *everyone*, my first reaction is to defend myself. "C'mon, it's a quiet county road. Everyone treats it like a yield." That wouldn't hold up in traffic court though, would it? No. The law is the law.

My second reaction is to realize how often I rationalize my actions with God too. He tells me to love my neighbor, and I say, "C'mon, but these people are so arrogant." He tells me to go and make disciples, and I say, "C'mon, this could get uncomfortable." He tells me to approach people when I'm offended, and I say, "C'mon, I'd rather just stew about it in private."

No. His Word is his Word. His love for me changes the way I look at what he tells me. I no longer think his commands limit my life. Instead, I get to love him back by obeying him. In fact, **"this is love for God: to obey his commands. And his commands are not burdensome, for everyone born of God overcomes the world"** (1 John 5:3,4).

Of what are you proudest?

Pastor Mark Jeske

Let's face it—the male spirit thrives on being seen as powerful. We men are terrified of being called weak or a loser. We know that we are graded and evaluated in society by how we project strength, and there are various ways we can do that: exhibiting physical strength, demonstrating mental sharpness by achieving graduate degrees, accumulating money, or by a lofty position in the business world.

Women often identify themselves by their relationships. A man needs to feel proud of his accomplishments. Guys, of what are you proudest? Are you proud of the right things? **"This is what the LORD says: 'Let not the wise man boast of his wisdom or the strong man boast of his strength or the rich man boast of his riches, but let him who boasts boast about this: that he understands and knows me"** (Jeremiah 9:23,24).

Taking care of your body, accumulating wealth, nailing the corner office, or attaining a PhD are all wonderful things, but they will not satisfy unless you are connected with your God through your Savior Jesus. You are nothing without him. You are everything with him.

If you had to write the final sentence for your own obituary, what would it say? How about, "He died and now lives in the Lord, grateful for grace, grateful for the opportunity to be useful to his Lord."

____

____

____

____

____

A whiff of Jesus

Jason Nelson

How do we share our faith with people at work? Sometimes we can be direct and tell them the wonderful story of Jesus' love if they don't know it. The circumstances may be right for it: Our relationships are genuine and open. We have gotten to know each other and have discussed other personal matters. Explaining the reason for our hope is the natural thing to do.

But sometimes there are limitations. It wouldn't help the cause of the gospel to force the issue. The decorum of the workplace might make it uncomfortable for everyone. The noise of the workplace might make it impossible to say *Jesus* without it sounding like cussing. Sometimes it's even against the rules.

Because we love him so much and have great respect for his Word, we want people to know. When there is no other way, we can always give people a whiff of Jesus. Even if the setting restricts talking about our faith, we can make sure people smell it on us. **"Wherever we go, God uses us to make clear what it means to know Christ. It's like a fragrance that fills the air"** (2 Corinthians 2:14 GW).

I think we know the implications. It's that whole salt and light thing: acting and speaking in a way that gives people a pretty good idea who is behind it.

May we pass the sniff test on a regular basis.

____

____

____

____

____

July 14

What are you looking for?

Pastor Mark Jeske

Enjoying spending time with old people is learned behavior. Young folks don't have the patience for it, but in time. . . . One of the things I have learned to appreciate about many older people is that they look for the best in others and celebrate it. They seem not to be as interested in condemning and judging. That serenity comes from many decades of people watching. They've learned that most of life is a mishmash of good and evil, noble and wretched, lofty and miserable. They have softened over the decades, becoming more patient, understanding, and accepting.

And they choose to see their glasses as half full. **"He who seeks good finds goodwill, but evil comes to him who searches for it"** (Proverbs 11:27). If my dear spouse wanted to itemize my faults, weaknesses, and sins over the years and then study that list each day, she would stay permanently angry. And vice versa, of course, but how much better if we look for and itemize only the good in our loved ones? It's there in abundance if we only look!

If you look at the events of your day today through goggles of pessimism, you will see one letdown and disappointment after another. Nothing and nobody will ever be good enough for you. If you look at people through the same glasses that Jesus uses to look at us, you will see goodness *absolutely everywhere*!

Bad decisions. Good stories.

Linda Buxa

I was driving down the main street of my town when I saw the guy's shirt: "Bad decisions make the best stories."

I got all high-and-mighty because I was pretty sure his shirt was trying to make sin sound like good fun. Perhaps it was an out-of-hand spring break. Maybe teenage rebellion earned a visit from the police. Or a bachelor party in Vegas where things stayed there.

Then I realized the shirt was pretty accurate. My dumbest decisions do make the best stories—of God's grace. So do yours, because you are **"convinced that neither death nor life, neither angels nor demons, neither the present nor the future, nor any powers, neither height nor depth, nor anything else in all creation, will be able to separate us from the love of God that is in Christ Jesus our Lord"** (Romans 8:38,39).

King David knew. He slept with Uriah's wife and then had Uriah killed in battle. God still called him a man after his own heart.

Abraham understood. Twice he tried to pass his wife off as his sister so he wouldn't be killed and have Sarah taken into a harem. God made him the father of many nations as he had promised.

Peter denied that he even knew Jesus, yet Jesus gave him the high privilege of feeding his lambs.

How about you? Jesus' sacrifice brought you back into a relationship with the Father. His love washes away your dumb decisions. His mercy takes away your shame. Thanks to Jesus, nothing—not even your bad decisions—can separate you from his love.

So much immorality

Pastor Mark Jeske

There's an old gag that says, "Marriage is a great institution, but who wants to live in an institution?" Hahahaha. Marriage is indeed a human covenant *instituted* by God on the sixth day of creation. It is a brilliant invention for the reproduction of the human race, guaranteeing that a child will have the protection, love, and access to life wisdom of both a female and male in the home.

It is an antipoverty mechanism, for two people can live more cheaply together than separately. It is healthy—if you marry as a virgin and stay loyal to your spouse, you will never have to fear sexually transmitted diseases. It is a tremendous advantage to face life's challenges as a lifelong team, with double the brainpower, double the imagination, double the talents, double the life experiences.

And it provides the only God-pleasing way that there is for sexual activity that does not offend against the Sixth Commandment. Pretty much everybody I know thinks we live in an insanely sex-drenched culture. St. Paul might give us an argument though: **"Since there is so much immorality, each man should have his own wife, and each woman her own husband"** (1 Corinthians 7:2).

Sexual immorality (i.e., sexual activity outside of marriage) not only can cause tremendous damage to people and their relationships; it incurs sinful guilt before God. Christian couples have a solemn obligation and thrilling mission to have an impact on the world and live their faith by making their "institution" look like a *great* place to live.

____

____

____

July 17

The Word works

Pastor Mark Jeske

Of all the reasons for world missionary reluctance, the last thing you'd guess is fear of success. But that's exactly what drove the prophet Jonah to a ship headed in a direction opposite from God's. He was called by God from the nation of Israel to bring the Word to Nineveh, capital city of the massive Assyrian Empire, towering to the north over little Israel. Jonah didn't want to go.

Some of his reasoning was poisonous. He had no love for Assyrians and could imagine no possible use for them in God's kingdom agenda. He hoped God would destroy them, not save them. But after a three-day weekend in a watery hotel, he agreed to go to Nineveh. Jonah had admirable qualities too: *he passionately believed that the Word works:* **"I knew that you are a gracious and compassionate God, slow to anger and abounding in love, a God who relents from sending calamity"** (Jonah 4:2).

Jonah was so confident in the power of the Word that he went all alone to bring a message of warning and repentance to strangers. He was right—his humble presence brought about a national spiritual renewal, reaching up all the way to the king. A critical mass of people did indeed repent and God indeed spared them the threatened destruction.

Our world today, more than ever, needs to hear both of God's coming judgment and of God's mercy in Christ. When you speak the Word clearly, it's as though God himself were speaking.

The Word works.

It's a girls' club

Linda Buxa

A few years ago, I joined what the women referred to as their old ladies' Bible study. They teased that I was too young to be in their group, but they welcomed me and taught me the way Titus 2:3,4 tells them to: **"Likewise, teach the older women to be reverent in the way they live . . . then they can train the younger women."**

They taught me about being a faithful pray-er, asking me later how God was answering those prayers. They taught me about friendship. They taught me that my future includes still being concerned about and praying for my children no matter how old they get.

Finally, they taught me that lovely countenances do not come from an easy life—they lived through tough times; however, all of them are strong and confident because their hearts are at peace with God and revere the God who made them, redeemed them, and loves them. Because they know this love, they love each other like family.

As important as this message was in Bible times, it's equally important today. The busier women get, the easier it is to feel lonely. The more we hear we should do it all, the less we feel we can hold it all together. God has put us on the same team to spend time together, encourage each other, build each other up, teach each other, and learn from each other.

Men, I know this devotion is more for women, but I bet you need mentors in your life too.

I don't know what to do

Pastor Mark Jeske

One of the reasons we like action movies is that the heroes are larger than life. They are not only handsome and brave and strong; they always seem to know what to do. They always have a plan; they are brilliant improvisers when the plot changes; they always look together and confident.

Here's the difference—they live in the movies, where the writers make them look clever, wardrobe sets them up with really cool clothes, stuntmen take their falls, and the bad guys make fatal mistakes and always lose in the end. You and I live in a place called reality, where our choices are murkier, the paths more confusing, and our relationships more complicated.

Life is full of human dilemmas: Which career track is right for me? Is this woman worth committing to? What do I do with an out-of-control child? You have a Friend in heaven who is waiting to be asked for his help: **"Trust in the LORD with all your heart and lean not on your own understanding; in all your ways acknowledge him, and he will make your paths straight"** (Proverbs 3:5,6). God is amazing! He can make a way out of no way. He knows when and how and who and how much. When asked, he will give us the information we need on a day-to-day basis.

Our part is threefold: *listen* to his messages, *acknowledge* him as we walk, and *trust* that the right path will become clear when God is ready to show it to us.

Money isn't everything

Pastor Mark Jeske

Would you believe me if I told you that money isn't everything? No, I didn't think so. In our culture everything's for sale. Money is the ultimate tool to get what you want. Indeed, it is an efficient and powerful tool, capable of much evil as well as much good. But the love of it is addictive, and men and women for millennia have sold their souls in pursuit of it.

How can you develop a healthy attitude toward money? How can you teach your children and grandchildren? First, help them see all their possessions as belonging to God. The earth is the Lord's, and everything in it. We are renters and employees in God's world, not owners and controllers. Second, we are managing God's stuff *for him,* to advance his royal and divine agenda, and our financial lives work best when we see ourselves as his managers. Third, worshiping God and serving other people are more important (and more fulfilling) than seeking your own power and comfort.

Money really isn't everything. In fact, it isn't even the most important part of a happy life. Even if you're not sure you can believe me, you would do well to believe God: **"Better a little with the fear of the Lord than great wealth with turmoil. Better a meal of vegetables where there is love than a fattened calf with hatred"** (Proverbs 15:16,17).

I know where you live

Pastor Mark Jeske

I've lived and worked in some pretty rough neighborhoods over the years. But my life has never been as tough as that of the Christians who lived in Pergamum in western Asia Minor. Satan owned that city, and the huge pagan altar to the Greek god Zeus built there (now in a German museum) was one of Satan's tools for confusing and misleading people.

The growing Christian presence in Pergamum brought a furious counterattack from Zeus' priests and Satan's demons. But God saw everything going on there, knew where every one of his believers was, and managed all events there, even their sufferings, in order to advance his kingdom of believers. **"I know where you live—where Satan has his throne. Yet you remain true to my name. You did not renounce your faith in me, even in the days of Antipas, my faithful witness, who was put to death in your city—where Satan lives"** (Revelation 2:13).

The Lord knows where you live too. He sees your dangers, grieves at your losses and hurts, sends his angels to protect you and your family, and watches to see how you handle temptation and stress. His great desire is that you remain faithful. Antipas' martyrdom did not cheat him out of his heavenly reward—in fact, it just propelled him into glory more quickly. His courageous example was repeated many times over and provided inspiration for the rapid growth of the Christian church.

Yes, family reconciliation is possible

Pastor Mark Jeske

It's a dog-eat-dog world out there. The dogs eat one another in families too, and sad to say this happens in Christian homes. I used to watch my own kids argue and fight and grimly called their abusing one another "family Darwinism" (you know, survival of the fittest). One of the older kids even explained it to me once: "Dad, we have to pick on the younger ones to toughen them up for the playground, or they'll be eaten alive."

There is much worse. The greatest hurts and abuse often come from those who are supposed to love us the most. How can you forgive someone who has hurt you deeply or often or both when no one was looking? Consider Joseph—his older siblings actually sold their mouthy little brother into slavery and told the old man that a wild animal had gotten him. In an amazing turnabout, Joseph was eventually promoted to vice pharaoh in Egypt at the very time that the brothers had to come to Egypt for food during a famine.

What would be Joseph's revenge now that they were in his power? **"Joseph said to his brothers, 'I am Joseph! Is my father still living?' But his brothers were not able to answer him, because they were terrified at his presence"** (Genesis 45:3). Perhaps because there had been so little mercy in their hearts, they found it hard to believe it could exist in another's.

Are old hurts keeping people apart in your family? Could you arrange a Joseph moment?

____

____

____

____

It's the Lord's fight

Linda Buxa

There they were, stuck between the Red Sea and the Egyptian army. On one side the Israelites faced death by drowning, on the other the army of their former captors was racing toward them, assuring them of a gruesome death. That's when the complaining started. Moses, their leader, stood up and told them, **"Do not be afraid. Stand firm and you will see the deliverance the LORD will bring you today. . . . The LORD will fight for you; you need only to be still"** (Exodus 14:13,14).

Frankly, you'll never find yourself between a body of water and a charging Egyptian army. But you can sympathize with the Israelites, can't you? As God allows challenges, even life-threatening ones, in your life, you know it's so easy to complain, asking him *why me* and *why now*?

Let Moses' words calm your heart. Place your worry at the feet of Jesus' cross. There Jesus fought—and won—the biggest battle of your life. Now you get to watch him work through your current struggle.

Maybe God fights for you by giving you the strength to keep going. Maybe he fights for you by giving you a complete rescue or a miraculous healing. Maybe he will fight for you by taking you home to heaven, because a temporary loss on this earth is his eternal victory.

No matter how he works, God's got this. Stand firm. Be still. See his deliverance.

How will you learn?

Pastor Mark Jeske

All education involves change. It changes the amount of data in your brain, changes your opinions, changes your perspectives and points of view, changes your behaviors, and changes your relationships. I have concluded that there are only two ways to learn: through words and through pain.

Children are great absorbers and great learners, but they have limits to how much they will accept through talk. You might consider a spanking an experiential learning opportunity for them, or as Ricky Ricardo might have said, "Now I get it, since you 'splained it to me."

God's preference is to educate us through words, especially his Word, but he has other means at his disposal. You've probably heard me refer to "God's two-by-four" when people go through hardships brought on by their bad choices. **"He who scorns instruction will pay for it, but he who respects a command is rewarded"** (Proverbs 13:13). This is as true of 50-year-olds as it is of 5-year-olds. Thus not all pain is bad—if it helps people see more clearly or repent more sincerely, it is *totally* worth it.

When you study the Ten Commandments, for example, do you see them as annoying restrictions on your freedom of movement and pursuit of personal fulfillment, or do you see them as God's profoundly loving principles that bring a happy life and a healthy community?

Heaven is a lake cottage

Jason Nelson

While Martin Luther was at a big meeting in Augsburg (1530), he wrote to his son encouraging him to be a faithful boy. He described heaven in terms Hans would find appealing: "I know a pretty, lovely, pleasant garden, where many children go; they wear golden coats and gather nice apples, pears, cherries, and plums from under the trees; they sing, jump, and are merry. They also have pretty little horses with golden bridles and silver saddles" (*Luther's Works*). Heaven is amazing, but the picture isn't complete. Envisioning our own perfect place helps us long to be there.

What is your heaven? My heaven is a lake cottage. The shore is studded with whispering pines, and a long pier goes out into pristine water. Weed beds nearby hold plenty of scrappy bluegills. Within reach of a long cast is a deep edge where walleyes beg to be caught. Loons call, and it's always a nice June evening with no mosquitoes.

John had a better revelation: **"Before me was a throne in heaven with someone sitting on it. And the one who sat there had the appearance of jasper and carnelian. . . . And I heard a loud voice from the throne saying, 'Now the dwelling of God is with men, and he will live with them. . . . He will wipe every tear from their eyes'"** (Revelation 4:2,3; 21:3,4).

Heaven is a perfect life with Jesus, and I know he likes to fish.

____

____

____

____

I know your love and faith

Pastor Mark Jeske

We are all hungry for recognition. Go ahead and admit it. When we do something well or help somebody out, we expect and long for an "Attagirl!" or "You're so awesome!" Most of the really great works of faith, however, are done with few witnesses, or maybe none at all. Who sees the hours spent with a cerebral palsy patient? Who sees you when you shovel the sidewalk of the elderly widow next door, when you do the taxes of your brother-in-law who is hopeless with numbers? When you get groceries for someone who's homebound? When you tutor a child struggling in school? When you spend an hour on the phone with a suicidal friend?

God does. You may assume that he sees it all and that every time you help someone else on his or her journey, the face of God lights up. He told the Christians at Thyatira, **"I know your deeds, your love and faith, your service and perseverance, and that you are now doing more than you did at first"** (Revelation 2:19).

When Jesus left the earth, he sent his Spirit to power us up for our promotion. He basically gave us his job—to proclaim the good news of the gospel and to back up the integrity of the message with a life that makes our talk believable. Don't worry if your service to other people sometimes seems unseen and unappreciated. The One you care about most is absolutely thrilled with what you're doing.

Don't take it personally

Pastor Mark Jeske

"Don't shoot the messenger!" That's what we holler when we get some major blowback to what we've said. When we are simply relaying someone else's decision, when we are just stating company policy, when we are only passing on the boss' instructions, we don't have to take personally people's attitudes about the content. It's not our content. Their real issue is with someone else.

On Maundy Thursday evening, in the darkened upper room, Jesus gave extensive last teaching to his disciples to prepare them for a lifetime of representing him. He didn't sugarcoat it—he gave it to them straight. They were going to take some major abuse for the message that they would bring to the world, that Christ Jesus is the only Savior of sinners like them.

But they shouldn't take that abuse personally. **"If the world hates you, keep in mind that it hated me first. . . . 'No servant is greater than his master.' If they persecuted me, they will persecute you also"** (John 15:18,20). When you speak about appropriate sexual behaviors today, for instance, and dare to suggest that sex belongs only in marriage, you may be mocked. When you state your belief that God made the world in six days, you may be lampooned as an unscientific buffoon. When you tell people that hell is real and that only Jesus can keep you out of it, some may snicker and roll their eyes.

Don't take it personally. You're only the messenger.

Believers' lives always end well

Pastor Mark Jeske

Not all movies have happy endings. Sometimes the guy doesn't get the girl. Sometimes the business fails. Sometimes the hero is killed. It is one of the exquisite pleasures of Christianity that absolutely every one of God's promises will be fulfilled, that every one of his chosen will make it to heaven, and that Satan not only will lose, but he has in fact lost already.

The middle chapters in the book of our lives are always the hard ones. But the ending is totally worth waiting for: **"Do not fear, O Zion; do not let your hands hang limp. The LORD your God is with you, he is mighty to save. He will take great delight in you; he will quiet you with his love, he will rejoice over you with singing"** (Zephaniah 3:16,17).

Here's what you have to look forward to: When you die, your physical body returns to the earth from which it is made. Your spirit joins the Lord and the souls of all the saints of the past. When Christ returns, your physical body will be raised from the ground and in soul and body you will witness the universe dismantled and re-created. In God's new world there will be no crime, no diseases, no starvation, and no war. These former things will pass away and become a faint memory. All of the saints will be gathered in one grand reunion.

Regardless of how hard the path had been, believers' lives always end well.

Don't talk so much

Pastor Mark Jeske

"When words are many, sin is not absent, but he who holds his tongue is wise" (Proverbs 10:19). Wow! Truer words were never spoken. Don't talk so much, people! "Listen first" is powerful advice for both business and home. When you pay attention to your customers first before pitching them your product or service, you are much more likely to win their respect and trust. They will feel that you are working for them, not manipulating them for your benefit.

"Listen twice before speaking once" is also a healing strategy for marriage. No husband ever got into trouble with his wife for listening too much. Think of all the dumb and hurtful things you've said when you were irritated or tired or angry or defensive. Think of all the misunderstandings that arose because you were too impatient with the conversation to listen, really listen.

We use barrages of words to control the conversation or vent emotion. But think about it—if you can keep your mouth shut during stressful times, things often look a lot different the next day. Words that you fire off to zing or punish will never be forgotten, and you will have to live with the backlash for a long, long time.

Most of us can barely resist the temptation to get in the last word. If you must, how about making the last word, "I need to think about what you've said, dear."

July 30

Is God bipolar?

Pastor Mark Jeske

Do you have any friends or loved ones who have been diagnosed as bipolar? This is serious business. The severe mood swings that characterize this form of mental illness can do a lot of damage. The individuals cannot manage their manic and depressive episodes and usually need therapy and mood stabilizer drugs.

Does it seem as though God swings back and forth between two different personas? The prophet Nahum described what God is like in these words: **"The LORD is a jealous and avenging God; the LORD takes vengeance and is filled with wrath. The LORD is good, a refuge in times of trouble. He cares for those who trust in him"** (Nahum 1:2,7). He is indeed a God of wrath and a God of mercy, but that doesn't make him bipolar.

He is in complete control of his actions, applying judgment and forgiveness always at the appropriate times and to the appropriate people. Those who have joined Satan's evil rebellion will reap the punishments promised for the devil, but those who repent and trust in their Savior will receive mercy. Believers find that God is filled with goodness, a safe place and refuge in times of trouble, and a steady provider and caregiver.

God himself once described himself to Moses in this way: **"The LORD, the LORD, the compassionate and gracious God, slow to anger, abounding in love . . . forgiving wickedness, rebellion and sin. Yet he does not leave the guilty unpunished"** (Exodus 34:6,7).

That's not a disorder. That's just how he is. Can you accept that?

Fathers and daughters

Jason Nelson

I have two daughters who stole my heart on day one. I also have two sons, and they're okay too. We're buddies. We work together, play together, laugh a lot, and engage in regular one-upmanship—everything dads do with boys when they become men. But it's a different kind of privilege to be the father of daughters.

God intends the father-daughter relationship to be the purest and most significant male-female relationship in the human experience. A father affirms the femininity and beauty of his daughter. He shows her affection without any sexual overtones. The father's integrity gives a daughter a moral compass. She knows what standards to hold other men to. A father is the best advocate for his daughter's competence and lets her know anything is possible. He coaches her in developing her talents to do what she thought was impossible. Christian fathers want their daughters to be full voiced in expressing their faith with self-confidence no matter the circumstances of their lives.

Rulers of old put their best foot forward when they sent daughters to represent them. It was a big deal if their daughters were there. **"Daughters of kings are among your honored women"** (Psalm 45:9). No one reflects what a man is all about better than his daughters do. My daughters will always have my heart. They make me feel like a king.

August

"JESUS ANSWERED, 'I AM THE WAY AND THE TRUTH AND THE LIFE. NO ONE COMES TO THE FATHER EXCEPT THROUGH ME.'"

JOHN 14:6

Sometimes there is no miracle

Pastor Mark Jeske

All Christians love the miracle stories in the Bible. We rejoice with the paralytics and lepers and blind as they jumped for joy with new health. If you live long enough yourself, you might just witness one of the Lord's absolutely supernatural reversals of the laws of nature in your own life.

But sometimes there is no miracle. A grieving *Time of Grace* viewer wrote in, "My sister-in-law is dying of cancer. She asked me, 'If there are so many people praying for me, why doesn't God let me live? How much power do these prayers really have?'"

It was John the Baptist's great charge and commission to herald the coming to earth of God himself. "The kingdom is near," he said. He was imprisoned because of the boldness of his prophetic witness, and after many weary days in the dungeon things got worse. Evil King Herod's niece/stepdaughter arranged to get rid of the prophet once and for all: **"Prompted by her mother, she said, 'Give me here on a platter the head of John the Baptist.' The king was distressed, but because of his oaths and his dinner guests, he ordered that her request be granted and had John beheaded in prison"** (Matthew 14:8-10).

Do you think John was praying for a miraculous jailbreak? the gift of invisibility? a host of angels? None came. He was beheaded. Sometimes we serve God best through our hardships. Sometimes his kingdom comes faster via our weakness. And that's okay.

____

____

____

____

August 2

Love your friends

Pastor Mark Jeske

You may never have heard of it. A day to celebrate friendship was proposed back in the 1930s by Joyce Hall, founder of Hallmark, but the idea never really got big in the U.S. People figured it was just a gimmick to sell cards in a dead spot between other holidays, which in fact it was.

But Friendship Day took off in South Asia; sales of "friendship wristbands" are big in India, Nepal, and Bangladesh. Thanks to an initiative by a Paraguayan doctor, the United Nations observes a day of international friendship each year.

Even without observing a recognition day, however, people value their social networks more than ever. Digital communication has connected people as never before, with instant messaging, texting, Facebook, and Twitter. Long before social media existed, friendship bound together people's lives. **"Jonathan said to David, 'Go in peace, for we have sworn friendship with each other in the name of the LORD, saying, "The LORD is witness between you and me, and between your descendants and my descendants forever"'"** (1 Samuel 20:42).

God made people to need people. Don't fight it. Embrace it. Love your friends, and let God's gifts to you flow through them: encouragement, scolding, sympathy, guidance, companionship, joy.

Troubles shared are only half as heavy. Joys shared are twice as good.

You are not a pawn

Linda Buxa

Every two years in September, a costumed human chess game is played in Marostica, Italy. In the town square, Piazza del Castello, the human chess pieces (complete with live horses for the knights) stand on a giant chessboard, waiting to receive their orders to move.

When your life looks nothing like the life you planned for yourself, it might seem like you are simply a pawn in God's giant chess game. You wonder if maybe he is only giving orders, moving you around this planet on a whim.

It's not only at Christmas that we need to remember Jesus' name: Immanuel, "*God with us.*"

Not God above us, not God watching us, not God vaguely aware of us, not God playing with us. We are not bit players in his game. Instead he got in the game with us; he came to play for us. He chose to leave heaven and become one of us, to walk with us, to live among us.

When Jesus went back to heaven after he won, he didn't leave us alone again to resume the game on our own. Instead, the Holy Spirit came and now lives inside of us. *God with us* is now *God in us*.

The news only gets better. While we wrestle with this imperfect world, we know a perfect version of it is waiting for us. Jesus' victory guaranteed it.

"I heard a loud voice from the throne saying, 'Now the dwelling of God is with men, and he will live with them. They will be his people, and God himself will be with them and be their God'" (Revelation 21:3).

I have a terrible boss

Pastor Mark Jeske

Johnny Paycheck got a lot of mileage out of his 1977 hit song "Take This Job and Shove It." The song resonated so deeply with people that the slogan appeared everywhere—coffee mugs, feed caps, and demotivational posters.

If you have some degree of control over your work environment, you can make adjustments to stay sane. But how can you keep going when your boss is the problem? He displays no integrity . . . she finds fault with your work constantly . . . he resents your Christian faith and picks on you because of it?

Bad leadership in your workplace, however, can become a tremendous platform for living your faith. Anybody can plot revenge, sabotage projects, bad-mouth leaders behind their backs, and nurse quitting fantasy scenarios. It takes a Christian to show grace to people who don't deserve it. What St. Peter wrote about to slaves applies equally well to employees: **"Submit yourself to your masters with all respect, not only to those who are good and considerate, but also to those who are harsh. For it is commendable if a person bears up under the pain of unjust suffering because he is conscious of God"** (1 Peter 2:18,19).

As an incentive toward that kind of undeservedly kind behavior, you might ponder how kind and merciful God has been to a selfish sinner like you. He will take care of judging and punishing on his own schedule and in his own way. In the meantime, let God's mercy come *to* you; let God's mercy flow *through* you.

____

____

____

Hope has a backbone

Jason Nelson

Despair looks the same everywhere. It looks the same in rough neighborhoods, little ghost towns on the prairie, and across rural wastelands. It looks the same in developed places way past their prime and emerging places struggling to locate the first rung on the ladder. Desperation wears people down and is worn on their faces with the same numb expression. I'm sure desperate people wish things would change for the better.

Desperation overwhelms best wishes every time. But it is no match for hope, because hope has a backbone. Hopeful people stand tall and look ahead. Goals, optimism, resources, and effort are the backbone of hope. Confidence in God's readiness to bless is hope's sure footing and generates amazing energy to persevere. **"Those who hope in the LORD will renew their strength. They will soar on wings like eagles; they will run and not grow weary, they will walk and not be faint"** (Isaiah 40:31).

Hope is a gift of God and fits nicely with faith and love. It is incredibly durable. It has an excellent track record and is very contagious. People catch hope from hope-filled people who show them a way forward and prop them up a bit as they take the first steps into a better future.

I won't wish you well. But my hope is that these few words put a little more backbone in yours.

Nobody can love me

Pastor Mark Jeske

"The Child is father of the Man." William Wordsworth wrote that in 1802, noting with quiet satisfaction how simple joys like gazing upon a rainbow will last well into adulthood. Alas, the dark side is true as well. Hurts and abuse suffered in childhood can still cripple adults many decades later. A broken Child can be father of a broken Man.

One of the most important jobs parents have is helping children to believe that they are lovable. Loving parents affirm a child's worth. They not only forgive children for their mistakes and misbehaviors; they teach the children to learn to forgive themselves.

A child who emerges from childhood not feeling loved may well believe that she is unlovable. That horrible fear will then lead her later in life to interpret the words and actions of others in the worst possible way, and she will find confirmation of that fear. She may find rejection everywhere.

Restoring one's confidence of personal worth starts at the cross of Christ. There on Calvary is unmistakable evidence that God thinks we are precious, worth saving, and valuable enough to ask his Son to become human like us, suffer because of us, die for us, all so he can take us to heaven to live with us. No one can say, "Nobody loves me, not even God," because **"God so loved the *world* that he gave his one and only Son"** (John 3:16).

____

____

____

____

____

Time to pray

Linda Buxa

"Remember those in prison as if you were their fellow prisoners, and those who are mistreated as if you yourselves were suffering" (Hebrews 13:3).

Beheadings, mass murders, rapes, and imprisonments. The news is filled with stories of Christians who are persecuted. The evil is beyond imaginable.

Even though they live thousands of miles away, they are part of our family because they believe in Jesus—who was mocked, beaten, spit on, and crucified. They are our brothers and sisters, and they are suffering for believing in our Brother.

It might seem easy to feel helpless. But there is so much we can do!

We follow the example of the believers in Acts 12 who were "earnestly praying to God" because Peter was in prison. We remember those who are suffering and mistreated. We speak up for them. We pray for their courage, strength, and comfort. We pray that their torture is used for God's glory.

We pray as if we are the ones being persecuted—because when one part of the body of Christ suffers, every part suffers with it.

Finally, we pray for the persecutors, because we have no idea the plans God has for them. Saul, who approved of Stephen's stoning, became Paul, one of the greatest dispensers of God's grace.

Jesus means it when he tells us, **"Love your enemies and pray for those who persecute you, that you may be sons of your Father in heaven"** (Matthew 5:44,45).

Children of the Father have an awful lot of praying to do. Let's get busy.

August 8

Work hard

Pastor Mark Jeske

It is a fantasy of lazy people that economic wealth and success occur for other people because of luck, destiny, or cheating and that their own personal effort, therefore, is pointless. They deny the cause-and-effect link between work and personal wealth and so as a life strategy try to devise ways of tapping into what others have built up.

The Bible's warnings about greed and materialism are always timely. The love of money will indeed always be a root of all kinds of evil. However, that doesn't mean that exerting energy, working hard, intentional and disciplined saving, and careful investing to accumulate wealth are bad things. In fact, Scripture teaches us, **"Lazy hands make a man poor, but diligent hands bring wealth"** (Proverbs 10:4).

The Lord has severe words of judgment about abusive and stingy rich people, and he most certainly watches out for the poor, but that doesn't mean he sanctifies poverty as a life goal. Laziness is sin. Work is godly, for God himself works every day, exerting his mind and power on behalf of people he loves. Accumulated wealth means your children and grandchildren won't have to beg for food and shelter, means that there is money for somebody else to borrow to finance a home, means that there is money to borrow for someone to start or expand a business.

Means that the next generation of young people can find a job.

All the nations are God's instruments

Pastor Mark Jeske

All the time that you have been a believer, you've been told that you are an important agent of God. You are encouraged to see yourself as God's change agent, both individually and as part of your congregation, bringing God's Word and God's love to your community and the world. Scripture tells many stories of how God was at work through families of believers like Abraham's and through the nation of Israel.

Does it surprise you to hear that God just as readily uses *unbelieving* kings and their nations in his agenda? **"Look at the nations and watch—and be utterly amazed. For I am going to do something in your days that you would not believe, even if you were told. I am raising up the Babylonians, that ruthless and impetuous people"** (Habakkuk 1:5,6). Perhaps King Nebuchadnezzar thought Babylon's rise was due to his military brilliance or mastery of organizational theory. Ha! God thinks it was he who raised the Babylonians to power.

God used them to humble the stubborn nation of Judah and sequester them in captivity for a 70-year resting time. At just the right time God raised up a new overlord for the Middle East—Persia—and he led the Persian king, Cyrus, to decree that the Israelites could return home.

Do you suppose that God is still at work behind the scenes today, moving things around to grow his kingdom?

____

____

____

____

Can you keep a secret?

Pastor Mark Jeske

Is there any such thing as a secret anymore? There are security cameras everywhere now, and their unblinking eyes see all and record it forever. The Internet has unlimited memory storage, it seems. Nothing that once flew through the wires and air is ever really lost—it is on a server somewhere and can be found and brought back. Every cell phone is now a camera and video recorder, silently absorbing everything going on.

Don't think you're brilliant because you caught somebody else in a sin. Everybody sins. Everybody takes a stupid pill on certain days and says and does things that are embarrassing or hurtful or wrong. **"A man who lacks judgment derides his neighbor, but a man of understanding holds his tongue. A gossip betrays a confidence, but a trustworthy man keeps a secret"** (Proverbs 11:12,13).

Blabbing information that makes other people look bad may give you a gossipy thrill or make you feel morally superior or get you attention and friends (you think). A more Christian attitude, however, is to work to build up people rather than to enjoy tearing them down. It is better to help mend a frayed relationship than to be a part of ripping it further.

Think of all the dark parts of your life that you hope never see the light of day. Think how much you appreciate that your friends in the know do not reveal embarrassing and humiliating information about you. You can show that same mercy.

Eventually

Jason Nelson

The most reassuring promise in the entire Bible just might be Romans 8:28: **"We know that in all things God works for the good of those who love him, who have been called according to his purpose."** It also might be the most readily challenged by anyone who is leery of God and skeptical of faith talk. Maybe you've had someone suggest exceptions to you from his or her experience. Maybe you've wondered yourself if this promise leaks like a sieve.

The promise isn't that everything will always be good for those who love him. He made that promise once at the very beginning. He can't make that promise again until the very end because what happens now is threatened by evil he has nothing to do with. The promise is that even under these difficult circumstances, God will not stop working to bring good into the lives of those who love him. He will honor the commitment he made when he called us to faith in Jesus Christ: "I will never leave you or forsake you." It will all be good, eventually.

It is inspiring to hear believers tell real stories that validate this promise because eventually they were able to see something good. Eventually they learned a lesson, overcame hardship, and were better off. There are people who have lived through their own hell and can guarantee you that nothing falls outside of this promise. It will be good eventually.

____

____

____

____

What's in your head and heart?

Pastor Mark Jeske

Without a doubt, receiving the Lord's Supper is the most profound encounter with God we are allowed this side of heaven. Think about it—you are being given the very body of Christ, once nailed to the cross for you. You are given the blood of Christ, the very price of your salvation. His body physically touches yours; you become part of his. Your forgiveness is guaranteed; your place at the heavenly banquet table is promised.

But you need to know what is going on for the Lord's Supper to have these blessed effects, and you need to believe what God is teaching you. **"Whoever eats the bread or drinks the cup of the Lord in an unworthy manner will be guilty of sinning against the body and blood of the Lord. Everyone ought to examine themselves before they eat of the bread and drink of the cup"** (1 Corinthians 11:27,28). What's in your head and heart really matters; that's why churches ask potential communicants to take the Bible studies first so that their participation will not be in an "unworthy manner."

What does this examination look like? Four things:

1) Admit that you are a lost and condemned sinner.

2) Rejoice that your Savior Jesus has lived, suffered, died, and risen for you.

3) Recognize in the Supper the true body and blood of Christ, given and poured out for you for the forgiveness of your sins.

4) Rededicate yourself to serving the Lord with your life.

___

___

___

Old John

Jason Nelson

Old John came to this country from Austria a long time ago. He worked in a factory in the city and then moved up north. He may have had a family but lives alone in a trailer in the woods. He is a slight man, probably a shrunken version of his former self. He has some scattered back teeth that peek out when he flashes his big open smile. Even in warm weather he bundles up in well-worn layers, grabs his carved walking stick, and navigates a little trail to check for his mail.

The day he turned 90 he shrugged off a wish for a happy birthday. He pointed heavenward and with a stubborn accent whispered, "I just want to go to the Lord." Old John spoke for many people his age. Ninety isn't the new anything. It's old age, and more of us may have to deal with it. It's likely to be a test of faith. It would have been insensitive to tell John he seems spry for a man his age or should be glad he can still live on his own. Only he knows what it's like to be in his body and feel what's in his soul.

Old John is ready to die and is enduring what is left of life by clinging to a promise that we can all cling to: **"I was young and now I am old, yet I have never seen the righteous forsaken"** (Psalm 37:25).

____

____

____

____

____

Spray-painted hazards

Linda Buxa

Each year in Finland there are 3,000 to 5,000 reindeer versus auto accidents. These cause 15 million euros in damage and kill about 4,000 reindeer.

Last winter, the Finnish Reindeer Herders' Association came up with a unique way to solve the problem. They painted the reindeers' fur with a water-soluble paint, and spray-painted the antlers with a more permanent reflective paint. This way, the animals reflect auto headlights, giving drivers time to slow down and steer around the danger.

Too often temptations are like unmarked reindeer. You don't see them until it is too late. The wreck leaves you with a huge pile of damage—emotional, spiritual, physical, and financial. God tells us to spray-paint the danger in our lives: **"Have nothing to do with the fruitless deeds of darkness, but rather expose them. But everything exposed by the light becomes visible, for it is light that makes everything visible"** (Ephesians 5:11,13,14).

Use the light of Jesus, the Light of God's Word, to know what is dangerous for your faith. Then mark it so you can spot it a mile away and avoid it.

By the way, this is a whole lot easier if you have a group of Christians in your life to help you. Find friends who are brave enough to speak up when you are toying with darkness, who hold you accountable when fruitless deeds seem like a good idea. These are the same friends who, when you have caused a wreck, will listen to your confession and offer Jesus' forgiveness to you.

Safe driving!

Resolving grief

Jason Nelson

The death of a loved one tears us apart. It's a free fall into sadness with a very hard landing. I'm sorry that you've lost people you love. I have too. And I'm sorry that more losses are going to come for all of us.

Losing people hurts so much because it wasn't supposed to be this way. Death was unintended by God and is an unwanted ending to our good lives. It's unavoidable and disrupts our sense of what we want to last forever. **"God has done everything at the right time. He has put a sense of eternity in people's minds. Yet, mortals still can't grasp what God is doing from the beginning to the end of time"** (Ecclesiastes 3:11 GW).

Jesus felt grief. His dear friend Lazarus died before his time. Jesus knows death throws us into emotional turmoil. He wept over this loss—a human thing to do with grief. We need to wash it from our spirit with tears. Lazarus' sister blamed Jesus for not getting there sooner or doing more to prevent Lazarus' death. That too is very human, dealing with anger and guilt in the grieving process. For grief to resolve, we must detach it from both.

Then eternity happened. Jesus ignored time and brought Lazarus back to life. He gave Lazarus the resurrection he and his sisters believed in. Jesus resolved their grief and his grief with his power over death.

____

____

____

____

____

Will Jesus claim you?

Pastor Mark Jeske

The greatest message in all of Scripture is that of *grace*—God's unconditional love for you expressed through the work of Jesus Christ. On Calvary, God declared the world "not guilty" of sin. St. Paul praises him as a "God who justifies the wicked." There is no merit in us worth claiming in God's court.

However, do not confuse God's *universal grace* with *universalism,* the idea that all people on earth are going to heaven regardless of how they lived. Scripture teaches with equal force that we are justified *by faith.* We need to hear and believe the message for its amazing promises to come true for us.

During his ministry on earth, Jesus radiated grace every day he walked in Israel. But in spite of his powerful words and actions, some refused to repent and believe in him. He told a sad story about skeptics who made up their minds too late: **"Later the others also came. 'Sir! Sir!' they said. 'Open the door for us!' But he replied, 'I tell you the truth, I don't know you.' Therefore keep watch, because you do not know the day or the hour"** (Matthew 25:11-13).

We leap into eternity either through our own day of death or the great day of judgment. We don't know the day or hour of either. The consequences of unbelief are terrible—Jesus refuses to let you in, and the angels of doom haul you away.

Keep watch!

God did me a favor

Pastor Mark Jeske

When a group of married guys is sitting around on the deck or at a bar, occasionally one of them will say something like, "I married above myself." Heads will nod, and somebody will chime in, "We all did." That doesn't mean that we say it or show it to our wives very often, but deep inside we know. We know.

We know that our wives tune us up to be better family members, better employees, better dads, better *men*. We have learned better manners, social graces, and the priceless art of thinking ahead as to how our words and actions will affect other people. We learn to listen a little bit first before plunging ahead into things. We get insights into how the other 50 percent of the human race thinks.

We get a life partner who can help interpret what happened at the office party or family gathering. We get a steady friend who will tell us the truth when we need to hear it, whether we like it or not. We get someone who will tend us when we've been bruised, clap and cheer for us even when nobody else is, and eagerly join us in life's adventures.

Men did not invent gender, sexuality, or marriage; God did. It might also surprise us to find out someday how much God had to get involved to connect us with our wives. **"He who finds a wife finds what is *good* and receives *favor from the Lord*"** (Proverbs 18:22).

August 18

We're almost there

Linda Buxa

When we lived in California, my husband and his brother climbed Mt. Shasta. The hike up this 14,000-foot volcano isn't for the faint of heart. It requires good planning and the right gear to make it safely to the top.

As they climbed, the elevation started getting to them. They couldn't walk, breathe, and chew food at the same time. They got tired so easily. At one point, my husband wanted to turn around, but my brother-in-law convinced him to keep going. Later on, the roles reversed and it was my husband's turn to say, "We're almost there."

The photo from the top of Mt. Shasta shows that the effort was worth it. It also highlights that if they had hiked by themselves, they might not have reached the top. It would have been too easy to quit.

Christians have a goal too: to reach heaven. The journey requires the right gear and good climbing buddies. **"Let us be self-controlled, putting on faith and love as a breastplate, and the hope of salvation as a helmet. For God did not appoint us to suffer wrath but to receive salvation through our Lord Jesus Christ. He died for us so that, whether we are awake or asleep, we may live together with him. Therefore encourage one another and build each other up, just as in fact you are doing"** (1 Thessalonians 5:8-11).

The view from heaven will be worth it. Hang in there.

Grandchildren

Pastor Mark Jeske

What is it that makes dignified and sober senior citizens get so giddy? Their grandchildren, of course. The kids' artwork is on the fridge, their framed pictures are all over the house, their birthdays are all in Grandma's datebook (and in her memory), and the old folks count the days until the next get-together.

Grandparenting is kind of a do-over for parents who are painfully aware of mistakes they made the first time 'round. Grandparents play more, tolerate more, listen more, spoil more, and stress less than when raising their own kids. They know that one of their main jobs is to make the grandkids feel important. It's the parents' job to do the boring stuff, like getting the homework done, teaching the importance of sharing in household chores, enforcing obedience, and levying punishments.

Grandparents bring profound value to their younger family members. They have a wealth of wisdom accumulated the hard way. They have stories from the distant past to help kids understand how our present came to be. They can demonstrate grace, class, and patience.

How blessed are the grandparents who live in the same town as their grandkids—they get to see them more than just once a year. It's win-win-win: the grandparents get to enjoy their grandkids, the parents escape for some blessed relief, and kids think the whole deal is a treat for their benefit. **"Children's children are a crown to the aged"** (Proverbs 17:6).

Grandparents, wear your crowns with pride!

August 20

How long?

Jason Nelson

I have never heard anyone say, "You know what I really love to do? *Wait*." I have never known anyone who is eager for checkout lines to be long because they love standing there. No one wants the restaurant to be swamped so they can wait for a table. Who wants the doctor running behind because they just love sitting in the waiting room? God made time, and he made it for us. We always hear the clock ticking. Whenever we are put on a list, we want to know how long it will take. How long will we be waiting? That tendency causes lots of stress for us during times of trouble.

David prayed like a man tired of waiting. **"My soul is in anguish. How long, O Lord, how long? I am worn out from my groaning; all night long I flood my bed with weeping and drench my couch with tears"** (Psalm 6:3,6). Waiting makes time drag. Waiting through suffering makes time stand still. That's hard to bear. It's also necessary when we are waiting for the Lord. What is best for us is the only thing on his schedule. His mercy is never on the clock. If you have ever waited for the Lord, you know from good experience that you don't want him to rush. With patience and faith, **"wait for the Lord; be strong and take heart and wait for the Lord"** (Psalm 27:14).

____

____

____

____

____

August 21

He'll make more

Pastor Mark Jeske

Some people shrug off hardship and adversity. They leave their "poverty days" in the rearview and go forward without looking back. Other people remember the lean days too much and have anxiety running in the backs of their minds all the time. They act out that fear by becoming pack rats and hoarders. ("Don't throw that out—I might need it someday.") They feel guilt when they buy something. They pore over their retirement savings often and groan that it's not enough. Every downturn in financial markets ricochets through their brains. They can't bring themselves to be generous givers to a ministry because they might run out of money.

Those fears and pressures are not unique to this modern era—Christians have always struggled with them. In early Christian times, people felt just as much financial stress as we do today. The terror of scarcity is rooted in the suspicion that God's active working in people's lives is mostly in the past and that we are marching forward on our own into an uncertain, treacherous, scary future.

St. Paul's wonderful words of encouragement resonate as much today as they ever did: **"God is able to make *all* grace abound to you, so that in *all* things at *all* times, having *all* that you need, you will abound in *every* good work"** (2 Corinthians 9:8). The God we worship loves to give you things, bless your efforts, grow your resources, connect you with friends, and help you succeed.

Don't be afraid of running out. He'll make more.

____

____

____

____

August 22

Are Christians the new counterculture?

Pastor Mark Jeske

Back in the 1960s it was fashionable to imagine that young people had created a new way to live and think, a "Counterculture" to the majority "Establishment." Sex, drugs, rock 'n' roll, and antiwar protests were badges of belonging. Radicals urged people to kick down "Victorian" and "Puritanical" restraints on their freedoms and behaviors. They won.

The irony is that those views are now in the majority. Homosexuality is now not only legitimized; gay marriage is legal in many states. Cohabitation and single parenthood are the new normal. Divorce is much easier to obtain now than it was in 1960.

Biblical Christianity is the new counterculture. We are becoming an underground resistance, because we worship a King bigger than fashion, follow moral principles that are timeless not trendy, and still believe in sin and redemption. The way St. Paul described living as a Christian in the pagan Roman Empire sounds so right now: **"I tell you this, and insist on it in the Lord, that you must no longer live as the Gentiles do, in the futility of their thinking. They are darkened in their understanding and separated from the life of God because of the ignorance that is in them due to the hardening of their hearts"** (Ephesians 4:17,18).

Can you stand being in the minority? Whose approval do you crave? What do you value most? Whom do you most admire? Whom do you most wish to imitate? What is the mission of your life?

____

____

____

Back to Sunday school

Pastor Mark Jeske

As Labor Day approaches, the newsprint advertising supplements are full of "Back to School" sales and coupons. Kids look forward to some new clothes, and parents can go back to their normal schedules. As the lazy days of August fade away, it's time to go back to class and step up to a grade higher.

People are not born literate and "numerate." Decoding language symbols and manipulating the decimal number system is learned behavior. It's hard work—nothing comes automatically. Knowing the ways of God doesn't come automatically either. It must be patiently taught by the mature to the immature, from the wise to the young.

God's Word has real answers for the most important questions: where we came from, the meaning of our present existence, and what happens after death. Only Scripture helps people discover their Creator; only Scripture helps people meet their Savior; only Scripture reveals the Spirit's agenda for our lives. King Solomon tells us that only those who know the Lord are truly wise: **"The fear of the LORD is the beginning of knowledge, but fools despise wisdom and discipline"** (Proverbs 1:7).

As you see to the schooling of your children and grandchildren, don't forget Sunday school. The teachers do not replace your own responsibility for discipling the young, but they are priceless partners in that crucially important endeavor.

Surrounded by blindness

Linda Buxa

"How, then, can they call on the one they have not believed in? And how can they believe in the one of whom they have not heard? And how can they hear without someone preaching to them?" (Romans 10:14).

Years ago I visited the Green Grotto Caves in Jamaica. These mile-long caves have a fascinating history. Christopher Columbus landed two miles from this spot in 1494. The Spanish hid there when the English took over the island in the 1600s. Runaway slaves used them as a hideaway. Pirates and smugglers have used them too.

In the middle of all this though, in the crystal-clear subterranean lake, fish have been swimming, blindly unaware of what's going on around them. Literally blind. Without light, these fish never developed the ability to see.

You may not know it, but you live in a whole lake of blind people. You might be involved in a bunch of church activities, but your neighbors still have never heard about Jesus. Your friends and coworkers might have heard but can't see how Jesus could impact their lives.

The enemy is doing everything he can to keep them blind: **"The god of this age has blinded the minds of unbelievers, so that they cannot see the light of the gospel of the glory of Christ, who is the image of God"** (2 Corinthians 4:4).

If you don't tell them, they will never know. If you don't show them, they might never see. It's a great privilege to help change their eternity.

____

____

____

In God's eyes I'm somebody

Pastor Mark Jeske

When they need to preserve an important bit of information in a hurry and don't trust their memory, some people have the cute habit of writing it on the back of their hands or their palms with an ink pen. Maybe it's a phone number, a key date, or an important name. We see our hands better than any other part of our body. You know the phrase, "Out of sight, out of mind"? Well, the reverse is true too: "In sight, in mind."

When God wanted to create a metaphor for helping believers know how precious they were to him, he took that custom of palm writing, which must have existed already for thousands of years, and applied it to himself as though he had hands. **"Can a mother forget the baby at her breast and have no compassion on the child she has borne? Though she may forget, I will not forget you! See, I have engraved you on the palms of my hands"** (Isaiah 49:15,16).

If there is some writing on your hands, you will see it and think about it many times each day. How amazing it is that God promises that he knows your name, remembers your needs, and thinks about you multiple times each day. He cares about you even more than a mother cares about her newborn (pretty much the gold standard for intensity of attachment). You are that important to him.

In sight, in mind.

In God's eyes I'm forgiven

Pastor Mark Jeske

Billy Crystal used to appear on *Saturday Night Live* doing a smarmy parody of actor Fernando Lamas that he called "Fernando's Hideaway." He would do "interviews" with celebrity guests, assuring them, "You look mahvelous, simply mahvelous. Remember, it's not how you feel but how you look."

In a strange coincidence, God could say that same thing about your relationship with him. I have talked to any number of people over the years who didn't seem to be following active Christianity in any serious way, but they assured me that they "felt good" about going to heaven someday. Feelings are often wrong. But what God *sees* is never wrong. He knows who the fakers and poseurs and hypocrites are. He also knows who the real believers are.

When you came to faith in Jesus Christ as your Savior, your appearance changed. Washed of your sins; wearing now the holiness of Christ as though it were a robe; connected by faith to Christ's suffering, death, burial, and resurrection; you are a new person. **"'Come now, let us reason together,' says the Lord. 'Though your sins are like scarlet, they shall be as white as snow; though they are red as crimson, they shall be like wool'"** (Isaiah 1:18). You can rejoice in your new identity. You have new strength and motivation to live your new identity.

You know, in God's eyes you look mahvelous, simply mahvelous.

In God's eyes I'm useful

Pastor Mark Jeske

Parents do their children an enormous disservice when they do everything for them. Pampering and spoiling may help insecure parents feel better, but that cripples children's ability to do for themselves and grow into competent adults. Children need to feel not only safe and secure but *useful*, that they are making a contribution to the family's progress. As soon as possible they need to learn to take out the trash, make their beds, haul laundry, do dishes, rake, dust, and vacuum.

Church leaders should not baby congregational members either. Christians are built to serve. Their baptism day is draft day into God's army. We all need to feel not only loved but *useful*: **"Each one should use whatever gift he has received to serve others, faithfully administering God's grace in its various forms"** (1 Peter 4:10).

An all-powerful God doesn't really need us, of course. Does that thought distress you? It shouldn't. The Engineer who designed and built California redwood forests doesn't *need* me. But he *chooses* to use me because it is his mission for his children to grow us up into miniature versions of himself. He doesn't like our injecting ourselves into his business, like judging. But he absolutely refuses to do things for us that he has equipped and commissioned us to do.

In your congregation, God treats you like grown-ups. He will handle the conversions. Your jobs include administration, outreach, education, fellowship, and care for people and property. Isn't it great to be useful?

In God's eyes I'm beautiful

Pastor Mark Jeske

It's a struggle to look good, isn't it? How hard we work at it; how constant the pressure. We all know that every day we are being evaluated on our appearance. Frankly, most of us aren't that hot. Age, gravity, and stress take a toll each year. Take a look around you next time you're sunning yourself at a crowded beach. Only a very few of those people should be wearing so little clothing.

We try to be brave about it and wear flattering clothes, paint the acne, color the gray, sneak out for liposuction or Botox, try to resist junk food, ask about Rogaine, and make a stab at working out. But I suspect that most of us are pretty insecure about how we look.

But we have acceptance, love, and even admiration in the arms of our heavenly Father. Here's the message his Son, Jesus, was commissioned to proclaim during his earthly ministry: **"The Spirit of the Sovereign LORD is on me, because the LORD has anointed me to preach good news to the poor. He has sent me . . . to comfort all who mourn, and provide for those who grieve in Zion—to bestow on them a crown of beauty instead of ashes"** (Isaiah 61:1-3).

Note the language—we receive a crown not of victory or rank or power (though those things are true), but a crown of *beauty* to replace the ashes of shame, loss, insecurity, and the ugliness of our sin.

In Daddy's eyes you look great!

____

____

____

____

In God's eyes I'm family

Pastor Mark Jeske

I would like to think I love mankind, but frankly I have time and energy to share with only a few. I drive by some blocks in my city and think, "Man, somebody should help you trim those overgrown bushes, pick up that trash, do some carpentry repairs, and get some paint on the place." But I don't pull over. I don't know the owners or have a personal relationship with them. Now, when my brother-in-law needs help roofing his garage, that's another story.

When God looks at your life, at your wounds, your needs, your struggles, he doesn't just drive by in his divine chariot. You're family! Through your baptism he has called you nothing less than his *children*: **"You are all children of God through faith in Christ Jesus, for all of you who were baptized into Christ have clothed yourselves with Christ"** (Galatians 3:26,27).

He has accepted all the obligations of fatherhood—protecting, providing, teaching, correcting, and rescuing. When you approach him, you don't have to adopt the tone and posture of someone seeking favors from a government official, mafia boss, or bank. You aren't begging. You may call on your heavenly *Father*, who loves you even more than human fathers love their kids.

All parents cherish the memory of cuddling with their small children right after their baths and then tucking them into bed. Remember that smell? Thanks to your baptism, you smell that good to your Father in heaven.

August 30

In God's eyes I'm perfect

Pastor Mark Jeske

You know, it's good to pay attention to details. It's good to finish what you started. It's good to be tidy. It's even good to aim for perfection, but some people are cursed at not being able to stop. They never seem happy with other people because they're so disappointed at their shortcomings. Nothing is ever quite good enough—the salsa was too picante, the roast was a little dry, the coffee not hot enough, and there was dust on the chair rungs.

They probably aren't happy with themselves either. Perfectionists just can't relax after a project and say to their helpers, "You did well," and think to themselves, "and I did too." There was always more that could have been done, flaws to fret over, and insecurity about what people may or may not have thought.

Here are words of encouragement for all perfectionists, and all victims of perfectionists, from the half-brother of our Lord Jesus himself: **"To him who is able to keep you from falling and to present you before his glorious presence *without fault* and with great joy—to the only God our Savior be glory, majesty, power and authority, through Jesus Christ our Lord"** (Jude 24,25). In God's eyes we're perfect, as perfect as Jesus himself!

That means you can look forward to your first face-to-face meeting with God completely without fear. He won't be disappointed in you. In fact, according to Jesus' own words, the first thing you will hear is, "Well done, good and faithful servant."

In God's eyes I'm immortal

Pastor Mark Jeske

Comedian Woody Allen said once that he didn't want to achieve immortality through his work. He wanted to achieve immortality by not dying. Behind that joke (as probably behind most humor) is a painful truth: we are all shuffling toward the graveyard. You can deny it, pretend, distract yourself, fantasize a different ending, or refuse to talk about it, but the hard reality is that we are *mortal* (from the Latin word for "death").

Not only are we doomed to live on this earth in a span measuring only decades; some have their short lives shortened even more by illness, accident, or crime. How quick the acts in life's theater! How soon we are broomed off the stage!

God doesn't look at our lives that way at all. He sent our Savior Jesus to conquer death, and now through faith in him believers connect with Jesus' *immortality* (i.e., "can't-die-itude"). **"I am the resurrection and the life. He who believes in me will live, even though he dies; and whoever lives and believes in me will never die"** (John 11:25,26). God sees us now as deathless. This present age is only a phase to be succeeded by a better one.

Freed by that empowering gospel good news, we can live each day to the full, enjoying it and all God has put there, serene in the confidence that whether our days are many or few, everlasting heaven and the grand reunion await.

September

"THE PEACE OF GOD, WHICH TRANSCENDS ALL UNDERSTANDING, WILL GUARD YOUR HEARTS AND YOUR MINDS IN CHRIST JESUS."
PHILIPPIANS 4:7

I'm afraid

Pastor Mark Jeske

Sometimes it's good to be afraid. Small children should be afraid of the danger of traffic on a busy city street. Carpenters should fear to be careless around the whining blade of their table saw. All Christians should be afraid to defy God, blow off his commandments, ignore his holy will, and thus incur his wrath.

President Franklin Roosevelt respected what a spirit of fear could do to sap a nation of its self-confidence and will. In his first inaugural address, in the pit of the Great Depression in 1932, he said that "the only thing we have to fear is . . . fear itself—nameless, unreasoning, unjustified terror which paralyzes needed efforts to convert retreat into advance."

Ministries and congregations sometimes attempt too little because they fear too much. Individual Christians never develop their ability to witness for their Savior because they are afraid of making a mistake. Laypeople fear being criticized for incorrect teaching, so they leave the "religious talk" to the clergy.

Satan wants to keep us afraid, weak, and disengaged from the world, huddled into our little cave-sanctuaries. Here is St. Paul's stirring call: **"God did not give us a spirit of timidity, but a spirit of power, of love and of self-discipline"** (2 Timothy 1:7). Call on that power! Be all God has made you and called you to be! Speak! Love! Serve! No fear!

Labor of love

Pastor Mark Jeske

The first Monday of September means different things to different people. To children it's a day off of school, if they've started the new school year. To frazzled employees it's the blessed relief of a three-day weekend, the unofficial end of summer. To northerners it's the day you take in the pier at the lake. To unionized workers it's a day to reflect on the movement for workplace safety and fair working conditions.

May I suggest a unique take on the day for Christians? The day for *not* working is a great time to ponder God's will *about* working. St. Paul helped the Thessalonian Christians see their jobs not as a necessary evil to survive and then quit as soon as they could: **"We were not idle when we were with you, nor did we eat anyone's food without paying for it. On the contrary, we worked day and night, laboring and toiling so that we would not be a burden to any of you. . . . We gave you this rule: 'If a man will not work, he shall not eat'"** (2 Thessalonians 3:7-10).

God *made* us to work. He himself poured all his creative design and engineering into the world he made, and he exerts himself on our behalf every day. The entire universe would collapse, incinerate itself, and grow dark and cold without his sustaining might.

We are called to look at work as he does—as our personal echo of his great labors. Love your job!

Seeing the crowds

Linda Buxa

A famous athlete just bought a house a few miles away from my home. The whole community is buzzing about it, wondering if they'll run into him at the grocery store or the gas station. He moved to the area to find some off-season peace, but now that he has become "somebody," everyone wants a glimpse of him.

A celebrity watch is nothing new. Two thousand years ago, Jesus could not move from place to place without a huge crowd following him, wanting healing and miracles. Rarely was there peace—even if he tried. **"Jesus went through all the towns and villages, teaching in their synagogues, proclaiming the good news of the kingdom and healing every disease and sickness. When he saw the crowds, he had compassion on them, because they were harassed and helpless, like sheep without a shepherd"** (Matthew 9:35,36).

Look at the people around you. They aren't hanging out with you because of your popularity but because God put them in your life for a reason. He knows they are harassed and helpless, needing a Shepherd. He knows you can help them find peace. You get to tell them firsthand about Jesus' grace, mercy, and compassion. You get to introduce them to the Savior, who takes the outcasts and makes them royalty.

If everybody in your life already knows about the Shepherd, start praying to meet more people. God loves creating opportunities for you to talk to other people.

____

____

____

Preach it, David!

Linda Buxa

I was reading Psalm 73 the other day and wanted to shout, "Preach it, David!"

"For I envied the arrogant when I saw the prosperity of the wicked. They have no struggles; their bodies are healthy and strong. They are free from the burdens common to man; they are not plagued by human ills" (Psalm 73:3-5).

He put to words the feelings in my heart. And he is spot on, don't you think? I look around and see businessmen who cheat their way to wealth, people who lie without consequence, bosses who treat their subordinates like trash but get promoted anyway. The people who love Jesus seem to get stepped on, ignored, mocked.

I was on an aggrieved soapbox when David got to the part of the psalm that stopped me short: **"When my heart was grieved and my spirit embittered, I was senseless and ignorant; I was a brute beast before you"** (verses 21,22).

I wanted David to stop preaching it, but he was right. Being jealous of people headed to hell just highlights my ignorance. Envying their temporary wealth just makes me shortsighted. Wishing for a burden-free life shows I still don't grasp how God refines me and draws me close to him.

So I listen as David keeps preaching it: **"You guide me with your counsel, and afterward you will take me into glory. Whom have I in heaven but you? And earth has nothing I desire besides you"** (verses 24,25).

Amen!

____

____

____

Care for your animals

Pastor Mark Jeske

Biblical Christians bristle at the notion that people descended from animals. We believe Genesis 1 and 2, that man and woman were made at the end of the six days, creation's crown. There is nothing in Scripture to suggest that animals have souls. Dogs can't believe in Jesus and won't face a personal judgment day. But that doesn't give us license to treat our animals poorly. Just because they aren't human doesn't mean they're disposable.

"A righteous man cares for the needs of his animal," says the Bible (Proverbs 12:10). Why would God have thought it necessary to include that admonition in Scripture? Perhaps because it is a characteristic of sin for the strong to take advantage of the weak, for people to get so wrapped up in their own agendas that they neglect the needs of others, including animals in their care. Perhaps mistreatment doesn't seem so bad because "it's just an animal after all."

We've come a long way from the days when horses provided most transportation and when many homes in big cities had chicken coops in the backyard. People today seem to have as many pets as ever. They provide valuable companionship and, in the case of larger dogs, home security. They are part of the wonderful web of life that God has provided in our world. We can show our respect for the Creator by how we take care of this part of his creation.

September 6

The mystery of the code

Jason Nelson

In 1953 James Watson and Francis Crick solved a mystery when they announced that every detail of living things is determined by an interwoven double helix of DNA. They discovered that organisms possess a genetic code and pass it along to future generations. My God, how great thou art!

Even more surprising is that genetic variation among all nations and groups of people is one-tenth of 1 percent (nature.com). All people on earth are 99.9 percent the same. There is one human race. That makes sense considering we have one Creator and a common set of parents. The differences among us are superficial. What shade of brown is our skin? What kind of round are our eyes?

The greater mystery is how we've made statistically insignificant differences monumental. We come to believe that nearly identical people are just not like us at all. Then minor differences get distributed geographically and become divisive.

Disciple Peter struggled with that kind of bigotry. He harbored resentment that the gospel was also for those filthy Gentiles. God told him, **"Do not call anything impure that God has made clean"** (Acts 10:15). God made all people and made them his children through the blood of Jesus. There is no genetic or Christian reason for racial hatred. All have sinned and fallen short. All are redeemed by God's love in Christ.

The most accurate label we can put on each other is brother and sister.

An outrageous request

Pastor Mark Jeske

If you know that you are in someone's will, it is considered very bad form if you appear to wish that the testator would hurry up and die. Even worse would be to ask for your inheritance before the loved one has actually expired. Jesus' opening proposition in his amazing parable of the prodigal son certainly made all of his hearers sit bolt upright.

"There was a man who had two sons. The younger one said to his father, 'Father, give me my share of the estate.' So he divided his property between them" (Luke 15:11,12).

I don't know which is more outrageous—the insolent cheek of the younger son or the incredible decision by the father to grant the request. I'll tell you what—if any of my kids would ask to cash out his or her part of my estate before I was dead, the strain on our relationship would be *severe*.

Jesus' parable highlights a central feature of human life on planet earth. God so desires that people's love for him should be given freely that he trusts us with a huge amount of freedom, thereby allowing the possibility of grievous failure. From God's point of view, there can be no true love without major risk.

He has entrusted you with enormous resources and allows you terrific latitude in how you use it. He is risking everything in the hope that you will love him back.

The struggle doesn't seem worth it

Pastor Mark Jeske

There's an old saying we urban dwellers have heard over the years: "You got to go wit' da flow." You know what that means. It's hard bucking the culture. It's hard being called a Goody two-shoes or a choirboy. It's hard living by a moral value system that seemingly nobody else follows. It's hard saying no to sin that is part of everybody else's lifestyle. It's hard to sacrifice when everybody else is having fun. The cost is now; the payoff seems so far in the future as not to exist.

The strain on European and American Christians is how to live lives of self-control and faith integrity in a post-Christian culture. Imagine the strain on African and Asian Christians who live under a government that is actively hostile to Christians and allows or even encourages persecution. Why go through all of this?

Here's why: **"Let us fix our eyes on Jesus, the author and perfecter of our faith, who for the joy set before him endured the cross, scorning its shame, and sat down at the right hand of the throne of God. Consider him who endured such opposition from sinful men, so that you will not grow weary and lose heart"** (Hebrews 12:2,3).

We're not in heaven yet. There is no heaven on earth. But the glimpses of the real heaven from the pages of God's Word and the touches of real love that we experience from people whom God has sent into our lives give us hope that the wait will be worth it. Hang on!

____

____

____

____

Running on empty

Jason Nelson

The gadget engineers are pushing wearable technology. Computers in eyeglasses and watches can keep us connected and our hands free. We can accessorize with wristbands to monitor our health. We can wear cameras on our foreheads so everyone can see the world from our perspectives. It's the Internet of everything. I think we should wear little dashboards with trouble lights so we know when to check our fluids. Sometimes we don't notice when everything is running low until we grind to a halt.

That's especially true of our spiritual life, which is the engine of our lives. There are many things that drain away our joy, and we don't notice it's too low until something breaks down. **"A miserable heart means a miserable life; a cheerful heart fills the day with song"** (Proverbs 15:15 MSG).

Nothing fills our hearts like all things Jesus. Meditating on his Word, his love, his presence replenishes our faith and keeps it strong. My tank runs empty too, and I chug along on mere fumes of happiness. I get a refill every time I sit down to write one of these devotions. As I try to imagine what you're going through, I confront what I'm going through. The privilege of bringing God's Word to you renews my faith. Thinking about what Jesus means to me fills me up again. That's the power of the gospel.

____

____

____

____

____

September 10

I can't forgive myself

Pastor Mark Jeske

Shoulda, coulda, woulda. Those three painful words are an anthem of regret that we sing to ourselves when we've failed, choked, blanked, blundered, or bungled something important. You know, it's good to accept responsibility for our own mistakes. Seriously! Blamers are no fun to be around because everything is always somebody else's fault. It is refreshing when others, and we ourselves, own up and claim what we did.

Except when the self-blaming doesn't stop. If you get into a time loop where all you can do is remember your failure, all you can do is feel ashamed, all you can do is beat yourself up, you will stay broken and on your knees forever. True repentance doesn't stop with acknowledgement of guilt. Truly repentant people lift up their eyes to Christ and his cross and allow his words of gospel love to penetrate the fog of blame.

Christ has already taken on himself the blame and punishment for all of our sins. Why would we try to take it back? He gives us that incredible gift purely out of mercy—we don't have to pressure ourselves with qualifying for it or meeting his minimum standards. Let go! **"There is now no condemnation for those who are in Christ Jesus"** (Romans 8:1).

If Jesus has forgiven you, you are forgiven indeed. If Jesus chooses to like you, you can like yourself. If Jesus has shown you mercy, you can lighten up on yourself.

____

____

____

Why?

Pastor Mark Jeske

The second week of September will forever bring a painful annual memory to every American. In our everyday language, *911* means both the number to call in an emergency and the date on which 2,996 people were killed by hijacked aircraft that were driven into three large buildings and crashed into a field.

By now we pretty much know the *what*. We still have a hard time with the *why*. Why would 15 Saudis plus an Egyptian, a Lebanese, and two men from the United Arab Emirates kill that many unarmed civilians? Our countries get along, don't they? Why do they hate us so?

Irrational persecution is nothing new. King David felt it: **"My eyes fail, looking for my God. Those who hate me without reason outnumber the hairs of my head"** (Psalm 69:3,4). These words were prophetic of the thoughts of the suffering Savior as well. Satan loves rage and violence, and he drives people both to rational and irrational violence. There will be more, much more, before the end comes.

David, Christ, and we all turn to the same source of security and comfort: **"But I pray to you, O Lord, in the time of your favor; in your great love, O God, answer me with your sure salvation"** (Psalm 69:13). God's mighty angels will shield us; God's superb global management guarantees that all things, even disasters, will work for our good; God's gracious purposes will all be achieved.

Look for the devil's mask

Linda Buxa

I know a man who served as a missionary in Brazil. As he walked along the streets, he saw the food and candles that were left out as an offering to spirits, which is part of the Umbanda religion. This religion combines African traditions, Catholicism, spiritism, and indigenous beliefs.

Having watched the religion in action, the missionary commented, "The devil takes off his mask in Brazil."

For the most part, in the U.S. the devil wears a mask. He disguises the ways he uses to take our attention off God. Our idolatry takes slightly more socially acceptable forms: sports, entertainment, work, busyness, comfort. We don't think about evil because we don't often see its face.

God wants us to take our blinders off, to remember **"our struggle is not against flesh and blood, but against the rulers, against the authorities, against the powers of this dark world and against the spiritual forces of evil in the heavenly realms"** (Ephesians 6:12).

Just because we may not see him outright, we can still see Satan's marks. The father of lies wears his mask as he ruins families, makes people feel alone, stirs up arguments, gets us comfortable, and distracts us from loving the people who don't know God.

It's not hopeless though.

Jesus **"disarmed the powers and authorities, he made a public spectacle of them, triumphing over them by the cross"** (Colossians 2:15).

The battle is still going, and it's time to get back in.

____

____

____

I feel so stupid

Pastor Mark Jeske

Everybody does dumb things. Even the people who seem to have perfect lives are just better at hiding their mistakes or getting them blamed on someone else. Our minds, hearts, spirits, and strength were broken in the fall into sin, and we must not put the burden of perfectionism on ourselves. We did not enter life pure and perfect, as did Adam and Eve. We were broken from the get-go.

But we can learn. We can grow in knowledge (facts), wisdom (meaning of the facts), and discernment (good judgment). As we recall, sometimes painfully, our misdeeds of the past, it is not helpful or productive to dwell on those memories too long. Confess them to God. Give the guilt to Jesus and let him carry it. Apologize to those you may have hurt, and do whatever you can to restore what you broke. And then move on.

Spend your energy looking to the future and making changes in yourself so you won't repeat the mistake, or worse, become addicted to a constant loop of the bad behavior. God is much more interested in your future than in your past. God's Word is your source of information and power: **"The fear of the Lord is the beginning of knowledge"** (Proverbs 1:7). Our failures in life come from not organizing our lives around God's agenda.

When we don't worship him, we will end up worshiping something else.

I know that you have little strength

Pastor Mark Jeske

"I know what you're going through." You may hear that from friends wishing to seem sympathetic. What you want to snap back at them is, "You have no idea what I'm going through," but instead you just say, "Yeah."

Our God tracks absolutely everything going on in our lives. He and the angels rejoice at our triumphs, and they groan at our struggles, intervening at strategic times to keep us on the path that leads to heaven, binding up our wounds, standing us back up on our feet, and giving us a little tailwind to keep going.

God knows that we're weak sometimes. He told the struggling Christians in the Asian city of Philadelphia, **"I know that you have little strength, yet you have kept my word and have not denied my name"** (Revelation 3:8). Whether it involves money, family relationships, health, or business, God has compassion on our human weaknesses. He does not despise us for not being supermen and women. He may even be allowing these hardships to draw us closer to him. What he is interested in most of all is our faith in our Savior Jesus. Have we given up on the gospel's promises? God urged the Philadelphia Christians, and he urges you too, to hold onto what you have so that no one can take away your crown of glory. Overcome, and he will make you a pillar in the heavenly temple.

You may die a debtor, but connected to Jesus you will wake up in heaven a spiritual millionaire.

The precious gift of unity

Pastor Mark Jeske

We are all a bunch of independent-minded individuals, aren't we? In our family discussions, there may be five of us in the room but there are six strong opinions. In our congregations, Satan doesn't have to work too hard to open up deep cracks in the plans and spirit of the ministry. Sometimes the longer you've known people, the worse it gets. Martin Luther was said to have groaned once, "God save me from my enemies . . . and my friends."

King Hezekiah was God's point man to bring about a huge spiritual reformation in Judah in the late 700s B.C. He sent emissaries through his realm, and also to the shattered kingdom of Israel to the north, inviting people to come to a huge national Passover feast in Jerusalem, neglected for ages. Some actually overcame their regional resentments and made the pilgrimage. What's more, **"also in Judah the hand of God was on the people to give them *unity of mind* to carry out what the king and his officials had ordered, following the word of the LORD"** (2 Chronicles 30:12).

Unity of mind and spirit doesn't happen automatically. It's a precious gift of God and must be tended by each of us. It is hard but worthwhile work for people in a Christian organization to develop agreement on a common mission, on values and philosophy, on clear lines of responsibility and authority, and on goals that are important.

And then pray for the hand of God.

____

____

____

____

I feel all alone

Pastor Mark Jeske

It's a common but understandable mistake to draw conclusions about our relationship with God from our relationships with people around us. When family life is happy and peaceful, it's easy to say, "Thank you, God." When we're enmeshed in a lot of conflict, we imagine him angry with us. When people we thought were friends start ignoring us, we think he's dumping us too. On top of everything, our guilty consciences make us ashamed to pray, assuming that he's too irritated to care about us anymore.

Jesus himself knew what it felt like to be alone. After some hard things in his teachings caused many followers to abandon him and drift away, he asked his disciples if they were going to leave too. They actually did abandon him in the Garden of Gethsemane. Jesus' suffering on the cross was utterly alone—even his Father forsook him there—so that Jesus could guarantee to us that his Father would never forsake us.

King David, sinner and saint, knew he was never alone: **"Though my father and mother forsake me, the Lord will receive me"** (Psalm 27:10). What a relief it is to be able to end a bad day with the prayer, "Well, Father, at least you're still here with me." Here is God's promise for you and for all believers: **"God has said, 'Never will I leave you; never will I forsake you'"** (Hebrews 13:5).

Sleep well tonight.

What happened to our relationship?

Pastor Mark Jeske

It is a miserable failing in many homes that the husband and wife take each other for granted. They figure that now that they're married, they don't have to try so hard any longer to be nice. They don't listen as well; they grow indifferent to the other person's needs; they talk less; they say "I love you" less. Before they know it, their love for each other has cooled off.

We should not over trust in God's grace. The fact that he loves us unconditionally and is phenomenally patient with us does not give us permission to ignore him until we want something. The Bible is crystal clear: God's grace goes first, revealing the great works of Christ. Faith comes next, worked by the Spirit, and our faith response of good works comes next, an absolutely nonnegotiable sign of true and genuine faith.

When our words of faith and deeds of love are iffy or absent, sirens should go off in our heads. God's words of warning to the Christians at Ephesus and to us come because he loves us and doesn't want to lose us: **"Yet I hold this against you: You have forsaken your first love. Remember the height from which you have fallen! Repent and do the things you did at first"** (Revelation 2:4,5). It *is* possible to lose your faith. It *is* possible to throw away your salvation. It *is* possible to choose things other than God to love and worship.

God would love to hear from you. It's not too late.

______

______

______

______

You find Jesus in the strangest places

Jason Nelson

If you've been following his career, you know you'll find Jesus in the strangest places. He's a bit of a mystery, and he admitted it. **"In a little while you will see me no more, and then after a little while you will see me"** (John 16:16).

He's been known to hover over a void, creating light and everything else. He is the Word of God, full of grace and truth. He was in a burning bush, a fiery furnace, and wherever the Angel of the Lord was needed. He tucked himself in a human embryo, slid through a birth canal, and landed in a feeding trough. Shepherds and Magi looked for him because the star meant he had to be somewhere. He wandered off during a festival and was found in the temple debating scholars. He ate with sinners, mixed it up with hypocrites, and went off alone to pray. He was crucified and buried but after three days was not to be found in his grave. He sits at the right hand of God and is in the midst of two or three who gather on earth in his name.

He is with us now and will come again to take us where he is. You find Jesus in the strangest places, and he invites us to seek him out. Come into my heart, Lord Jesus. It's a strange place, and I need you there.

____

____

____

____

____

That's my story and I'm sticking to it

Pastor Mark Jeske

In Jesus' parable of the talents, the story ends on a sour note. The master is calling in his main accounts: **"Then the man who had received the one talent** (i.e., a valuable gold or silver bar) **came. 'Master,' he said, 'I knew that you are a hard man, harvesting where you have not sown and gathering where you have not scattered seed. So I was afraid and went out and hid your talent in the ground. See, here is what belongs to you'"** (Matthew 25:24,25).

The "one talent" manager shows why the master had trusted him the least—he had the bad judgment to embarrass the master and call him a shady dealer *publicly*! But his first action was worse—he buried the money instead of doing the minimum, i.e., at least just walking it to the bank.

Why would he hide the money? Well, to steal it, of course. If he buried it, there would be no paper trail. Nobody would know he had it. If the master never returned, in time he could pretend that it was his.

How easy it is for us to play mind games like Mr. One Talent. How easy it is to look at God's stuff and say, "Mine." How easy it is to forget that we were created for his service and his agenda. How good it is for you and me to have this conversation before God returns and it is too late.

____

____

____

____

____

September 20

You can plagiarize God

Jason Nelson

Stealing the ideas and words of another is a crime against humanity. Content-filled websites and copy/paste computer functions make it easier and easier to get away with. Students need to fight the temptation. So do writers. Teachers must watch for the theft of intellectual property. So must editors. Always give credit where credit is due. But you *can* plagiarize God. It's not a sin to make his words your own.

The prophets made a career out of "plagiarizing" God. It was his idea. **"I will raise up for them a prophet like you from among their brothers; I will put my words in his mouth"** (Deuteronomy 18:18). God wanted prophets to take his message and run with it. He wanted his words in the public domain and accessible to everyone. Sometimes they acknowledged the source: "This is what the Lord says." And they taught people how to recognize a fraud. **"'How can we know when a message has not been spoken by the Lord?' If what a prophet proclaims in the name of the Lord does not take place or come true, that is a message the Lord has not spoken"** (Deuteronomy 18:21,22).

This is the screen for authenticity. You know it is originally from God if it rings true, no matter who says it. So go ahead and speak his words like they are yours and use his teachings like you own them.

____

____

____

____

____

You've got a friend

Pastor Mark Jeske

"You just call out my name, and you know wherever I am, I'll come running . . ." Carole King got a lot of mileage out of that song, as well as the honor of hearing it covered by a lot of other singers. How can you listen to it without feeling warm inside?

How many friends do you have? I mean real friends, the ones you can count on? Friends who like you even when you can't do anything for them? Who like you when you're broke? crabby? stranded? unemployed? divorced? in jail? **"A friend loves at all times, and a brother is born for adversity"** (Proverbs 17:17).

You know, we'd all like friends like that in *our* time of need. Maybe we aren't quite so quick to be there for somebody else. Ever hear the old joke, "A friend in need is a friend to avoid"? Here's one of God's gospel principles: you get what you need and want by giving it away first. Just as a spirit of generosity in your heart stimulates God to be even more generous with you, so the more you take care of people around you the more friends you will have.

True friends are God's gifts to you. They are brothers (and sisters) born for times of adversity, yours and theirs. Take a little friend inventory right now. Who are your top three? What could you do or say today that would make them feel important?

____

____

____

____

____

Cling to your refuge

Linda Buxa

On Christmas Day 2004, supermodel Petra Nemcova was in Thailand when a tsunami hit.

Dragged under the water, she thought she was going to die. Somehow she popped up and grabbed onto a palm tree. As the water raged around her, she heard the screams of people who were being swept away by the ocean. In all about 230,000 people died that day.

Even though her pelvis was shattered and she was going in and out of consciousness, Petra clung to that tree for eight hours, waiting for a rescue. It finally came. Today she uses her experience to reach out to others, running a foundation that builds schools in areas hit by natural disasters.

You may not have experienced a literal tsunami, but you know a figurative one, don't you? Your marriage is falling apart. Your baby died. You lost your home to a fire. Your teen became addicted to heroin. Your mother died tragically in a car accident.

As troubles swirl around you, you cling to your God for however long it takes because you know he is your refuge. Then you use your experience to tell others to hang in there because their faithful Rescuer is coming. **"Praise be to the God and Father of our Lord Jesus Christ, the Father of compassion and the God of all comfort, who comforts us in all our troubles, so that we can comfort those in any trouble with the comfort we ourselves received from God"** (2 Corinthians 1:3,4).

____

____

____

Do religious sacrifices still exist?

Pastor Mark Jeske

With the fall of Jerusalem in A.D. 70 came the total destruction of its temple, the place where Jesus and his disciples came often to worship and pray. As the great altar in the courtyard was destroyed, the sacrifices also ceased once and for all and have never been resumed.

Animals no longer need to be ritually slain. Jesus Christ was chosen by his heavenly Father to be the great Lamb of God, whose death on Calvary took away the sin of the world. The deaths of animals were only advance shadows of the real thing, and Good Friday's awesome events made them no longer necessary.

So has the concept of sacrifice gone away? No, not at all! St. Paul has a challenge for you: **"I urge you, brothers, in view of God's mercy, to offer your bodies as living sacrifices, holy and pleasing to God—this is your spiritual act of worship"** (Romans 12:1). Man-made religions are transactional—you perform good works or religious rituals in order to get something from a deity.

Only in Christianity did God go first, essentially reestablishing a relationship with his lost children through the birth, life, suffering, death, and resurrection of his Son. Christ's total commitment to us invites our total commitment back to him. He trusts us with that gift. Our lives of worship and service back to him are our sacrifices, living sacrifices that help other people and please him.

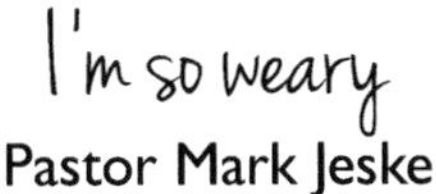

Pastor Mark Jeske

Some fatigue comes because you have given your body and mind a good workout that day. You are physically and mentally tired, but your soul is content because you got a lot done. Then there's the fatigue that comes from worry, unresolved conflict, and the dread that your life is wasting away without much to show for it. It's hard to charge into the day's work when you don't think you're accomplishing anything good, when you dread confrontations that you know will be unpleasant, or when you expect another barrage of criticism. Unresolved stress is *exhausting*!

There was a miserable stretch in King David's life when he was king in name only. His throne had been usurped by his rebellious son Absalom, and David had to flee Jerusalem for his life. He was so taken by surprise by this treachery that his flight was haphazard and somewhat disorganized. If Absalom's army had caught up with him at that early stage, the father and all taken with him would have been killed.

But David didn't panic. He wrote a poem about the experience: **"O LORD, how many are my foes! To the LORD I cry aloud, and he answers me from his holy hill. I lie down and sleep; I wake again, because the LORD sustains me"** (Psalm 3:1,4,5). When you are carrying a huge load of evening stress, give it to God during your prayers, let it go, and sleep well.

God will work on things for you overnight.

It's the little things

Linda Buxa

In Matthew 10:8, Jesus sends out the disciples with this message: **"Heal the sick, raise the dead, cleanse those who have leprosy, drive out demons."**

I get a little jealous of that sometimes. Wouldn't it be awesome to be one of the Twelve, walking around performing miracles in Jesus' name? I know I won't be healing leprosy, but still my pride loves to do the big things. You know, the things that allow people to see my good deeds and praise my Father in heaven. In my more honest moments, however, those things make me feel better about myself because they bring me praise too. (There goes the "good" part of those deeds!)

Just 34 short verses later, Jesus readjusts my thinking: **"If anyone gives even a cup of cold water to one of these little ones because he is my disciple, I tell you the truth, he will certainly not lose his reward"** (verse 42).

Quiet, unseen deeds are also works that God loves. They may not get attention, but they are prized. These ordinary moments are chances to serve him too. The person too frail to leave home is strong enough to pray. The stay-at-home parent who gives cup after cup of water to his or her toddler is serving God's children. The text you send to a friend, reminding her of God's faithfulness, is a way that you encourage the people he has given you.

Every so often, you might get to do The Big Thing. Day in and day out though, it's the little things.

September 26

Why me? I deserve better

Pastor Mark Jeske

Parents can spot certain inborn behaviors in their children. One is an intense radar for anything that smacks of unfairness. "Mom! That's not fair! You didn't let *me* do that!" is the kind of talk every home hears. Grown-ups think and act like that too. When something bad happens, we groan, "Why me? This isn't fair! I've had more than my share of bad luck already this year. I *totally* don't deserve this!"

People who say that are right, actually, but for the opposite reason. We don't deserve this, but in fact deserve something far worse. If we received from God what our daily moral thoughts and behaviors deserved, we would be packed off to hell immediately. Psalm 130:3,4 says, **"If you, O Lord, kept a record of sins, O Lord, who could stand? But with you there is forgiveness."**

Abraham had a far better posture before the Lord. On one occasion he had a big ask to make of God, but he didn't talk about what he had earned or deserved. He made no demands; instead, he approached the throne with humility: **"Abraham spoke up again: 'I have been so bold as to speak to the Lord, though I am nothing but dust and ashes'"** (Genesis 18:27).

When we Christians are trying to make sense of our misfortunes, let's not descend into indignation or bitterness. Let's accept what the Lord has chosen to allow in our lives and seek how our troubles can become an opportunity for God's saving agenda.

Walk in the light

Jason Nelson

The Maori people of New Zealand have a proverb: *Turn your face to the sun and the shadows follow behind you.* There is a lesson in that simple observation. We are better off heading into the light and leaving darkness behind. If we do the obvious play on words, this is more than the saying of an indigenous tribe. It is the truth of God. Turn your face toward the Son of righteousness and walk in the light.

There is a lot of darkness out there. All of it is the shadow of evil. Some gets promoted to us in certain kinds of television programs, movies, music, video games, and art. Some folks will even tattoo very dark images on their skin. It seems like a statement. They prefer the dark side. It speaks to their souls. We are kidding ourselves if we don't think heavy exposure to darkness takes its toll. It pushes the light right out of us.

But, **"God is light; in him there is no darkness at all. If we claim to have fellowship with him and yet walk in the darkness, we lie and do not live by the truth. But if we walk in the light, as he is in the light, we have fellowship with one another, and the blood of Jesus, his Son, purifies us from all sin"** (1 John 1:5-7).

Friend of Jesus, face the Son and let's walk in the light.

Let it go

Pastor Mark Jeske

Simon Peter once came to Jesus with a pretend question. He was really bragging about his perceived magnanimous spirit, but he pretended to ask Jesus for the outer limits of what could be expected in the area of forgiveness in response to some injury from another person. **"'Lord, how many times shall I forgive my brother when he sins against me? Up to seven times?' Jesus answered, 'I tell you, not seven times, but seventy-seven times'"**(Matthew 18:21,22). In other words, there is no limit.

Forgiveness is the beginning move in how human relationships are healed. Then why is it so hard? Why are we so reluctant to forgive?

Well, we can say that we don't want to enable bad behavior by letting scoundrels off the hook. If we forgive, we lose moral leverage—after all, if we were hurt by someone else, that makes us better than that person, and we can silently enjoy our superiority. Being owed a debt is like an asset—why would you *give* it away without demanding something for it?

Do it anyway. Holding onto anger and old wounds keeps you in anger prison forever. It cleanses your soul to let it go, because that is the way of Christ. He went first to buy your forgiveness—you and I can certainly learn how to forgive the far smaller debts others owe us. Let it go.

Aren't you glad Jesus knows no limits in his willingness to forgive you?

September 29

The ministry of kind words

Pastor Mark Jeske

"The mass of men lead lives of quiet desperation." Henry David Thoreau wrote that in *Walden* in 1854, and he meant women too. Thoreau's sad observation hasn't changed much. If you look around you at the supermarket, bleachers, workplace, parking lot, or even church, you will see people who look normal and placid as they go about their tasks. Inside they are probably stressed and miserable—their son is in prison, their spouse has been cheating, they fear being fired, their credit card debt is in the stratosphere, they are terribly lonely, they can't get over the sexual abuse suffered in childhood, and they know they drink way too much.

Assume that the people you talk to each day live in the land of desperation. **"An anxious heart weighs a man down, but a kind word cheers him up"** (Proverbs 12:25). Just think—you can change the trajectory of a life by a few words. Such a small thing! What does it cost you to talk a little? When someone is walking through a desert, parched for lack of encouragement, your kind words are sips of cool water.

What does it take? 1) Turning outward, getting over obsession with self, looking at other people and listening; 2) Remembering with gratitude the people with kind words whom God has sent into our lives; 3) Finding joy in making other people feel important.

Pick one person you will see today and start your new ministry of kind words.

____

____

____

____

Choose not to hear

Pastor Mark Jeske

Back in the day, when I was teaching daily catechism class to middle school students, their clowning used to drive me crazy. It was like playing endless whack-a-mole—I tried to get on top of every misbehavior and scold them back into silent submission. One day a wise parent pulled me aside and told me, "They're doing it on purpose because they enjoy watching you get upset." That comment changed my life. I calmed down in class and became partly deaf and blind—some things I just chose not to respond to. They calmed down too.

You know, you don't have to try to field every ball that's hit your way. Some you let whizz past your ear out into the outfield. **"A fool shows his annoyance at once, but a prudent man overlooks an insult"** (Proverbs 12:16). That's one of the secrets of parenting. You don't have to go and dig out of your kid everything that she has mumbled under her breath. Let it go. Pretend you're hard of hearing. You don't have to react emotionally to everything your spouse says in the heat of the moment either. Let it go. Some hard words are best overlooked.

That's not to make light of bad behavior. God's Proverbial point is that people on their own will later come to regret their bad manners, or as their temper cools they will realize they didn't mean it. If you act deaf when an insult comes your way, it's one less argument.

October

"IF GOD IS FOR US, WHO CAN BE AGAINST US?"
ROMANS 8:31

God, why have you rejected me?

Pastor Mark Jeske

"Are you mad at me?"

How many hundred times have you heard somebody say that to you? She misinterpreted the look on your face and jumped to conclusions because she hasn't heard from you in a while, or he didn't understand something you did or said. His own inner turmoil led him to assume that you were angry.

God is not surprised to hear murmurs of fear from his children. He doesn't always feel that he has to explain himself, and he knows we don't always grasp either his wonderful objectives or figure out the details as we go along. Each day he hears prayers with content like this: **"You are God my stronghold. Why have you rejected me? Why must I go about mourning, oppressed by the enemy?"** (Psalm 43:2).

We all have sin with us all the time, and not just in our deeds. Sin is in our minds and leaves a greasy residue of guilt. If left untreated, that guilt will eat away our spiritual self-confidence and depress us into thinking that we must be unlovable to God. We then assume that whatever affection he ever had for us must be gone and start interpreting everything bad in our lives as divine judgments and punishments.

It is at just such times as these that we need to look up at Jesus' cross. There is the source of all grace; there is the source of a love that is unconditional; there is mercy far greater than all our failings piled together.

Ah, you still love me

Pastor Mark Jeske

Ask any wife. It's not enough for a husband to assume that because he said he loved her five years ago he doesn't need to say it again. The magnetic force that holds a loving and trusting relationship together decays a little every day and needs to be refreshed often. It *must* be refreshed if it is to last.

Tired, disappointed, guilt-laden, and fearful believers—you too need to pay attention to God's love messages to reenergize your certainty of his favor. It's the best and most powerful reason to read your Bible, go to church, and have family devotions. The gospel of Christ, which comes to you through the pages of Scripture or the food of the Lord's Supper, reassures you that you still matter to God. He loves you even more than you love your children. Yes, that much!

The Bible lays out many stories of people just like us and shows how God works in their lives for good *every time*! There is no limit to his power, patience, or generosity. He who didn't flinch at sending his Son to die for us and then raised him from the dead will not hold back the many smaller things we need as well. **"Many are the woes of the wicked, but the LORD's unfailing love surrounds the man who trusts in him. Rejoice in the LORD and be glad, you righteous; sing, all you who are upright in heart"** (Psalm 32:10,11).

How about singing a song to the Lord right now?

Lessons of the lost and found

Pastor Daron Lindemann

Jesus told three parables of the lost being found in Luke chapter 15. A lost sheep. A lost coin. A lost son. Found! Ponder the following:

Why did the shepherd leave 99 sheep to look for 1 that strayed? Can you imagine the risk? Must have been a very special sheep. And a determined shepherd.

Why did the woman throw a party because she found a simple coin? Can you imagine being invited to a "lost coin found" party? Must have been a very meaningful coin. And a joy-filled woman.

Why did a grown man kiss his long-lost son instead of curse him for his rebellious behavior? Can you imagine the confused relief of the son? Must have been a very loved son. And a merciful father.

The cost and effort of pursuing the lost is not an issue compared to the joy of the celebration when they are found.

These stories do not reflect normal human behavior, but they do describe the normal behavior of a gracious God.

The joy of the ones who seek and find the lost contrasts with the grumbling of the Pharisees who dismissed the lost in Jesus' day.

Jesus' critics accused him of welcoming sinners. And they were right.

"Now the tax collectors and 'sinners' were all gathering around to hear [Jesus]**. But the Pharisees and the teachers of the law muttered, 'This man welcomes sinners and eats with them'"** (Luke 15:1,2).

He welcomes you and me too.

____

____

All believers are God's communicators

Pastor Mark Jeske

One of the most misleading words in the English New Testament is *preach,* as in "preach the gospel." Everybody knows what "preaching" is—it's what paid pastors do in church from their pulpits on Sunday. It is a restricted activity that only a very small number of Christian leaders do. The word *preach* makes people think of getting a long-winded scolding, being talked down to, bored to death.

But that's not what the original Greek words say. When the resurrected Christ commissioned his disciples to continue his work, he was not speaking only to the clergy but to all believers. All Christians, children too, are part of the nation of God's proclaimers and heralds. The prophet Joel joyfully anticipated that aspect of the New Covenant, which came true on Pentecost Sunday: **"I will pour out my Spirit on all people. Your sons and daughters will prophesy, your old men will dream dreams, your young men will see visions. Even on my servants, both men and women, I will pour out my Spirit in those days"** (Joel 2:28,29).

All believers are God's communicators with a spiritual mission in life. The day you were baptized is the day you were drafted into God's army. Pastors indeed perform a valuable function. They receive special training to be your coaches and teachers, but they must not be allowed to steal from you your joy at telling people what a wonderful Savior we have in Jesus Christ.

You have the Spirit too.

Part of the answer

Pastor Daron Lindemann

Ever find that your prayer for someone or something is answered sooner than you thought or closer than you'd like?

Jesus urged his disciples, **"Ask the Lord of the harvest, therefore, to send out workers into his harvest field"** (Matthew 9:38). No doubt they did ask. They shared Jesus' concern. The very next verse in Matthew's gospel reports that Jesus **"called his twelve disciples to him"** (Matthew 10:1) and sent them out.

They asked the Lord to send out workers. And then they were sent. Their prayer was answered in them.

When you pray for a friend to be blessed by God, be prepared for God to send that blessing through you. When you pray for more stable income, you'll probably miss it if you watch for money to grow on trees, but you just might find a unique employment opportunity or career option you hadn't previously considered. When you pray for patience, just watch, God will put you in circumstances that allow you to practice patience. When you are praying humbly and honestly for a better marriage, you notice your own shortcomings, and through your repentance the Designer of marriage works.

God loves it when you pray to him. He also loves making you part of his answer. Sometimes prayer doesn't just change things. It changes you.

Beggars' banquet

Pastor Mark Jeske

God loves to describe a peaceful and happy relationship with him as a great feast. Who wouldn't want to gain entrance to God's mansions and sit down at that fabulous table? Admittance to God's feast is counterintuitive, however. All the normal ways you may have developed for getting hold of scarce and in-demand tickets to a hot Broadway show won't work with God.

You can't flatter your way in, fake your way in, sneak in, or work your way up and in. You can't toady up to influential people who will slide you in. You don't have the juice to force your way in. You can't buy your way in with your money. You know why not? Because it's a beggars' banquet. Tickets are free, but only to people with the right attitude: **"Come, all you who are thirsty, come to the waters; and you who have no money, come, buy and eat! Come, buy wine and milk without money and without cost. . . . Your soul will delight in the richest of fare"** (Isaiah 55:1,2).

Admit your spiritual poverty. Stop pretending that the rags of your soul are black tie and tails. Confess your sins and let the sweet message of Jesus' forgiveness fill you up. Put on his gorgeous clothes, the robes of his holiness, and enter God's dazzling palace of light. Eat the richest of fare.

And then we dance.

October 7

Don't look back

Diana Kerr

Have you ever considered how much you have in common with Abraham's nephew Lot and with his family's escape from Sodom and Gomorrah? I'm guessing you haven't. So let me pose a few questions:

How many times have you hesitated when God urged you to flee, to follow his lead elsewhere? Even when he's doing it for your own good? **"When** [Lot] **hesitated, the men grasped his hand and the hands of his wife and of his two daughters and led them safely out of the city, for the LORD was merciful to them"** (Genesis 19:16).

On top of your resistance, how many times have you tried to negotiate with God or convince him to change his plans like Lot did? **"But I can't flee to the mountains; this disaster will overtake me, and I'll die. Look, here is a town near enough to run to, and it is small. Let me flee to it—it is very small, isn't it?"** (verses 19,20).

And *then*, when you're finally on the run, turning your back on that thing you know you need to leave behind, how often do you look back with longing and sadness? **"Lot's wife looked back, and she became a pillar of salt"** (verse 26).

I'd rather be like Lot's Uncle Abram instead. In Genesis chapter 12, God tells Abram to pack up and move to a mystery destination. The next thing we read is, **"So Abram went"** (Genesis 12:4). No whining, resisting, or doubting. That's God's kind of obedience.

October 8

Church on the move

Pastor Mark Jeske

Any believer who's paying attention to the well-being of the Christians in the Middle East these days must be grieving. The military and political upheavals in that troubled region have made Christians vulnerable to both political tyranny and to the constant violent religious conflict going on between Sunni and Shiite Muslims. And then there are the hard-line Islamic right-wingers who want to establish a new worldwide caliphate. Iraq has lost over half of its Christian population in the last two decades; Syria's Christian losses are similar. Does this look as though God is not providing adequate protection for his people?

Or is it that God is more interested in people than in territory? It has happened often in history that God uses migrations of believers to bring the gospel to new places, and their hardships bring blessings to others. Consider the outcomes of the first large-scale persecution to break out in the New Testament era: **"On that day a great persecution broke out against the church at Jerusalem, and all except the apostles were scattered. . . . Those who had been scattered preached the word wherever they went"** (Acts 8:1,4).

From God's point of view, he can replace any material possessions his people may have lost. On judgment day, everything will be consumed anyway. What matters is being connected to our Savior in faith, connecting to each other, using our gifts to serve and help one another.

The church is people, not buildings or places.

____

____

____

Living in fear

Pastor Mark Jeske

When we're small children, we have too little fear. Parents have a lot of work to do to build an appropriate fear level in their little ones—they want the kids to be afraid of electrical outlets, hot stoves, sharp knives, broken glass, and traffic. As we get older, we discover other fears that prey on our minds—being fired, running out of money, growing old, being alone.

The most horrible of all fears is to be afraid of God. There are many strategies that people try to get rid of guilt—rationalizing away either God's rules or punishments, hanging around only with unbelievers, immersing yourself in atheistic or agnostic literature, staying really busy, or sedating yourself with drugs or alcohol. But those are all just various forms of hiding when we know we're naked. "[Adam] **answered, 'I heard you in the garden, and I was afraid because I was naked; so I hid'"** (Genesis 3:10).

When we let God's Word speak to us, when we ponder the immense promise of baptismal cleansing, when we savor the warmth and fellowship of the Lord's Supper, we find the exquisite relief of the forgiveness of our sins. Only through Christ does the guilt go away; only through Christ will the fear go away. With Christ we are as pure and holy as he. With Christ we enjoy our Father's daily providing, protection, and love. With Christ we enjoy the sure promise of immortality of soul and body.

Sweet. No fear.

___

___

___

___

Get out of the way

Diana Kerr

Full disclosure: I frequently doubt my ability to carry out the work God has given me to do. Writing devotions and blog posts that thousands of people read and running a life-coaching business is challenging and terrifying. I experience moments of inadequacy *a lot.*

I bet you doubt yourself too sometimes. I bet at times you feel incapable to lead a large team of employees, to organize that huge event at church, to serve as a teacher to the young children who are our country's future, or to raise your *own* children without messing them up. You question why God put you where he did and try to convince him you're not fit for the job.

Moses tried the same thing. (Spoiler alert: God didn't buy it.) **"'O Lord, I have never been eloquent, neither in the past nor since you have spoken to your servant. I am slow of speech and tongue.' The LORD said to him, 'Who gave man his mouth? Who makes him deaf or mute? Who gives him sight or makes him blind? Is it not I, the LORD? Now go; I will help you speak and will teach you what to say'"** (Exodus 4:10-12).

Moses made it all about himself, when it was actually all about *God.* It's easy to doubt when you focus on *yourself.* God reminds us to get over ourselves, to be obedient, and to let him work through us, inadequacies and all.

Limits to Satan's power

Pastor Mark Jeske

Some weaknesses we don't mind admitting. There's no shame in being tempted by chocolate, shopping, sports cars, or celebrity magazines. Other weaknesses are terrible and no one must ever know—extreme alcohol consumption, reckless gambling, violence in the home, embezzlement at work, or the urge to betray your spouse in an affair.

It's not just other people who have to struggle with seductive evil. Every one of us is flawed and cracked, and Satan is at us every day with a crowbar, trying to get the tip in. He wants to turn the cracks into gaping fissures. He wants to tempt us into acts and thoughts of rebellion so often that we give up our faith and assume that we are his helpless slaves.

What a relief it is to find out that our kindly Father knows that we are weak and doesn't despise us for it. Not only has his Son purchased forgiveness for our sins of the past, but he sends his Spirit to help us with temptations of today and tomorrow: **"No temptation has seized you except what is common to man. And God is faithful; he will not let you be tempted beyond what you can bear"** (1 Corinthians 10:13). Think of it—God actually sets limits to how Satan can come at us. He keeps the temptations within our range of coping with them with God's help. His Word and Spirit within us give us both the knowledge and power we need to resist the devil so that he will flee from us.

Yesss! (fist pump here)

Control freak

Diana Kerr

A Christian devotion seems like a highly inappropriate place to lie, so I'll be honest with you: I like control. There, I said it. I do! I like things to go my way and to go according to my plans. Seriously though, how many people can *genuinely* say that they prefer to let others dictate their lives? Or that they hope any intentions for their day get thrown out the window by unexpected circumstances?

Today's world gives you lots of opportunities for control. Be honest with yourself—don't you love all your options and the ability to dictate your life according to what *you* think is best? These days, you can control when you have kids; when you watch your favorite TV shows; and whether you want 2%, skim, soy, almond, or coconut milk in your latte.

Honestly though, controlling everything gets exhausting. Deciding all your plans for yourself doesn't always go as well as you think it should.

Reality check: breathe a sigh of relief, because God's got an agenda for your life even if your own agenda is falling apart. Plus, his plan is *way* better. **"In him we were also chosen, having been predestined according to the plan of him who works out everything in conformity with the purpose of his will, in order that we . . . might be for the praise of his glory"** (Ephesians 1:11,12).

Hmm, *my* plans versus the plans of a God who knows everything and is working everything out for his glory? I'll take God's plans, please.

Accept what you can't control

Pastor Mark Jeske

Everybody should work on a farm at some point in his or her life. Even if you have no interest in farming as a career, you will learn patience, among many other fine attributes. Crops refuse to be rushed. They refuse to grow without the right combination of fertile soil, rain, and sunshine. And they have their time and seasons. Crops refuse to grow to your dictates. You have to wait for harvesttime regardless of how badly you need the money. Crops ripen on their schedule, not yours.

Farming can teach you some helpful life attitudes. **"Be patient, then, brothers, until the Lord's coming. See how the farmer waits for the land to yield its valuable crop and how patient he is for the autumn and spring rains"** (James 5:7). We all fantasize about controlling every aspect of our lives, but that fantasy never comes true. Much of our lives is simply beyond our ability to control, as is the weather to farmers.

You can't choose your parents—they were given to you, as was your unique mix of skills and gifts. Instead of resenting your environment or your personal makeup, take inventory of all the good things you do have. Instead of assuming that your prayers are all unheard, give God some time to do his work. Instead of forcing things in your life, let God steer for a while.

Curb your impatience. Think like a farmer.

A change in the weather

Pastor Daron Lindemann

This morning a damp haze shrouded the front yard. It filtered the early morning sunrise into dirtied, graying tones of orange. The morning then developed into a bright, autumn day of sunshine. And it preached these words of God: **"I have swept away your offenses like a cloud, your sins like the morning mist. Return to me, for I have redeemed you"** (Isaiah 44:22).

A change in the weather can really change a person's outlook, can't it? Or at least change the appearance of life circumstances from blah to bright. And if that's what God can do to you with the weather, well, it gets even better!

Think of the billions of tiny vapor droplets in a cloud of morning mist that God sweeps away with his sunshine and wind. Think of the numerous mistakes you've made, promises you've broken, and words you regret. God sweeps them away "like the morning mist."

God the Son shines his bright promises on your blah day, and the fog disappears. God the Spirit breathes his words of truth and transformation into the shadows of your soul and it comes to new life.

It has cleared up for you to return to God without a cloud of sin hanging over your conscience. With sharper focus you can see more possibilities for today that demonstrate your love for God and others. It's a beautiful day!

October 15

God loves sex

Pastor Mark Jeske

Somehow engaging in conversations about love and human sexuality has been difficult for the church. I think one reason is that it's hard for pastors to get too close to the subject in Sunday messages because there are usually children around. What's more, when we do talk about sex, all people come away hearing is what we're against. The very word *sex* acquires a negative connotation in faith-talk because pastors have so many warnings to give.

That may be the reason why God made sure to put the Song of Songs in the Bible. When you read it for the first time, you might be confused. It looks like a love story about a very hot romance, with very passionate and sometimes erotic imagery. Does it surprise you to know that's exactly what it is? **"How beautiful you are, my darling! Oh, how beautiful! Your eyes are doves. How handsome you are, my lover! Oh, how charming! And our bed is verdant"** (Song of Songs 1:15,16).

Who do you think built all of the mystery and desire and urgency and passion in sex and romance? Of course! God did! He invented all those things to make marriage the most intimate and fulfilling and enduring voluntary human relationship possible. He invented all those things to make you happy. If you like sex too, get married. Stay married.

God loves sex. It's the adultery he can't stand.

The hidden life

Pastor Mark Jeske

Normally it's not good to lead a double life. That usually means that somebody has a mistress or is embezzling funds from her employer or is running some kind of illegal business.

You and I *do* lead double lives, you know. The indwelling of the Holy Spirit in our hearts, our angelic protection, our saintly halos are all invisible to others, and frankly we don't perceive them either. We don't *see* the filth of our sins being rinsed away in baptism; we *see* only humble bread and wine in the Lord's Supper; we don't *see* any evidence of immortality at a Christian funeral as we lay a lifeless body in the ground.

But our second life is there, and it's real. **"You died, and your life is now hidden with Christ in God"** (Colossians 3:3). Your faith in Christ, though invisible in the wave spectrum available to your eyes, has made you a new creation, cleansed you of all sin, made you an heir of heaven, and changed your way of thinking. In short, you have gone from death to life. You are loved, forgiven, and immortal.

But for now we have to wait for all those things to be revealed to all. We believe them now as an article of faith, guaranteed by God's Word. Soon, soon, all that is hidden will be revealed and glorious. When you think of the riches that Christ holds in trust for you, people will wonder what you're smiling about.

October 17

Easy come, easy go

Pastor Mark Jeske

One of the most wonderful experiences that a parent can provide a child is employment. I'm kind of skeptical about the value of free money (i.e., allowances) but very positive about wages. When a child is able to accumulate a little money, it's because she saved it up and didn't blow it on something stupid. She will respect that money a lot because she had to work for it and because she held onto it. She will respect it in proportion to the effort she had to expend. No effort, no value.

Everybody knows the proverb "easy come, easy go." Those four words apply equally well to money, fame, and popularity. And inheritances: **"An inheritance quickly gained at the beginning will not be blessed at the end"** (Proverbs 20:21). I know parents who have accumulated some wealth who are terrified to leave it to their kids. They love them too much to drop a big load of money on them all at once that they did not earn. Easy money easily distorts people's value systems, *even if they are nice people.* These parents actually plan to give the bulk of their estate away before they die.

As you are pondering how to leave the legacy of your property, the assets that you spent a lifetime putting together, you might consider spreading the bequests out over multiple years. You would hate to have it said that these bequests "weren't blessed at the end."

____

____

____

____

A few thoughts about fools

Pastor Daron Lindemann

"He who trusts in himself is a fool" (Proverbs 28:26).

Sometimes I think I am so wise, God, so smart and on top of things. By your blessing, that is sometimes the case. But most often it's only because I foolishly convince myself that I am wiser than I really am. I fail to consider your point of view, fail to measure my plans by your immeasurable promises, fail to acknowledge that faith is the beginning of real wisdom.

You have been so patient with me in my foolishness, dear God. You have stooped down and lowered yourself to connect with me on my level, all because you love me—fool that I am. Some would call you a fool for that. In our world you're not supposed to love people who can't do anything for you. But you are not a creature of this twisted world. You are the eternally gracious Savior. My Savior.

I need your love and your attention, God. So that I can keep from being a fool. So that I can apply spiritual wisdom to my problems and feel the load lighten because your promises will do their work.

They always do.

All things must pass

Pastor Mark Jeske

"The brother in humble circumstances ought to take pride in his high position. But the one who is rich should take pride in his low position, because he will pass away like a wild flower. For the sun rises with scorching heat and withers the plant; its blossom falls and its beauty is destroyed. In the same way, the rich man will fade away even while he goes about his business" (James 1:9-11).

How can the *lowly* in society possibly take pride in their *high* position? The point is not that people are saved through poverty or their own pain. Rather—those who have few earthly treasures and who have suffered a lot are less likely to view life on earth as paradise and more likely to be interested in the promises of the gospel. In Jesus' parable it was not Lazarus' poverty that carried him to Abraham's embrace but faith; his suffering stripped away all the comfortable illusions about life on earth, all the illusions that money can buy.

In the same way, some believers are rich in worldly wealth (Abraham, David, Solomon). But they have a special burden, because money easily turns people's heads, inflates their sense of self-importance, distracts them from godly priorities, and leads to a false sense of security. Wealth cannot much delay a sinner's death nor give him or her acquittal in God's court. A rich believer's true treasure lies in recognizing one's natural spiritual poverty and in utter reliance on the true righteousness that Christ alone gives.

Claymation

Pastor Mark Jeske

The mythologies of heathen religions all have strange and fantastic stories and doctrines behind their temples. What makes them attractive to people is not how logical their systems are or how believable the claims of their priests, but the fact that they offer manageable ways to control your relationship with a force stronger and wealthier than you. "Worship" of these deities is a transaction—you do something or give something to get something you want. For example, Baal worshipers were farmers who desperately wanted rain for their fields and fertility for their animals, so the priests of Baal portrayed him as the deity who controlled rainfall.

Christianity is the opposite. God is the one who did something to get what he wanted. He offered up his Son in order to win his lost children back. The first sacrifice was his. The redemption of the human race came at massive cost to Jesus Christ. Thus our worship, prayers, rituals, building projects, service, and stewardship are not manipulations to gain wealth for ourselves; they are just natural responses to a love that big.

We Christians realize that we aren't trying to control a transaction. **"O Lord, you are our Father. We are the clay, you are the potter; we are the work of your hand"** (Isaiah 64:8). The point? Everything about our faith is about him—it's his workshop, his design, his purpose, his agenda, his software, his environment.

We're just his clay. Lord, please make me into something useful for you today.

October 21

Mt. Moriah

Pastor Mark Jeske

Psalm 121 urges believers to lift up their eyes to the hills, for that is where their help comes from. It's not that God has something against valleys. But when God knew he was going to do something really significant, he chose mountaintops.

Abraham one day got the heaviest message ever: **"God said, 'Take your son, your only son, Isaac, whom you love, and go to the region of Moriah. Sacrifice him there as a burnt offering on one of the mountains I will tell you about"** (Genesis 22:2). That command must have seemed so wrong in so many ways to Abraham. For one, it was murder. God hurled curses on the Canaanite religions that advocated child sacrifice. Second, Abraham and Sarah had waited their entire lives for this miracle son—he was the most precious thing in their lives. Third, Isaac was the key to the chain of promises God had repeatedly made. If Isaac died, it all collapsed.

In spite of everything, Abraham obeyed. He still believed all of God's promises, figuring that he would get to witness a resurrection. God was thrilled. Abraham had passed his test, and so God provided a ram replacement for Isaac and the young man was spared.

What God would not let Abraham do, he did for us. This same Mt. Moriah later became the site for the Jerusalem temple, where animals were ritually slain in anticipation of the great sacrifice of the Son of God. And it was in Jerusalem that God's own Son was slain for us.

October 22

Mt. Sinai

Pastor Mark Jeske

Six months after the great exodus from Egypt, as the giant columns of marchers slowly straggled eastward through the wilderness, God called a halt near the base of Mt. Sinai. The Israelites who lived through that experience would never forget it. It was there that God formed his covenant relationship with them. It was there that this ragtag mass of ex-slaves became the nation of Israel, bearing the name of the Lord.

To gain their respect, God created dark, billowing clouds over the mount. Thunder boomed and lightning bolts cracked down from the summit. Eerie trumpet blasts split the air and the earth quaked. The Israelites were terrified. Then they heard God speak his Ten Commandments in a voice so overwhelming that they begged Moses to ask him to stop. Moses went up the mount to intercede.

But the Sinai experience was not all intimidation and law. Even before the earth began to shake, Moses had gone up the mount to speak with God: **"The LORD called to him from the mountain and said, '. . . Although the whole earth is mine, you will be for me a kingdom of priests and a holy nation'"** (Exodus 19:3,5,6). That's how God thought of the Israelite nation—royalty, priests, holy. They were the future princes and princesses of heaven; they were chosen for priestly service; and they were holy, sanctified by the blood of lambs representing the Lamb.

You are God's holy, royal priests too.

October 23

Mt. Ebal

Pastor Mark Jeske

Moses knew from the Lord that he was within days of his death. He spent most of his remaining time teaching the Israelites in the mammoth farewell addresses called Deuteronomy in the Bible. As prompted by the Lord, he instructed the people to carry out an unusual but dramatic learning exercise.

Moses would be buried east of the Jordan, but their future lay on the other side. **"When you have crossed the Jordan into the land the LORD your God is giving you, set up some large stones and coat them with plaster. Write on them all the words of this law. . . . And when you have crossed the Jordan, set up these stones on Mount Ebal"** (Deuteronomy 27:2-4). Mt. Ebal, at 3,084 feet towering over the city of Shechem to the north, would have the shrine of God's law. Six tribes were to stand on Mt. Ebal; as the Levites shouted God's curses on evil behaviors, the people of Reuben, Gad, Asher, Zebulun, Dan, and Naphtali would cry out, "Amen!"

Even the people who were not able to possess a written copy of the Torah (Scriptures) would have this shrine as a point of reference for the commandments of God. Today the Bible is our Mt. Ebal. Anyone who can read or even listen will hear the living voice of God today as powerfully as any Israelite ever did.

Disobedience to the will of God brings his curses now as then.

____

____

____

____

Mt. Gerizim

Pastor Mark Jeske

In some of his very last words to the Israelites, Moses gave instructions for a powerful religious drama he would not be alive to see. Six tribes were to ascend the slopes of Mt. Ebal. The other six tribes—Simeon, Levi, Judah, Issachar, Joseph (i.e., Ephraim and Manasseh), and Benjamin—were to ascend Ebal's twin. Mt. Gerizim rose 2,849 feet to the south of the city of Shechem. As the Levites shouted God's curses on sinful behavior, others located on Mt. Gerizim would answer antiphonally with God's blessings on obedient behaviors.

The Lord takes no pleasure in administering punishment. How eager he is to open up the faucet of heaven and pour out prosperity on believers: **"All these blessings will come upon you and accompany you if you obey the Lord your God: You will be blessed in the city and blessed in the country. . . . The Lord will send a blessing on your barns and on everything you put your hand to. . . . If you pay attention to the commands of the Lord your God that I give you this day and carefully follow them, you will always be at the top, never the bottom"** (Deuteronomy 28:2,3,8,13).

That stirring instruction in holy living would have made a powerful impression on all, especially the children. Truly when Israel gave God its obedience, there was no limit to his generosity. At King Solomon's time, there was so much gold in circulation that silver was considered of little value.

Say it with me: "Lord, I love to do your will."

Mt. Nebo

Pastor Mark Jeske

"Moses, I have good news and bad news. The good news is that you will be able to see how beautiful the land of Canaan is. The bad news is that you will die where you are standing." **"Moses climbed Mount Nebo from the plains of Moab to the top of Pisgah, across from Jericho. There the LORD showed him the whole land. . . . The LORD said to him, 'This is the land I promised on oath to Abraham, Isaac and Jacob when I said, "I will give it to your descendants." I have let you see it with your eyes, but you will not cross over to it'"** (Deuteronomy 34:1,4).

You really can see a long way from Mt. Nebo. Located just east of where the Jordan River empties into the Dead Sea, the Nebo ridge rises 2,680 feet. On a clear day, you can see much of the Jordan River Valley to the north and all the way to Jerusalem to the west. Moses must have been thrilled that the terrible 40-year march in the Sinai wilderness was over. He must also have been terribly sad not to see the Promised Land in person. At least he got the bird's-eye view. His poor leadership and bungled proclamation of God's Word earned him an early retirement (see Numbers 20).

You and I, like Moses, will not see the Promised Land on this earth. We live and die in hope.

Mt. Carmel

Pastor Mark Jeske

The steep ridge that runs at an angle through Israel all the way to the Mediterranean was the scene of a showdown much bigger than the O.K. Corral. It was high on Mt. Carmel, 1,800 feet above sea level, that the true God was given glory once again and the heathen god Baal and his priests were soundly defeated.

A huge crowd gathered around priests of Baal as they pleaded with their god all day to ignite a sacrificial altar. It was in vain. Nothing happened. Then **"Elijah went before the people and said, 'How long will you waver between two opinions? If the LORD is God, follow him; but if Baal is God, follow him.' . . . The fire of the LORD fell and burned up the sacrifice, the wood, the stones and the soil, and also licked up the water in the trench. When all the people saw this, they fell prostrate and cried, 'The LORD—he is God! The LORD—he is God!'"** (1 Kings 18:21,38,39).

What a thrill! Finally the Lord God of Israel had declared himself. The euphoria didn't last long. Elijah soon was on the run again, afraid for his life at the hands of the evil king Ahab and his loathsome wife Jezebel. As you continue your long and hard walk by faith and not by sight, let your mind imagine a sizzling lightning bolt from heaven zapping an altar on Mt. Carmel. Just smile. And keep walking.

Mt. Calvary

Pastor Mark Jeske

Of all the shapes and configurations that a hill could be, how extraordinarily perfect is it that the place where Jesus Christ was crucified should have looked like a human skull. And that's what *calvaria* means in Latin. His place of death looked like a place of death.

The site where the Roman soldiers headed had surely been used for public executions many times before. Possibly the passersby that day had witnessed the sad spectacle of dying criminals before. This execution was different. The "great exchange" was taking place. The innocent Son of God willingly accepted the blame for a world of sins and sinners so that a world of sinners might be called forgiven and holy. **"Just as man is destined to die once, and after that to face judgment, so Christ was sacrificed once to take away the sins of many people; and he will appear a second time, not to bear sin, but to bring salvation to those who are waiting for him"** (Hebrews 9:27,28).

On Mt. Calvary the purest grace of God was shown and given to the world. On that dark day, as the nails were pounded into his sacred body, the Son of God became the Lamb of God who takes away the sin of the world. All those who believe in Christ's wonderful forgiveness have it. Those who don't, don't.

And now—your eternal future is riding on what you do with this information.

Mt. of Olives

Pastor Mark Jeske

Just east of the royal city of Jerusalem, across the Brook Kidron, is the gentle rise of the Mt. of Olives. It really was a mount of olives at Jesus' time. Late in the night of Maundy Thursday, Jesus spent some time in prayer in its olive grove—the Hebrew words *gath shemen* ("Gethsemane") mean "olive oil press." His disciples experienced the double shame of falling asleep when they should have been praying and of running away when they should have been staying.

On another Thursday six weeks later, the resurrected Christ gathered his disciples on that same mount one last time and shocked them one last time: **"When he had led them out to the vicinity of Bethany, he lifted up his hands and blessed them. While he was blessing them, he left them and was taken up into heaven"** (Luke 24:50,51). They felt as if they were being abandoned. Jesus encouraged them to see his ascension as a promotion for them—they now had his job of evangelism and teaching. He charged them with their mission of making disciples, first in Jerusalem, then in Judea and Samaria, and from there to the ends of the earth.

For centuries the lower areas of the mount have been used as a burial ground—there are over 150,000 graves, every one of which will yield its body on the great day of judgment when Christ returns.

The disciples' Great Commission now belongs to us. We've got work to do.

October 29

Mt. Zion

Pastor Mark Jeske

The term *Zion* has multiple layers of meaning and metaphor. It referred originally to the steep, narrow ridge of King David's original capital city of Jerusalem. Fortified with tall walls and blessed with a secure water supply, it was almost impregnable. When the temple was built on an old threshing floor to the north of that ridge, the term *Zion* stretched to include the temple precincts.

Zion can also refer to the entire city of Jerusalem and the "Daughter of Zion" to its inhabitants. The term grew in New Testament times to refer to all believers, that is, the church. It became a favorite congregation name among Christians in the 1800s. Also in those years Jews longing to return to the land of Israel coined the term *Zionism* to articulate strategies for how they might reconstitute their ancient land after many centuries of diaspora.

The most beautiful of all the uses of the name Zion is as a metaphor for heaven itself, the gathering of the people of God in the heavenly temple of God in the city of God: **"But you have come to Mount Zion, to the heavenly Jerusalem, the city of the living God. You have come to thousands upon thousands of angels in joyful assembly, to the church of the firstborn, whose names are written in heaven"** (Hebrews 12:22,23).

October 30

Win-win

Diana Kerr

Have you noticed that when you're busy or stressed, one of the first things to go is the time and energy you spend on others? In an effort to get through a busy season of life or a stressful day, we turn inward and focus on ourselves to try to get by.

Unfortunately, that tendency can be rather counterproductive. Studies show that those who encourage or compliment others, who volunteer, or who give away money or resources become happier as a result of those others-focused acts. Proverbs 11:25 seems to back up that data: **"A generous man will prosper; he who refreshes others will himself be refreshed."**

Dear family of believers, isn't that so true? *"He who refreshes others will himself be refreshed."* I'm sure you can think of a time when doing something for someone else lifted not just his or her spirits, but your own as well. (It probably made God smile too.)

My husband and I have been having fun being more generous lately. When it comes to deciding how much to spend on a gift for someone or whether we should pay for a friend's meal, he likes to say, "Will we miss that extra $20?" We never do.

Everyone needs boundaries, and no one can give and give of themselves endlessly without ever filling themselves back up. Thankfully, the beautiful truth is that if we're intentional about how we pour into others, God often fills us up with even more than we just poured out.

Spirits of the afterlife

Pastor Mark Jeske

Halloween is one of the biggest nights of the year, at least if you run a bar, sell candy, or rent costumes. People are endlessly fascinated with the legends and mythology of death, spirits, and the afterlife. Trick-or-treat, jack-o-lanterns, cobwebs, and the colors of black and orange dominate stores for the entire month of October.

Some of it is harmless fun, and some of what goes on is evil—the vandalism and fascination with black magic and satanic powers. We have no word from God that the spirits of those who have died will return to earth (with the possible dramatic exception of the spirit of Samuel in 1 Samuel 28). The souls of unbelievers are already in hell, not free to roam the earth and haunt houses and people but pent up in prison (1 Peter 3:19,20).

But the souls of the believing dead are in heaven in the Lord's presence, alive and alert, and like the angels they eagerly await the unfolding of God's plans. **"I saw under the altar the souls of those who had been slain because of the word of God and the testimony they had maintained. They called out in a loud voice, 'How long, Sovereign Lord, holy and true, until you judge the inhabitants of the earth and avenge our blood?'"** (Revelation 6:9,10).

When Christ returns to earth, they will get their bodies back. And they will see and approve the great judgment.

November

"I HAVE SET THE LORD ALWAYS BEFORE ME.
BECAUSE HE IS AT MY RIGHT HAND,
I WILL NOT BE SHAKEN."
PSALM 16:8

Standing on shoulders

Pastor Mark Jeske

We're spoiled.

Christians in the West today never had it easier. There are active congregations near where we live, abounding in worship opportunities, programming, schools, and staff just waiting for us to call or show up. Print, audio, and video resources surround us. This enormous network, however, rests on the shoulders of many generations of heroic and generous workers and leaders of the past. We owe a special debt to the martyrs, those who refused to give up their faith in Christ even at the pain of death.

Even before the fall of the Roman Empire, in the midst of the time of government persecution of the early church, Christians wanted to commemorate their leaders of the past, especially the martyrs, with an annual day of remembrance. By long custom, November 1 is the Feast of All Saints, along with its vigil the night before, the "Hallow E'en" (holy evening).

This year make a little pledge not to let the opportunity slide past to give God the thanks he deserves for providing the sainted people of the past who built the ministries that we enjoy today. Christian parents and grandparents, Sunday school teachers, camp counselors, pastors, choir directors, seminary professors, authors, and composers over the centuries have taught us, inspired us, and modeled true Christian behaviors for us.

"Remember your leaders, who spoke the word of God to you. Consider the outcome of their way of life and imitate their faith" (Hebrews 13:7).

____

____

November 2

Spirit at work: God's utterance

Pastor Mark Jeske

No one has ever seen the Holy Spirit, or any spirit for that matter. Spirits can see us; we can't see them, unless they use their powers to assume human form. Much of the work of God the Holy Spirit is hidden from our eyes. But that doesn't mean he's been absent from the earth. On the contrary—the Spirit of the Lord has been carrying out his holy agenda throughout human history.

It is the Spirit's grand mission to connect people with their Savior through Word and sacrament. Everything good in our lives ultimately comes from God's Word, and the Spirit uses his prophets to convey the very utterances of God himself. King David, anointed of the Lord, was aware of being a channel for information from heaven: **"These are the last words of David: 'The oracle of David son of Jesse, the oracle of the man exalted by the Most High, the man anointed by the God of Jacob, Israel's singer of songs: The Spirit of the Lord spoke through me; his word was on my tongue'"** (2 Samuel 23:1,2).

Without the Spirit's utterance, you would be completely on your own to try to find truth in the world's swirl of competing philosophies. You would never know anything for sure. But when you read the Bible, you can have complete confidence in its power, its truth, and its applicability to your life, for you are experiencing the Holy Spirit's information and power directly.

You can *know.*

____

____

____

____

Spirit at work: God's creativity

Pastor Mark Jeske

The Holy Spirit has always been connected with the stories of God's incredible creativity. In the first verses of Genesis, at the very beginning of the Bible itself, we hear that the Spirit hovered over the unformed watery mass. And then came the explosion of order and beauty and diversity, the explosion of *life* on earth.

The Spirit lives also in the hearts of men and women, bringing his divine spark to the children whom he has made. When God chose the time for his first house to be built, the movable tabernacle, he wanted it beautiful. So he sent the Spirit: **"The Lord said to Moses, 'See, I have chosen Bezalel son of Uri . . . and I have filled him with the Spirit of God, with skill, ability and knowledge in all kinds of crafts—to make artistic designs for work in gold, silver and bronze, to cut and set stones, to work in wood, and to engage in all kinds of craftsmanship'"** (Exodus 31:1-5).

God invented color and perspective and form and metals and wood and fabric. He loves pattern and shape and complexity and line and shadow. In nature he built incredible designs that steal your breath away. And he takes great delight in seeing the artistic creations that his children produce, especially those that are created to honor him and communicate the splendor of his creation.

Children of God, imagine! Paint! Draw! Weave! Sculpt!

Spirit at work: God's power

Pastor Mark Jeske

Commercial buildings and homes are lit from power plants, which derive their energy from burning coal or gas, nuclear reactions, giant wind turbines, or from solar arrays.

People need power too. We need food as the daily fuel for our bodies, but we need strength for our spirit as well—the strength to make the right choices, to stand up for what is right, protect those weaker than we, admit our mistakes and take responsibility, carry our own load plus help with somebody else's, finish a job, and keep our promises.

We need power also to fight Satan, who plants the seeds of doubt, fear, rebellion, lies, suspicion, paranoia, impatience, quarreling, and hypocrisy every day. St. Paul had something even better than money to bring to his brothers and sisters in the Ephesus congregation: **"I pray that out of his glorious riches he may strengthen you with power through his Spirit in your inner being"** (Ephesians 3:16). Powered up by the Spirit we can be gentle when others want to fight, kind even when treated unfairly, truthful even when it will cost us, hardworking even when nobody is watching, and generous even when we have little.

Doing for ourselves comes naturally. Spending of ourselves to make somebody else's life better never happens by itself—it is acquired behavior. It needs to be learned from the Spirit's words and powered by the Spirit's power.

May the Spirit strengthen you today in your inner being.

November 5

Spirit at work: God's wisdom

Pastor Mark Jeske

Wisdom is not the same thing as knowledge.

People with knowledge may have acquired a load of facts and information. They may be unbeatable masters of Trivial Pursuit or history nerds who know the dates and names of every battle in the Civil War's Peninsula Campaign. But that doesn't mean that they know what that information means, or more important, what to do with it. Having wisdom means that you can *interpret* the facts to know their significance, to be able to extract what is really important from the pile and leave the rest, and to know what to do next.

In matters of faith, just knowing religious facts is not enough. St. Paul wrote: **"I keep asking that the God of our Lord Jesus Christ, the glorious Father, may give you the Spirit of wisdom and revelation, so that you may know him better"** (Ephesians 1:17). Knowledge means that you can recite the names of the people in a Christmas manger scene; wisdom means that you can believe and confess that the baby in the manger is your Savior Jesus Christ, God come in human flesh to rescue the earth's people.

True spiritual wisdom is a Spirit gift. It comes from exposure to God's Word, whether read or heard. It comes from prayer, from hard experience, and from paying attention to what God is up to. Godly wisdom helps us know what to hang onto and what to let go of. Godly wisdom helps us distinguish the treasures from the trash in our lives.

Stairway to heaven

Pastor Daron Lindemann

The Lord promises to do for you what he did for Jacob, a man fleeing from the troubles he had made for himself. As Jacob wondered whether or not the Lord—the God of his fathers—was with him, angels appeared to him in a dream, ascending and descending a stairway to heaven (Genesis 28:12). The faithful Lord God was still with Jacob, and he didn't need to be afraid.

We take comfort in that truth, and we believe that Jesus is the stairway to heaven who connects heaven and earth as the Son of Man in human flesh. **"I tell you the truth, you shall see heaven open, and the angels of God ascending and descending on the Son of Man"** (John 1:51).

Those with self-sufficient dreams, convinced that they can climb their own ladders of success, fall miserably short. Those full of self-centered decisions, too busy looking out for themselves, miss seeing a Savior or hearing his calling.

Jesus has the power to open the kingdom of heaven to send angel armies on their missions. In his grace and mercy, he opens the kingdom of heaven to receive all believers, connecting them to him now. On the Last Day, he will send his angels to gather all believers, connecting them to heaven forever.

Jacob learned, through the gracious call of God atop a stairway to heaven, that the faithful promises of God comfort us in our sinful foolishness.

____

____

____

____

Yes, it is possible to lose your faith

Pastor Mark Jeske

Of all the risks that God has taken in his creation of the world and its people, the biggest is in his desire to be loved. Love, you see, cannot be coerced. It must be given. In order for love to be given freely, people must have the ability *not* to give it.

Through his Old Testament prophets, God opens up his aching heart over people who should know better yet who are abandoning the faith they once had. What's not to like about being God's child? What's not to like about enjoying complete forgiveness of your sins, daily Fatherly blessings, the protection of the angels, and immortality in heaven?

Well, Satan found life with God resistible, and he persuades God's children to abandon him as well. Sad to say, it is possible to be a believer and then later in life to throw your faith away. Paul gave young Pastor Timothy some sad examples: **"Avoid godless chatter, because those who indulge in it will become more and more ungodly. Their teaching will spread like gangrene. Among them are Hymenaeus and Philetus, who have wandered away from the truth"** (2 Timothy 2:16-18).

Jesus himself told Peter that he was praying his disciple's faith wouldn't fail (Luke 22:32). These solemn and serious warnings come to us so that we won't become arrogant or careless or distracted. We need to be alert to Satan's temptations so that his spiritual suicide won't be ours.

Precious Lord, take my hand

Pastor Mark Jeske

Thomas Dorsey grew up playing blues and jazz piano, sometimes in pretty disreputable places. But he underwent a religious conversion, and things really began to come together for him. He formed his own music publishing company, got married, and had just accepted a prestigious new job as choral director at Pilgrim Baptist Church in Chicago.

He accepted an invitation to play at a revival in St. Louis, leaving his pregnant wife in Chicago. While on the road he got a message that his wife had died in childbirth. He hurried back to Chicago, and his infant son died a few hours after his arrival. He was devastated. He related that he buried both of them in the same casket; only his faith sustained him in that bleak period. **"Teach me to do your will, for you are my God; may your good Spirit lead me on level ground"** (Psalm 143:10).

Later that year he wrote a song to express both his grief and his faith, in appreciation to the God who had carried him along in his time of sorrow. The hymn has brought comfort to many millions of people; Mahalia Jackson sang it at the funeral of Dr. Martin Luther King, Jr.

The hymn was "Precious Lord, Take My Hand." Are you familiar with it? If not, check it out in a hymnbook or online.

____

____

____

____

____

November 9

So many choices

Diana Kerr

A few years ago, researchers at Cornell University found that we make 226.7 decisions about food *in a single day*. I'm not sure how they came up with that number, but we humans make *a lot* of choices.

Often, we make choices rather unconsciously. In some cases, that's fine. I would hope you don't expend a lot of mental energy trying to decide whether to use a spoon or a fork to eat your cereal or whether to use your car's turn signals on the way to work.

However, some decisions are more important. Some of them *do* require at least a moment of thought. Are you going to jump in on the gossip about your boss after the meeting or make an excuse to head back to your desk? Are you going to allow an argument with your spouse to escalate or change the tone of your voice and speak gently instead?

The people of Israel made a lot of poor choices throughout Bible history. Jeremiah encouraged them to acknowledge the two paths before them and choose wisely. **"Stand at the crossroads and look; ask for the ancient paths, ask where the good way is, and walk in it"** (Jeremiah 6:16). Why? To honor God and to live in obedience, yes, but as Jeremiah continues, **"You will find rest for your souls."**

As you make hundreds of choices each day about which path to take, some may be insignificant, but others may have more serious implications. Choose your path wisely.

____

____

____

____

November 10

Idol talk

Pastor Daron Lindemann

Wood is created by God, and then sometimes people carve idols out of it. Animals and planets are created by God and in some cultures represent mythological gods. The imaginative power of the human mind is created by God, and with it we engineer our own saviors.

As he watches us flirt with false gods, something in our Maker and Redeemer clicks, making him wish we were giving *him* our attention instead. After God found his special people Israel dancing around a golden calf, he said, **"They made me jealous by what is no god"** (Deuteronomy 32:21).

What worthless idol can put a smile on your face by spinning a meteorite across the sky or painting a sunset in your corner of the world? What imitation savior knows your fears before they develop in you emotionally? These are acts of courtship by a loving God competing with selfish idols. **"He has shown kindness by giving you rain from heaven and crops in their seasons; he provides you with plenty of food and fills your hearts with joy"** (Acts 14:17).

Surely there is "no god" who can compare to the creating and providing of God Almighty. Once this captures a person's attention, well, the redeeming of the Son and sanctifying of the Spirit's breath set apart the true God as the one and only Savior.

Fear, love, and trust in God above all things. Nothing else compares.

November 11

Schizophrenic faith

Pastor Mark Jeske

One of the characteristics of bad movies is that they make cartoons out of people—their characters are either all pure or all evil. The reality is that all of us are walking contradictions. Sometimes we are courageous, sometimes cowardly. Sometimes we are noble, sometimes weak and selfish. Sometimes we are generous, other times miserly. The best movies illustrate how even villains have some admirable qualities and how hard even "good" people have to strive against their weaknesses.

Our faith lives can be schizophrenic too. Jesus met a man once whose son was being tormented by demon possession. He begged for Jesus' help, but confessed that his faith was pretty shaky: **"'But if you can do anything, take pity on us and help us.' '"*If* you can"?' said Jesus. 'Everything is possible for him who believes.' Immediately the boy's father exclaimed, 'I do believe; help me overcome my unbelief!'"** (Mark 9:22-24).

Jesus did not despise the man for his weaknesses, and he does not despise you either. He knows you inside and out—he knows you are a bundle of contradictions. His Word brings both encouragement and forgiveness—his love amplifies your good qualities and his great patience bears with your weaknesses. He knows that sometimes you are as strong as an ox in your faith and sometimes you wilt like a six-day-old cut flower.

Jesus' mission on earth is not to pin medals on the perfect, but rather to rescue the flawed.

____

____

____

I'd like to teach the world to sing

Pastor Mark Jeske

Anyone can get into a fight. It takes no brains to fight, only glands. Growing up as a Christian involves many learned behaviors, like telling the truth, putting others ahead of yourself, and deferring gratification. It also involves learning how to be a peacemaker.

Harmony between people, even between Christians, never just happens, because our natural state is fighting. The apostle Peter grew up a lot from the first time he laid down his fishing nets to follow Jesus: **"Finally, all of you, live in harmony with one another; be sympathetic, love as brothers, be compassionate and humble. Do not repay evil with evil or insult with insult, but with blessing, because to this you were called so that you may inherit a blessing"** (1 Peter 3:8,9).

Living in harmony with other people means enjoying their successes without envy or resentment. It means being willing to bear some of their pain. It means helping them in their projects at least as much as you are trying to get them to help you. It means making them feel important, listening to their ideas and problems first before airing your personal philosophies.

Peacemakers refuse to play the retaliation game; they let the Lord take care of vengeance. Our job is simply to broker to others the same mercy from heaven that the Lord has first given to us. There is a sweet reward for this heavenly work—God is watching, and he blesses the blessers.

The Last Day is the Lord's day

Pastor Daron Lindemann

Do you feel just a little anxiety about where you will be on judgment day, how you will respond to the global chaos, and what kind of forms you will need to fill out at the pearly gates? What if you choose door number two instead of door number three? What if you mess it all up and miss out on heaven forever?

Similar to a promotional brochure for the perfect vacation, the Bible answers any anxiety about judgment day and heaven, not with every specific detail but with a few select pictures and truths. So don't worry about it.

God will not miss the slightest technicality when it comes to taking believers to heaven. Your perseverance through earthly life, as well as your perpetual heavenly life, are both in God's hands. **"You will be counted worthy of the kingdom of God."** How? Well, it's **"God's judgment,"** not yours. And, by the way, his judgment is **"right"** (2 Thessalonians 1:5).

Judgment day is the "day of the Lord" (1 Thessalonians 5:2). It's not the day of the most powerful nation on earth or the day of a flu epidemic that fatally puts an end to the world's population or the day of your worst fears. It belongs to the Lord. He will take care of all who, by faith in his promises, want his help. He will raise the dead. He will send his angels to escort all believers everywhere safely through the chaos.

The Lord God will not mess it up. That's a promise.

____

____

____

____

Just as I am

Pastor Mark Jeske

Charlotte Elliott was the daughter of an English silk merchant. She had a happy childhood and a great life ahead of her until she experienced a physical breakdown in 1821 that left her an invalid for the rest of her life. Even worse for her was the spiritual fear and feeling of unworthiness that she daily experienced.

A Christian evangelist gave her much comfort and encouraged her to keep writing her poetry. One of her poems so impressed her sister-in-law that she arranged to have it published in the *Invalid's Hymn Book* in 1836. The musician and publisher William Bradbury (who also composed the famous children's song "Jesus Loves Me; This I Know") was so struck by Charlotte's poem that he composed the perfect tune for it. "Just As I Am, Without One Plea" had John 6:37 as its header: **"All that the Father gives me will come to me, and whoever comes to me I will never drive away."**

This little song, written by one so small and weak, has brought blessed peace of mind and heart to many millions of Christians. Through Jesus Christ all may know that they are loved and forgiven and those who believe it have it. If you lack Jesus, you have nothing. If you have Jesus, you have everything.

Just as I am, without one plea
But that thy blood was shed for me
And that thou bidd'st me come to thee,
O Lamb of God, I come, I come.

November 15

Lies of busyness: "My busyness pleases God."

Diana Kerr

Look at my calendar and you'll see a *lot* of stuff—deadlines, commitments, responsibilities. I'm sure some people would be impressed at all the "important" things I keep myself busy with.

In the United States, our society prizes busyness. "How are you doing?" our friends ask us. *"Busy!"* we reply, waiting for the sympathy or gold medal we think we deserve as a result of the chaotic life we've built for ourselves. Who cares if other people are impressed though? The question is, Does our *Creator* approve?

Why are you busy? What's the point of it all? Psalm 39:6 sums up one of my greatest fears for us Christians in our hectic world: **"We are merely moving shadows, and all our busy rushing ends in nothing"** (Psalm 39:6 NLT). Doesn't that almost give you chills? *Merely moving shadows. Busy rushing that ends in nothing.* The last thing I want is for most of my life to be pointless in the scope of eternity, but the truth is that much of my busy rushing is pretty pointless.

Busyness by itself isn't wrong, but busyness requires intention. Pray that God will guard you from pointless busyness and that if you *are* busy, that you'll live *busy with a purpose.*

____

____

____

____

____

November 16

Lies of busyness: "Work and ambition are wrong."

Diana Kerr

"Mary has chosen what is better," Jesus said in Luke 10:42 when he visited Mary and Martha's home. While Mary was listening to Jesus, Martha had gotten distracted with housework. We Christians hear this story and often hang our heads in shame, heaping guilt on ourselves for being productive.

In the previous devotion, we looked at the problem that results from *pride* in our busyness. On the flip side, many of us suffer from *guilt* over our busyness as well.

The truth is that work is one of our God-given functions. Countless people praise God through various types of hard work. They use the intellect and circumstances God has provided them with to preach, teach, build companies, raise families, and on and on. Numerous Bible verses praise having a strong work ethic. Work or ambition in and of itself isn't the problem. What the issue comes down to is heart, motivation, and priorities.

If our motivation is to serve God with our work but *also* make time with him our number-one priority, we're on the right track. There's a time to be still and to be in God's presence, and there's also a time to work and get stuff done. In those times when we're doing work, let's approach it according to Colossians 3:23: **"Whatever you do, work at it with all your heart, as working for the Lord."**

____

____

____

____

____

Lies of busyness: "There aren't enough hours in a day."

Diana Kerr

Have you ever said something like that? I totally understand. Sometimes life feels like you're running on a treadmill while someone keeps pushing the button to increase the speed faster and faster.

Twenty-four hours never feels like enough. If only we had more time! A couple extra hours a day would make all the difference! Or maybe an extra week to be able to catch up, right? (How do I know your thoughts? Because I have the exact same thoughts myself.)

The truth is that God will accomplish through you what he needs to accomplish in the time available. Our almighty God is the one who came up with 24-hour days after all. If God thinks that's good enough, it is. I love the end of the book of Job when God challenges Job's frustrations and puts him in his place for questioning God: **"Where were you when I laid the earth's foundation? Tell me, if you understand. . . . Have you ever given orders to the morning, or shown the dawn its place?"** (Job 38:4,12).

In other words, God's the boss man and he knows what he's doing. You can wish for more time, but you're not going to get it. You can't make your days longer. What you *can* do is your best and leave the rest in God's hands. After all, if everything in life depended on *us*, no amount of hours would ever, *ever* be enough.

____

____

____

____

____

Lies of busyness: "I don't have time to rest"

Diana Kerr

A couple years ago, I heard about how one of my former professors makes a conscious effort to seek Sabbath rest on Sundays. I was intrigued. How did she manage to "give up" so much precious time on Sunday and still get all her errands and cleaning and to-do lists done? I started reading up on the Sabbath and its value for today's Christians.

What I learned surprised me. Numerous books and articles I read pointed to a biological need for consistent, weekly rest. Could it be possible that God actually designed our bodies to *need* a day off each week? Was the scientific evidence true—that mental and physical rejuvenation for one day a week actually causes people to get significantly more done in six days than they can in seven days when they *don't* make time to rest?

Mark 2:27 indicates that the Sabbath is something God intentionally created for our good: **"Then Jesus said to them, 'The Sabbath was made to meet the needs of people, and not people to meet the requirements of the Sabbath'"** (NLT). Jesus isn't explicitly clear what those needs are, but we know that we humans need rest. We need refreshment. Most of all, we know that we need to stop and pause and fill our cups with God, even if it's not on Sundays or for an entire day.

Making time to rest in the Lord can be really challenging, but the benefits of that rest are worth the effort.

____

____

____

____

November 19

Lies of busyness: "I need to fix this on my own."

Diana Kerr

Now that we're on the final day of this series on busyness, you might be feeling there are some areas of your life you want to change. You might be thinking that the solution is to somehow find a way to do better than you're doing now—to set goals to spend your time more wisely, alter your thinking, or challenge your motivation.

When you think about how to actually make those goals happen though, your stress level rises. It feels daunting to think about tackling those overwhelming changes on your own.

Don't underestimate God's role in your busyness and the changes you want to make. Yes, you can make a lot of progress with strategic prioritization and some valuable time-management tips, but that doesn't mean you shouldn't turn to God for help. God invites us to come to him over and over throughout the Bible, to call on him in all circumstances. If you're overwhelmed with the current state of your busyness, go to God. **"Do not be anxious about anything, but in everything, by prayer and petition, with thanksgiving, present your requests to God"** (Philippians 4:6).

Ask God for his guidance as to how to move forward, for his wisdom in setting your priorities, and for his help in keeping your motivation in check. Remember that you don't have to be perfect. God's love for you does not depend on what's on your calendar today. Enjoy peace and rest in that precious truth.

Shortcuts

Pastor Mark Jeske

"This time it's different." You and I can rationalize almost anything with those words. We can ignore time-tested principles of investment to make risky bets. We can trust the wrong people with our business and savings.

How tempting it is to take forbidden shortcuts when God is just not acting in a timely manner! King Saul had marshaled Israel's troops for war with the Philistines, but the prophet Samuel was not showing up to offer sacrifices to the Lord. Saul was neither priest nor Levite and knew that he had no business acting like one. But this time it was different, so he took a shortcut: **"Saul remained at Gilgal, and all the troops with him were quaking with fear. He waited seven days, the time set by Samuel; but Samuel did not come to Gilgal, and Saul's men began to scatter. So he said, 'Bring me the burnt offering and the fellowship offerings.' And Saul offered up the burnt offering"** (1 Samuel 13:7-9).

Samuel arrived in time to see the smoke and smell the burning. The kingship would be taken from Saul's family and given to another from that day forward.

You want your business to succeed, but God is not blessing it as fast as you want. So you falsify some records and accounts to "speed things up." You love this man and know you want him forever. He hasn't proposed, but you invite him into your home to live with you to "speed things up." *Hmm . . .*

____

____

____

____

November 21

You have lots of company

Pastor Mark Jeske

Sufferers often feel very isolated. Everybody else seems to be doing fine. They look back and keenly regret the loss of their mobility or of sharp eyesight or hearing or memory for faces and names. It is a comfort to be with other people who suffer disabilities whom you can perhaps help, and it is an even greater comfort to know that even the mighty apostles of the Lord, the champions of the gospel of the first century, knew hardship personally. John the Baptist wasted away in Herod Antipas' dungeon until the time of his beheading. Think of the beatings and imprisonment that Paul endured.

St. John wrote that his hardships bonded him with all believers who suffered: **"I, John, your brother and companion in the suffering and kingdom and patient endurance that are ours in Jesus . . ."** (Revelation 1:9). John had to endure exile on the island of Patmos when he wanted to continue serving his circuit of congregations in western Asia Minor. He is still our brother and companion—in *suffering,* in the (building up of the) *kingdom,* and patient *endurance.* Like marines in boot camp, the fatigue and stress and hardships we experience in service to our mission only makes us tougher and more useful to our King.

When you suffer hurt or loss, you do not have to fear that you are being punished or that you have fallen from favor with the Lord. You have company. Good company!

November 22

Masks

Pastor Mark Jeske

One of the first casualties of the nightmare of alcoholism is the truth. Heavy drinkers lie—to their families, to their bosses, but first to themselves. They cultivate a fantasy world to enable their drinking to continue. Long after everybody else is on to them, they continue to pretend to themselves that everything is fine.

People can try to fool God, but they will never succeed—he sees through us like a pane of glass. If Satan cannot keep you from Christianity and church life, he will try to hollow out your heart and let you pretend that your old passion and integrity are still there. In the days of the early church, a man named Ananias wanted the benefits of pretending to be a paragon of generosity while keeping the money for himself.

The apostle Peter was on to his scam: **"Ananias, how is it that Satan has so filled your heart that you have lied to the Holy Spirit and have kept for yourself some of the money you received for the land? Didn't it belong to you before it was sold? And after it was sold, wasn't the money at your disposal? . . . You have not lied to men but to God"** (Acts 5:3,4).

Does it terrify you to realize that God searches the human heart? Then give up your games. Be honest with him and with yourself. Confess your sins to him. Embrace Jesus' forgiveness. And then live a life of integrity—say what you mean, mean what you say.

Finding paradise

Pastor Daron Lindemann

Now this is paradise. The Bible tells us that after **"the heavens and the earth were completed in their vast array. Now the LORD God . . . planted a garden in the east, in Eden; and there he put the man he had formed. And the LORD God made all kinds of trees grow out of the ground—trees that were pleasing to the eye and good for food. . . . A river watering the garden flowed from Eden"** (Genesis 2:1,8-10).

However, Adam and Eve didn't consider the Garden of Eden paradise at all, but prison. Instead of thanking the Lord God for creating a luxury home for them, they cursed him for not making it better.

So Adam and Eve took the fruit that God had prohibited and the devil had promoted, eagerly anticipating the paradise that would become theirs. What they chewed and then swallowed was not paradise at all, but poison.

After their disobedience, Adam and Eve wanted to be as far away from God as possible, to hide from him, blame him, and shut him out of their lives. In his mercy, the Lord wanted to be closer to Adam and Eve than ever. He sought them in the garden. He loved them and would not let them go. Instead, he punished the serpent. And he also punished the seed of the woman, his own Son, who died as our substitute and Savior.

God has given his best for us. Look no further than his love to be perfectly content.

Joy and sorrow entwined

Pastor Mark Jeske

"It was the best of times; it was the worst of times," is how Charles Dickens began *A Tale of Two Cities.* Have you ever noticed how joys and sorrows are constantly intertwined in our lives? Even at the bottom of the pit there are still good friends to help lift you up; even at the peak of triumph something is unraveling.

Someone is in a car accident on the way to a wedding. Grandma is too sick to come to your graduation. You finally get the house painted but a big rain causes basement flooding.

Toward the end of his life, Moses composed a poem on the ways joy and sorrow were mingled in earthly life; after listing some hard features of life, he wrote: **"Satisfy us in the morning with your unfailing love, that we may sing for joy and be glad all our days. Make us glad for as many days as you have afflicted us, for as many years as we have seen trouble"** (Psalm 90:14,15). Moses knew the heartbreak and sorrow were givens; his hope was that God would ration out happiness in the same measure of pain that his children would have to bear.

What wonderful hope is in those words! What a comfort it is to know that God will keep sending blessings to lighten our load. Someday *all* tears will be wiped from our eyes. In the meantime, Lord, we depend on you to wipe away some of them.

November 25

Left behind

Pastor Mark Jeske

Husbands and wives sometimes joke with each other as to who will most likely die first. It would be nice, wouldn't it, if they could both live to old age and then go to heaven about the same time? Alas, it doesn't usually work out that way. Someone is usually *left behind.*

Like Anna. **"There was also a prophetess, Anna, the daughter of Phanuel, of the tribe of Asher. She was very old; she had lived with her husband seven years after her marriage, and then was a widow until she was eight-four"** (Luke 2:36,37). It was her exquisite joy to be in the temple the day Mary and Joseph brought the infant Savior for his ceremonial presentation. **"Coming up to them at that very moment, she gave thanks to God and spoke about the child to all who were looking forward to the redemption of Jerusalem"** (Luke 2:38).

Anna could have become a bitter woman with a shriveled soul, cursing her life, blaming God, and resenting other "happy" couples. Instead she thanked God for the time she did have with her husband and then looked for ways to worship and serve. Even at age 84 her evangelism testimony was powerful.

We would all like to write the script for our own lives. We can't, and the more we try to force things the more unhappy we'll be. How much better it is to accept the script God gives us and then see how he can use us.

Even when we're left behind.

Don't even start

Pastor Mark Jeske

Have you ever stood at the edge of a hydroelectric dam and marveled at the immense volume of water pent up behind it? To withstand the tremendous pressures—45,000 pounds per square foot at the bottom of Hoover Dam, for instance—the dams have to be built almost like pyramids, with wide bases for strength and stability.

Human emotions are like the waters of a river upstream from a dam—managed and released well, they can be very productive. Losing your self-control, however, is like a flood bursting through closed spill gates: **"Starting a quarrel is like breaching a dam; so drop the matter before a dispute breaks out"** (Proverbs 17:14). Large volumes of angry water are among Earth's most destructive forces.

Are you self-aware enough to know which are your hot buttons? Can you feel anger coming on, or does it surprise even you? Are you blurting hurt words before you even realize what's happening? In which kinds of situations do you find yourself losing your temper?

Once past your teeth, words simply cannot be pushed back down your throat. Once you have attacked or abused or ridiculed or cut someone, your words will be remembered forever. It takes ten times more work to undo your verbal damage than simply to clamp your jaw shut before it started flapping the first time.

Where are the cracks in your emotion dam?

___

___

___

___

November 27

Now thank we all our God

Pastor Mark Jeske

Martin Rinkart was a young pastor when he received the position of archdeacon in Eilenburg, a town northeast of Leipzig, just as the brutal Thirty Years' War erupted between Protestants and Catholics. Much of Germany was torn up. Eilenburg was overrun several times by different armies, and in 1637 a terrible plague ravaged the town. Rinkart was the only pastor still alive in the town and buried thousands of its inhabitants, including his own wife.

Rinkart lived just long enough to know that the Peace of Westphalia ended the war and his hymn of confidence and thankfulness even under severe tribulation was sung all over Germany to celebrate. It is still sung today and is a favorite on Thanksgiving Day.

It's hard enough to remember to thank God when life is peaceful and good. **"Be joyful always; pray continually; give thanks in all circumstances, for this is God's will for you in Christ Jesus"** (1 Thessalonians 5:16-18). How much more important is it to thank God in *all* circumstances! Sometimes he spoils us with his generosity, but often his best work is done when his people are suffering hardships. We win either way.

Now thank we all our God with hearts and hands and voices,
Who wondrous things has done, in whom his world rejoices,
Who from our mother's arms has blessed us on our way
With countless gifts of love and still is ours today.

____

____

____

November 28

It's okay to be last

Pastor Daron Lindemann

Supposedly, former professional boxer Muhammad Ali, in his prime, got on an airplane and was asked kindly by the flight attendant to buckle his seat belt. "Superman don't need no seat belt," Ali boasted, to which she replied, "Superman don't need no airplane either." Ali thought he was pretty great. Are you and I any different?

"I am the greatest," I claim when I consistently dismiss the doctor's warnings or disobey mom or dad's clear instructions.

"I am the greatest," I claim when I win a competition followed by a letdown performance as a result of thinking I'm invincible.

"I am the greatest," I claim with thoughts of superiority over other ethnic groups, social classes, or religious denominations.

"I am the greatest," I claim when I deny God's right to be God *over* me and *instead* of me every day. **"Such 'wisdom' does not come down from heaven but is earthly, unspiritual, of the devil"** (James 3:15). Sinful pride is deceptively, dangerously connected to the devil. Kill it before it kills you!

Jesus already killed sinful pride, and it will stay dead unless summoned to life by your selfish desires. To prevent this, Jesus taught, **"Anyone who wants to be first, he must be the very last, and the servant of all"** (Mark 9:35). Of course, Jesus didn't just teach this. He lived it, died it, and then rose as the firstborn from the dead to fulfill it. He also fulfills it in you.

November 29

Oh, come, Emmanuel

Pastor Mark Jeske

Oh, come, Emmanuel, and ransom captive Israel
That mourns in lonely exile here until the Son of God appear.
Rejoice! Emmanuel shall come to you, O Israel!

The melancholy plainsong of this ancient Advent hymn is a perfect setting for a cry from the heart of the suffering and waiting nation of Israel. Once enslaved in Egypt and a millennium later taken in chains to Babylon, the Israelites had to wait and wait some more to see their destiny as a nation fulfilled. Finally God sent the liberator Moses to Egypt; finally he sent the Persian king Cyrus to enable some of the captive Jews to leave Babylon and return to their ancient land.

As you wait for Christmas this year, as you wait for God's help in the stresses and pains of your life, as you wait for Christ to return and bring us Home, you can use your Advent month not just for shopping or killing time till the festivities. Sing this hymn with confidence—God keeps his promises. Sing this hymn with hope—your future will be better than your past.

Rejoice! Emmanuel, "God with us," came once in a manger as promised. Rejoice! Emmanuel comes to us now in Word and sacrament. Rejoice! Emmanuel will come soon to open heaven's gates.

"Therefore the Lord himself will give you a sign: The virgin will be with child and will give birth to a son, and will call him Immanuel" (Isaiah 7:14).

Leaders pray

Pastor Mark Jeske

The prophet Samuel was pretty glum. After a long career riding a ministry circuit, advising Israel's leaders, organizing resistance to the invading Philistines, and struggling with the people's spiritual indifference, his time was coming to an end and he knew it.

The Israelites wanted a king like the other nations. They grew impatient with judges and priests as leaders. Samuel wished that they had simply let God be their king. He would have provided everything that they needed. In his farewell address, he reviewed some of their history, gave them some thoughtful advice, and added some warnings about pitfalls ahead. And he prayed for them. He really cared for those people. **"The Lord was pleased to make you his own. As for me, far be it from me that I should sin against the Lord by failing to pray for you"** (1 Samuel 12:22,23).

Spiritual leaders pray for the people whom God has called them to lead. Pastors pray, parents pray, teachers pray, and church board members pray. They know that in some way God has even more good things to bring to people's lives—protection, resources, vision, abilities—and that just by asking they will release these blessings. Prayer reaches across great distances and connects us with God's great agenda. People who pray often know that God is giving them a little of his influence on how things will go in the future.

Who needs your prayers today? How about right now? Yes?

December

"BUT YOU, BETHLEHEM EPHRATHAH, THOUGH YOU ARE SMALL AMONG THE CLANS OF JUDAH, OUT OF YOU WILL COME FOR ME ONE WHO WILL BE RULER OVER ISRAEL, WHOSE ORIGINS ARE FROM OF OLD, FROM ANCIENT TIMES."

MICAH 5:2

Mi casa es su casa

Pastor Mark Jeske

One of the features of the first-century church that was exciting and appealing to people was the love and spirit of generosity that the Christians showed toward one another. They looked after one another and took care that no one suffered for lack of shelter, food, or clothes.

Christian fraternal organizations arose before there was a government safety net. They looked after widows and orphans and responded when families suffered disasters like fires or the death of the breadwinner. They pooled resources to make sure no one would suffer a debilitating financial blow.

In a dog-eat-dog world, genuine kindness really stands out. It is irresistible. If you want to make Jesus look good, and if you want people to feel drawn to your church, show unconditional love and generosity among yourselves. **"Offer hospitality to one another without grumbling"** (1 Peter 4:9). It always thrills my heart when I see Christians take in a foster kid, take in a child of relatives who are going through severe financial and personal stress, help an unemployed person find work, or make sure a lonely person has a place to eat a Thanksgiving dinner. It always thrills my heart when I see members of my congregation inviting not only their long-time friends to their gatherings but also drawing in the newbies and strangers.

How often do you have people over at your home? Would people describe you as hospitable?

Where did the devil come from?

Pastor Mark Jeske

The Bible presents a wealth of information about our world completely unavailable from any other source. It goes back in time before recorded history to describe the creation. It peers ahead into the future and gives us glimpses of what lies ahead and the glories of heaven. And it peeks behind the scenes of day-to-day life to see what is going on in the world of spirits and demons.

Some of the Old Testament prophecies of the coming Messiah use the life and experiences of King David as a jumping-off point. God used the same literary device to show us the sad transformation of Lucifer, the "light bearer" angel of glory, into our hellish foe Satan. The evil nature of the king of Babylon leads Isaiah prophetically to describe the evil nature of the devil: **"How you have fallen from heaven, O morning star, son of the dawn! You have been cast down to the earth, you who once laid low the nations! You said in your heart, 'I will ascend to heaven; I will raise my throne above the stars of God; I will sit enthroned. . . . I will make myself like the Most High'"** (Isaiah 14:12-14).

Satan's original sin was to grow weary of serving God and to desire to be a god himself. His mad revolt cost him his place in heaven and guaranteed an eternity in hell for himself. Now for a short while he and his demons roam the earth, seeking to seduce God's children into joining his rebellion.

Now you know.

Fighting in church?

Pastor Mark Jeske

If anything drives suspicious unbelievers away from the fellowship of a congregation, it is the perception of hypocrisy on the part of the members. Supposedly a church is portraying a superior way to live. Supposedly congregations and their leaders have figured out divine secrets to a happier life. Outsiders assume that church people consider themselves more moral than the average Joe.

So when sin and Satan invade the sanctuary, news gets around. In the Macedonian city of Philippi, the unreconciled bitterness of a conflict between two women was not only making the two of them look bad; it was making the whole congregation look bad. Where was this harmony Christ talked about? Where was the spirit of forgiveness? **"I plead with Euodia and I plead with Syntyche to agree with each other in the Lord"** (Philippians 4:2).

Notice that Paul didn't go into the reasons he may have heard of the conflict. He just urged them to figure it out. Paul would have agreed with James that "faith" without appropriate good works must be dead faith. We have received mercy from the Lord not just to comfort our own hearts but to enable us to become more merciful to others. We are forgiven in order to forgive, loved in order to love.

Are there any dysfunctions in your congregation right now that are hurting your reputation in your community? How are you positioned to bring about healing?

____

____

____

____

December 4

Enslaved by choice

Diana Kerr

Growing up, I *loved* historical fiction novels. Series like the *American Girls* or *Dear America* intrigued me with their historically accurate stories of girls my age who lived in earlier time periods in our country's history.

Whenever I would read a book about a slave girl in the 1800s, her story would fill me with emotion. I could feel just a *fraction* of her bondage and frustration and hopelessness. Still, I longed desperately for her freedom. In her case, there really was no way out of that slavery.

That kind of slavery is so unfamiliar to us, yet we experience our own bondage internally thanks to sin. Slavery to sin is a very different kind of bondage, but it stirs up some of the same emotions in us, doesn't it? We feel trapped, frustrated, and hopeless.

Unlike literal slavery, however, there is a way out. Isaiah 9:4 reminds us of Jesus' great emancipation: **"You have shattered the yoke that burdens them, the bar across their shoulders, the rod of their oppressor."**

Too often we feel weighed down with the burden of the poor choices of our past, or even those of our present reality. We allow sin and Satan the oppressor to keep us captive, when in reality we are free.

Friends, Jesus didn't just remove your burden and oppression, he *shattered* it. There's no need to live in slavery when you're actually free.

____

____

____

____

December 5

What if you believed God's promises?

Diana Kerr

Do you believe the entire Bible? Most of us would say, "Yes. Of course." But do you really? When it comes to God's promises, do you *believe* and *internalize* them deep down in your gut?

I once heard a pastor say that most of our Bibles are missing some pieces. They're incomplete. Why? Failing to believe the promises of God is like ripping out chunks of the Bible.

We don't always believe God will never leave us or forsake us. We don't always believe God's Word will not return to him empty. We don't always believe we are forgiven. We don't always believe God cares about our insignificant problems, or even about us. We don't always believe God will work out problems for our good.

We claim to believe the Bible, but we doubt the validity of God's promises. It's not always a conscious, blatant doubt, but more so a doubt that shows itself in our worries, anxieties, frustrations, and guilt.

Joshua spoke some beautiful words about God's promises during his last days on earth that are just as true for the Israelites as they are for us today: **"You know with all your heart and soul that not one of all the good promises the LORD your God gave you has failed. Every promise has been fulfilled; not one has failed"** (Joshua 23:14).

Read that verse over and over. God has a flawless track record. We have good reason to be confident in believing his promises.

___

___

___

December 6

What child is this?

Pastor Mark Jeske

What Child is this who, laid to rest, on Mary's lap is sleeping?
Whom angels greet with anthems sweet
while shepherds watch are keeping?
This, this is Christ the King,
whom shepherds guard and angels sing.
Haste, haste to bring him laud, the Babe, the Son of Mary!

If "Oh, Come, Emmanuel" is a plainchant from the Middle Ages, "What Child Is This?" is a romantic ballad from Renaissance England. The tune is lively enough in its triple time to dance to, and the content of William Dix's beautiful stanzas helps every singer figure out just what Christmas is all about. As fans of the New Orleans Saints would say, "Who dat?"

The Christmas miracle—God made man, omnipotence and weakness, vast reach and tiny fingers—is absolutely the most perfect example of God's upside-down way of getting his agenda accomplished. In the smallness of a baby, our God has come to earth. This tiny Child has come to our world to do nothing less than do battle with sin and Satan.

But he's big enough. Because in that little head is the mind of God, and in those little hands is power to heal and protect. He became incarnate to have a life to live in our place and to have a life to give in our place. *That* is what Child this is.

"Who, being in very nature God, did not consider equality with God something to be grasped, but made himself nothing, taking the very nature of a servant, being made in human likeness. And being found in appearance as a man, he humbled himself and become obedient to death—even death on a cross!" (Philippians 2:7,8).

Why did God make people?

Pastor Mark Jeske

No one could fault the ancient Greeks for being atheists. As St. Paul looked around him in Athens, he could see religious temples, shrines, and statuary of gods and goddesses everywhere. And yet in all that religious clutter people did not really know for sure where they came from, what the purpose of their existence was (if there was any purpose at all), nor what lay ahead after death. Their only strategy was to set up altars for absolutely every deity they had ever heard of, including one to "The Unknown God," just in case they had missed one.

Paul complimented the Athenians on their evident piety, but he let them know that the unknown God could be known, as could their origin and destiny: **"From one man he made all the nations, that they should inhabit the whole earth; and he marked out their appointed times in history and the boundaries of their lands. God did this so that they would seek him and perhaps reach out for him and find him, though he is not far from any one of us"** (Acts 17:26,27 NIV 2011).

People today struggle just as intensely with the great questions of human existence. They still see no design and purpose to their lives—all they have is the cold, dry wind of Darwinism that tells them they are accidents of billions of years of blind, random mutations and natural selection through survival of the fittest.

Aren't you glad to know that you are designed and loved, forgiven and immortal?

___

___

___

Better than Santa Claus

Pastor Mark Jeske

At best, the story of the jolly man in a red suit in December is a harmless legend with which to amuse and delight small children. At worst, it is a terrible twisting of the Bible's actual revelation about our miraculous provider.

The 1934 song by Coots and Gillespie, "Santa Claus Is Coming to Town," is much-loved, extensively recorded, and gets heavy radio airplay each year. But it is a drag on the Christian faith, because Santa, who supposedly sees and remembers all, promising to punish the naughty and reward the nice, actually does no such thing. Everybody knows it's a scam—you get presents every year regardless of how you lived. The implication is that God can't do those things either and that you can ignore his Word and warnings as you do Santa's.

In reality, **"The eyes of the LORD are everywhere, keeping watch on the wicked and the good"** (Proverbs 15:3). God really does keep track of all human behavior, yours and mine included. He knows you've been naughty; and to spare you from the terrible consequences of your misdeeds, he arranged the incarnation of his Son, Jesus. He knows also when you've been nice, and your deeds of love make his heavenly smile light up. The Holy Spirit whom he sent to live within you is your guide and inspiration to love one another, and not just at Christmastime but all year 'round.

So be good for Jesus' sake.

____

____

____

____

God, how long?

Pastor Mark Jeske

One of the best things about living in this century is the speed. I love the speed! I can get to any major city in America in a couple hours on a plane, journeys that used to take months of hard travel. I can send electronic messages anywhere on the planet instantaneously. I can video conference with anybody on earth that has the right equipment. I can send and receive pictures and video in seconds. I love how businesses cater to me, trying to get my attention and money through quick solutions to all my needs and wants.

One of the worst things about living in this century is the speed. I'm losing my ability to be patient. Years of experiencing immediate gratification make me fidget and complain when I don't get what I want *right away.* I'm embarrassed to say that this spills over into my spiritual life as well. When God doesn't jump to my wishes like an eager salesclerk, I get some attitude. King David did too: **"How long, O Lord? Will you forget me forever? How long will you hide your face from me?"** (Psalm 13:1).

How long indeed. We operate on the assumption that we pretty much know everything, and we can't imagine any reason why we should have to limp when God could so easily make us run. Why should I have to wait when I'm such a busy person? I've got things to do—can't God see that?

Please, Lord—teach me why patience is so important.

You can't miss Christmas

Pastor Daron Lindemann

To their surprise, church members in Poettmes, Germany, found a real, newborn baby in the manger of their nativity scene near the altar. The mother was located but said that she couldn't care for the baby. She left him there, hoping that someone else could.

God sent his newborn Son into the world not with the hope that people would care for him, but with the promise that he'd care for us. Yes, save us. **"For the grace of God that brings salvation has appeared to all men"** (Titus 2:11).

Look into the manger with faith and you'll see that Christmas is not what you make it to be. Christmas is what makes you God's own redeemed, forgiven, and loved child. Christmas is a gift. *To us* a child is born. *To us* a Son is given (Isaiah 9:6). God's final target in sending his Son, Jesus, isn't the manger. It is people. God enters the world and enters our lives.

You may miss your family this Christmas. You may have missed saying good-bye to a loved one who died and now lives with Jesus in heaven. You may have missed an application deadline or purchasing just the right gift for a friend. But you can't miss the grace of God that appeared in a manger.

Because the grace of God has not missed anyone.

____

____

____

____

____

Parting is such sweet sorrow

Pastor Mark Jeske

Juliet could barely tear herself away from Romeo. "Good night! Good night! Parting is such sweet sorrow, that I shall say goodnight, till it be morrow." Going their separate ways is a great way to heighten anticipation between two lovers. It is also a high stress moment though, because we all know how many things can go wrong before the two might be able to meet again.

Parting involves risk. Love sometimes cools off. Things change. One lover might lose interest or find a better offer or leave town. You might never see each other again. That was the fear in people's minds as members of the congregation in Ephesus gathered at the harbor to say farewell to their dear apostle Paul. He gave a stirring exhortation to them all to be strong, take care of each other, and stay true to their mission.

Then: **"When he had said this, he knelt down with all of them and prayed. They all wept as they embraced him and kissed him. What grieved them most was his statement that they would never see his face again. Then they accompanied him to the ship"** (Acts 20:36-38). Paul of course meant only that they wouldn't see him this side of the grave. In heaven comes the Grand Reunion.

You know, it's one of the most wonderful things about being a Christian—all separations are only temporary.

___

___

___

___

___

December 12

When plans blow up

Pastor Mark Jeske

You weren't planning to spend all day in an auto repair shop. You weren't planning on a connector flight getting canceled and having to fork out for an unexpected hotel stay in a city you didn't want to stay in. You weren't planning on another child, on having to find a job again, on having to be single again so soon.

Life happens. We try so hard to be organized and control things, but our plans sometimes just blow up. St. Paul had a wonderful vision of how beautifully his next Jerusalem visit would go: **"Pray that I may be rescued from the unbelievers in Judea and that my service in Jerusalem may be acceptable to the saints there, so that by God's will I may come to you with joy and together with you be refreshed"** (Romans 15:31,32).

What actually happened was that a riot broke out in Jerusalem, he was arrested, detained in a Caesarean prison for two years, and then shipwrecked. But God ironically did get him to Rome, and his prisoner status actually got him a hearing before governors and developed relationships in the Praetorian Guard in Rome that would never otherwise have happened.

God sometimes gets his best work done when there is chaos in our lives. Don't panic when your plans blow up. It may just be a platform for God to do something significant. Keep your eyes open to see what he might be up to.

December 13

Oh, come, all ye faithful

Pastor Mark Jeske

Yea, Lord, we greet thee, born this happy morning;
Jesus, to thee be all glory given,
Word of the Father, now in flesh appearing.
Oh, come, let us adore him, Christ the Lord.

"In the beginning was the Word, and the Word was with God, and the Word was God," says St. John in the prologue to his gospel (1:1). And what a mighty Word he is! Words communicate important information. In person Jesus came to reveal the true God to mankind: a God who is kind, wise, omnipotent, and who loves people.

When Satan outs himself, when he and his demons take possession of a human being, they abuse and destroy. Jesus' humble presence in his little manger is a foretaste of his humility on the cross, the mighty work through which God's wrath was diverted from us onto himself, and through which God's favor was diverted from him onto us. By faith, all ye faithful, ye can experience this amazing swap—you give Christ all your sins and he gives you the Father's forgiveness.

What can we say in response to this but glory be to God in the highest! What can we do but worship him. Oh, come, let us *adore* him, Christ, the Lord!

____

____

____

____

____

December 14

Build yourselves up

Pastor Mark Jeske

Only a few energetic and disciplined people over the age of 30 like how their bodies look. The rest of us need help. By now you've encountered Hans and Franz, two (comic) Austrian bodybuilders in lumpy gray sweats, who have one goal in life: they want to pump . . . you up.

Your spiritual life will sag at times during your life as well. The apostle Jude (not a comic at all) was aware from personal experience how out of tune he had been with God's Word and true plan of salvation. Though he was Jesus' half brother, he did not believe in Jesus as his Savior until after the resurrection.

The people who first read his letter needed a workout—badly—and Jude wanted to pump them up.

"But you, dear friends, build yourselves up in your most holy faith and pray in the Holy Spirit. Keep yourselves in God's love as you wait for the mercy of our Lord Jesus Christ to bring you to eternal life" (Jude 20,21). Push-ups and Pilates will help your abs and pecs, but to build your faith you need to be in the Word and in prayer.

Like bodybuilding, faithbuilding does not happen by itself. Only you can decide to attend a worship service or a Bible study group. Only you can crack open a Bible and listen. Only you can sing Christian hymns in your home and listen to Christian radio.

Only you can choose to read a devotion (like this one).

____

____

____

____

No doubts

Pastor Mark Jeske

"If any of you lacks wisdom, he should ask God, who gives generously to all without finding fault, and it will be given to him. But when he asks, he must believe and not doubt, because he who doubts is like a wave of the sea, blown and tossed by the wind. That man should not think he will receive anything from the Lord; he is a double-minded man, unstable in all he does" (James 1:5-8).

It is heartening to pray to a God who gives generously to all "without finding fault." When repentant sinners are forgiven by their loving Savior, they really are forgiven—God is no longer interested in accusing. The sin that once separated them has been nailed to the cross with Jesus and is gone. Gone! And so God's forgiven children don't have to feel stupid or guilty when they come to their Father for help, because he is interested in helping them, not in finding fault with them.

"And don't doubt," says James. Christian prayer expresses full confidence in God's unlimited love, God's unlimited power, and God's unlimited wisdom. According to James, if we doubt any of those aspects of God, we are double-minded, spiritually schizophrenic, unstable, and unlikely to receive anything at all from the Lord. Prayer is all about relationships—Christian prayer is a celebration of being children of our Father "who art in heaven."

If you're going to pray for rain, bring an umbrella.

Filled up

Diana Kerr

It's crazy how deeply empty a lot of people feel these days. Do you pick up on that emptiness? Do you notice it around you? You probably feel it yourself to some degree. We have so, so much that fills every piece of our lives—things that fill our closets, time, pantries, minds, attention, inboxes, garages, and on and on. Unfortunately, the more we try to fill ourselves with those things, the more empty we feel. No amount of earthly stuff can make the void go away.

We strive so hard to make our lives feel full, but the true solution requires no striving. True fullness comes from knowledge of a simple, beautiful truth. **"I pray that you, being rooted and established in love, may have power, together with all the saints, to grasp how wide and long and high and deep is the love of Christ, and to know this love that surpasses knowledge—that you may be filled to the measure of all the fullness of God"** (Ephesians 3:17-19).

"Wide and long and high and deep." Paul's not talking about the dimensions of a boat or a garage. The message he sends is this: Christ's love is expansive enough to fill our void.

"That you may be filled to the measure of all the fullness of God." This is Paul's prayer to the Ephesian Christians, and it's my prayer for you—that you allow God, through his fullness, to make you truly full.

___

___

___

___

___

Okay, I can wait

Pastor Mark Jeske

One of God's strategies for curing me of my chronic terrible sin of impatience is the same strategy he used for the people of Israel in the centuries before Christ. By asking his children to wait a while for his better time, he gives us far more than we could have done on our own. On my own, with my resources, at my speed, I could generate a trickle. By waiting for God, by dialing into his agenda and timing, by waiting for his formidable resources, I will experience a gusher.

Israel's history shows how powerful that operating principle is: **"I am the Lord your God, who brought you up out of Egypt. Open wide your mouth and I will fill it"** (Psalm 81:10). Think how long the Israelite slaves in Egypt groaned under their yoke. Think how Satan tempted them to assume that they'd been abandoned, that their covenant relationship with the Lord was in shambles, that there was no hope.

But at just the right time God called and trained Moses and Aaron, and they announced God's liberation for the Israelites and judgment upon Egypt. Ten hammer blows from heaven reduced the most powerful economy in the world to rubble, and somewhere around three million slaves walked away free.

Waiting for them in Canaan was a land of milk and honey. Waiting for you and me: more milk. More honey. Open your mouth and let God fill it.

December 18

Busy at rest

Pastor Daron Lindemann

One of the most feared statements of Jesus has nothing to do with taking up a cross or the dangers of sin or the sacrifices Christians face. It is this statement: **"Come to me, all you who are weary and burdened, and I will give you rest"** (Matthew 11:28).

As a time-conscious society, it's difficult for us to find the time to rest. We're so busy. We value the power of productivity.

Yet right now here you are, enjoying Jesus while the dirty dishes aren't cleaning themselves and the work project is making no progress without your attention and the messages pile up unanswered. Here you are, enjoying Jesus because you believe, you appreciate, that Jesus is never too busy for you.

He's never late when you need his help, never out to lunch or napping so that he doesn't notice your problems. He's always updated in his answers to your prayers, forgiving every sin, and filling every minute, every sunrise, and every sunset with his promises kept.

Jesus busies himself with you, and that's fulfilling for him. He enjoys you.

Rest doesn't necessarily mean doing nothing. Involve Jesus in your busyness, spend your minutes with faith, and set aside special moments like reading this devotion or prayer time or going to church for special enjoyment of Jesus. Being busy is okay, as long as Jesus is in it. Even Jesus is busy, but not too busy for you.

___

___

___

December 19

Mother Mary

Pastor Mark Jeske

When the angel Gabriel came to a woman named Mary with the world's most unusual birth announcement, it may have sounded a little glamorous. "Son of the Most High God, throne of his father David, reign over the house of Jacob forever . . ." Whew! Mary must have been giddy at first.

But her role was going to cost her. Bearing the label of unwed mother was no treat in a small town. Neither was deciding to go with Joseph to register in Bethlehem for the imperial census. **"Joseph also went up from the town of Nazareth in Galilee to Judea, to Bethlehem the town of David, because he belonged to the house and line of David. He went there to register with Mary, who was pledged to be married to him and was expecting a child"** (Luke 2:4,5).

Would you like to walk or donkey ride 80 miles over some very hilly dirt roads while very pregnant? No? I didn't think so. I don't know if Mary mistimed her due date or simply decided that she couldn't bear to stay alone in Nazareth. Either way, she made the trek nine months pregnant.

What about the trauma of going into labor in a barn, in the dark, with your carpenter/fiancé as your midwife? This courageous and faithful young woman played a huge role in God's plan to rescue the human race. All generations indeed shall call her blessed.

December 20

Silent night! Holy night!

Pastor Mark Jeske

Silent night! Holy night! Son of God, love's pure light
Radiant beams from thy holy face
with the dawn of redeeming grace,
Jesus, Lord, at thy birth, Jesus, Lord, at thy birth.

This powerful little carol has so worked its way into people's hearts all over the world that it isn't really Christmas unless you sing it at least once, preferably on Christmas Eve, preferably with the lights down low, children's faces lit only by the lights on the Christmas tree.

An Austrian village priest wrote these beautiful words in 1816, and a schoolteacher/organist quickly penned a simple tune to fit, although probably it was played for the first time on guitar in 1818.

Deep theology radiates from these simple words and pure pictures. The incarnation of Christ was not the actual blood-redemption, but it was the dawn. With the arrival of God's Son on earth, the long centuries of waiting were over and God's plans were in motion.

Possibly all was not so very calm nor bright 'round yon virgin mother and child. In fact, if Jesus was like almost every other baby, he squawked *just like us* when he needed food or fresh diapers. In your mind's eye, just look at God's Son and Mary's son lying there. Imagine the heavenly radiance that glowed from his little face and be certain of this—God must love me very, very much.

"For to us a child is born, to us a son is given, and the government will be on his shoulders. And he will be called Wonderful Counselor, Mighty God, Everlasting Father, Prince of Peace" (Isaiah 9:6).

December 21

Don't insult the Creator

Pastor Mark Jeske

Do roosters really think that they control the rising of the sun by their crowing? Perhaps. Did the great wealth and power of the Egyptian pharaohs really seduce them into believing their own mythology, that they were deities on earth who formed Egypt and its mighty river? God thought so: **"I am against you, Pharaoh king of Egypt, you great monster lying among your streams. You say, 'The Nile is mine; I made it for myself'"** (Ezekiel 29:3).

We would not dream of such arrogance today. Or would we? Do you think that the Colorado River formed the Grand Canyon? Do you think that the Himalaya mountain range was formed by billions of years of stress along the earth's tectonic plates and formed itself as it extruded upward? Do you think that the fantastically complex human being that is you had no designer? That over time, a lot of time, organisms changed themselves from one-celled amoebas into something like you?

There is an enticing allure behind the theory of evolution. If you are God's creation, living in God's world, then you are subject to him. You owe him. If you reject God's creation, you can declare yourself a sovereign, independent agent and live any way you want. You can create your own morality and need fear no accountability to a higher power.

Rejecting God's creation and ownership of the universe is spiritual suicide. Those who do so will hear a voice from heaven thunder, "I am against you."

Owning up to our sickness

Diana Kerr

At age 17, I was diagnosed with rheumatoid arthritis. Finally, I had an explanation for my many years of joint pain. But I was in denial. I begged my mom not to tell people about my diagnosis. If I thought about my disease or talked about it, I knew it would be *real.* I just wanted to pretend to be normal instead.

Maybe you've tried the same tactic. You ignore a sickness or pain thinking it will go away. Sometimes it works, but often you can't wish away a health problem. When you finally admit your body's weakness, you can take steps to get better and seek help.

I'm not in denial about my physical illness anymore, but being the very flawed person that I am, I fall into a similar state of denial sometimes about my sin and imperfection. Matthew 9:12 shames me and blesses me all at once: **"Jesus said, 'It is not the healthy who need a doctor, but the sick.'"** It shames me because I feel unjustifiably "healthy" in my spiritual life too often. It blesses me because it reminds me that I *am* sick, but I have Jesus.

When I talk with friends, it sounds like many of us feel that confession is one of the weakest areas of our prayer lives. We want to improve in that area because it's *crucial.*

If we're too proud to admit that we're sick, we don't need Doctor Jesus.

December 23

Shut your mouth

Diana Kerr

I have a love-hate relationship with the wise instructions of the book of Proverbs. Do you know what I mean? One minute I'm feeling a little smug as I read the verses. "Well, *that* verse doesn't apply to me," I think. Then, if I'm *really* feeling full of myself, my thoughts might wander to the kind of people to whom I think the verse *does* apply.

Inevitably, the next verse I read always stings me with a lesson I need to hear.

Proverbs 13:3. Ugh. A lesson I need to hear. **"He who guards his lips guards his life, but he who speaks rashly will come to ruin."** At first glance, we might read that verse and think of a time when someone said something awful to us. "I still can't believe she said that to me," we think. (Have you noticed how Facebook and the online world make it really easy for people to go after each other and be downright nasty?)

Let's try the reverse. Can you recall a situation when you opened *your* mouth and wish you hadn't? When you spoke rashly? Any type of poorly chosen words apply, and all of us are guilty to some degree. Angry words, prideful words, words of gossip, or any other hurtful words—even if unintentional—all cause big problems.

All of us can think of *other* people who need to guard their lips more carefully, but it's better for everyone if we remember that *we* fall into the "needs improvement" category as well.

The gift of God made flesh

Pastor Mark Jeske

Much of what keeps you busy this month is not really Christmas but Santamas. A lot of that is harmless fun—green and red decorations, office parties, white elephant gifts, and lit reindeer on your front lawn.

But when you actually pay attention to the Bible's account of the real Christmas, you are confronted with a game-changing story: a virgin conceives through the direct intervention of the Holy Spirit and then gives birth in a barnyard birthing room. But that's not even the biggest part of this big deal. The real miracle is that on Christmas Eve it was revealed to mankind that the Son of God had permanently taken on human flesh.

It was the most significant day since creation. Jesus came in person to relive our lives for us. To do that he needed to be not merely *like* us; he needed to *be* us. Every Christmas gift you've ever given, even the biggest one, pales in comparison with the gift the Father gave you—his Son, wrapped in strips of cloth and lying, of all places, in a manger.

His birth makes your immortality possible: **"The wages of sin is death, but the *gift* of God is eternal life in Christ Jesus our Lord"** (Romans 6:23). That's how valuable God thinks you are; that's how much he loves you. Thank you, God!

____

____

____

____

____

December 25

Joy to the world

Pastor Mark Jeske

Joy to the world, the Lord is come! Let earth receive her King;
Let every heart prepare him room and heaven and nature sing.

Nobody would have expected the great King of all to arrive like that. All the royalty in *Grimm's Fairy Tales* arrive in carriages drawn by a team of white horses. Can you believe that your Lord and Master arrived on earth through the birth process? And had nothing to wear but strips of cloth? And was laid in a manger (i.e., an animal's feed trough)?

Does the humility of the divine entrance disappoint you? discourage you? offend you? Were you expecting trumpets? armies? silks, ermine, golden mace, jewel-studded crowns? If you were near that cattle pen that night, would you have bowed down in worship?

Yes, we would! If God helped frantic parents and shocked shepherds and wealthy Magi from the East to see their Messiah in the Baby, he would have found a way to turn on the lights in our brains as well. People of earth, receive your King! Each Christmas is practice for the moment of Christ's second coming, when every knee will bend, either in worship or terror.

Prepare a place for Christ in your heart. Sing! Let everyone in your world know that you are happy that Jesus came all that way to claim you.

"Glory to God in the highest heaven, and on earth peace to men on whom his favor rests" (Luke 2:14).

December 26

Our world is so violent

Pastor Mark Jeske

It sure seems to me that our world is getting more violent all the time. Knuckleheads with guns drive around the city, taking their revenge on their enemies right out in the open. Innocent people get shot on their porches and in their homes. Children get caught in the crossfire. Thieves steal anything unsecured; robbers look at people as their private banks and make their "withdrawals" whenever they see an opening. Worse, so many thugs seem to get away with their evil deeds. On top of that, our government authorities over the decades have been shown to practice discrimination and abuse of their use of force.

And yet, the more things change, the more they stay the same. The prophet Habakkuk many centuries before Christ grieved over how much violence and wrong there was in his world. He demanded of God, **"Why do you make me look at injustice? Why do you tolerate wrong? Destruction and violence are before me; there is strife, and conflict abounds. Therefore the law is paralyzed, and justice never prevails"** (Habakkuk 1:3,4).

The world we live in is broken. We will never live in the Garden of Eden again this side of judgment day. The best we can hope for is some level of restraint on the forces of Satan and his demons. O Lord, deliver us from evil! Send your mighty angels to protect us and our children. Bring us home safely.

Perfect peace awaits us in heaven.

Unnatural grace

Pastor Daron Lindemann

To those who explain that Mary gave birth to Jesus naturally, I say: the virgin birth of Jesus is as unnatural of a birth as you can find, as the very grace of God itself is unnatural. That's something to contemplate at Christmastime.

"This is how the birth of Jesus Christ came about: His mother Mary was pledged to be married to Joseph, but before they came together, she was found to be with child through the Holy Spirit" (Matthew 1:18). Joseph and Mary hadn't yet come together sexually in marriage, so Mary couldn't be pregnant—except, she was! Mary became pregnant miraculously by the power of God the Holy Spirit. She gave birth not just to a human being but to a human being who was also God.

That's unnatural! Virgins don't give birth. And God is not a person. Except when the grace of God is involved. Because the grace of God is so unnatural.

It's unnatural for people who let God down too much to receive his faithful, forgiving love. It's unnatural for people who forget about God too often to have God answer a prayer when they suddenly remember they need something. It's unnatural for people who carelessly go through the motions of everyday Christian behavior or Sunday worship to believe in repentance that God—because of his grace and forgiveness—smiles with delight even at these half-empty expressions.

Grace is not logical, explainable, or subject to formulas. It's a miracle. Even in you.

____

____

December 28

I can't forgive

Pastor Mark Jeske

Do you ever ponder why it's so hard to forgive other people? I know why. Holding onto the grievance makes you feel righteous, morally superior. Forgiving someone takes the risk of enabling more bad behavior. The worse you can make somebody look in your own mind, the easier it is to overlook your own weaknesses and failures. And—if you hold onto your anger, you have powerful weapons to use in the next argument.

Jesus had severe words for any disciple of his who refused to show mercy to a fellow sinner. He told a story about a servant who had had a huge debt forgiven by his master: **"But when that servant went out, he found one of his fellow servants who owed him a hundred denarii. He grabbed him and began to choke him. 'Pay back what you owe me!' he demanded"** (Matthew 18:28). Isn't that pathetic? And yet that's how we look to God when we refuse to let go of our anger.

We've been forgiven so much! The amount we owe God because of our own sins and shortcomings is far greater than what any other person owes us. Let it go! Staying angry only keeps you locked in anger prison. Let God's mercy flow through you. Retaliation and threats and resentment and criticism only make people angrier and more defensive. Only kindness and love can change another person's heart.

To power up for that kind of sacrificial act, just think about the love it took for Christ to pay the price of your forgiveness.

The sound of soul

Pastor Daron Lindemann

I remember when one of my sons started taking guitar lessons. The enthusiastic melodies would echo down the hallway with such a rush that my wife and I would respond, "Keep it down!" Our other son was the singer. At the table. On his bike. And sometimes singing instead of otherwise getting ready, so that my wife and I would interject, "Stop singing!" We became the sound police, but then wondered if it was right to be squelching such abounding enthusiasm.

"With joy you will draw water from the wells of salvation" (Isaiah 12:3). Dropping a bucket into a well of fresh water is no chore, and there is no grumbling to be heard, only abounding enthusiasm, whistling a happy tune, fully expecting the bucket to return. Filled. This is joy. Joy is not a perspective shaped by circumstances. Joy shapes circumstances.

Like two young boys strumming or singing but definitely not uptight about the world's problems. Or like the cancer patient who can smile on the same day she receives a radiation treatment. Or like the lonely widow who can laugh about special memories on the anniversary of her husband's death. Or like the professional who says, "It's okay; God has other things in mind," after he loses his job. **"Shout aloud and sing for joy, people of Zion, for great is the Holy One of Israel among you"** (Isaiah 12:6). The Lord gives us abounding enthusiasm. That is the sound of soul.

God, I don't understand your ways

Pastor Mark Jeske

Everybody knows that children chafe at adult ways. They resist growing up because of all the hard work, self-sacrifice, and chores that adulthood entails. They resent being told no. They don't like waiting and deferring to others when their own wants seem so urgent. They just don't understand the adult world.

Here's an insight—the maturing process doesn't stop at age 16. In fact, we will be in God's school of maturation our whole lives. I don't care how old you are—you are probably *still* learning service to others above self, the importance of truth over lying, the virtues of patience, and the value of listening before speaking.

If you have ever questioned the wisdom of God's ways, you have a lot of company: **"How long will the enemy mock you, O God? Will the foe revile your name forever? Why do you hold back your hand, your right hand? Take it from the folds of your garment"** (Psalm 74:10,11). Every parent has heard the word *why* ten thousand times from inquisitive children. God hears it a lot too.

In time you may learn his rationale for how he is managing things in your life. But even if you don't, you can trust his kind heart and eternal wisdom. He's been tending his children a long time. He has your best interests at heart; he thinks big picture; he thinks long term.

It's all good. You'll see.

But I trust your wisdom

Pastor Mark Jeske

Dear God, I don't want to seem childish and whiny, but I'm so tired of struggling. My patience is wearing out; I don't understand what you're doing or where you are, and I'm frustrated. My sister still has MS, I have bills to pay and no money, my mom is disabled, the IRS is after me for my tax return of two years ago, and my son was arrested last week.

But you've always been there for me in the past. As I look back, I can see your gifts and blessings. Don't be angry with me—I have to vent somewhere. I know that my personal wealth and comfort are not of first importance. Help me! **"Your ways, O God, are holy. What god is so great as our God? You are the God who performs miracles; you display your power among the peoples"** (Psalm 77:13,14).

I know you have a plan for me. You always do. I have so much—don't let my fears make me think I have little. Thank you for my friends and pastor. Thank you for my family—I love them so much. I know you will send relief—help me expect it and watch for it. Show your power in my life! I know your answer to my needs may come in little pieces instead of one big piece. I know your heavenly rescue may come in the form of earthly helpers.

Forgive me, Lord. I trust your power and your heart. I trust your wisdom too.

Devotions for Special Days

Easter: The big deal

Pastor Mark Jeske

The magnificent pyramids of Egypt were actually constructed as burial vaults for the pharaohs: the bodies of Djoser, Khufu, and Khafra, carefully mummified and wrapped, were interred there. The burial chambers today, however, are empty. Jesus Christ was executed like the worst criminal, but he was buried like a prince in a newly hewn rock mausoleum. His vault is empty also, but for a completely different reason. Grave robbers looted the tombs of the pharaohs. Jesus walked out of his tomb alive again.

You would expect that non-Christians do not believe the Easter story. But it might surprise you to know how many Christian teachers are busy spreading the idea that the resurrection of Christ involves something other than the revivification of his corpse. In fact, our Savior was really, really dead. No pulse. No respiration. No brain waves. In fact, our Savior is now really, really alive.

This is a big deal. The bodily resurrection of Jesus Christ is the Father's very public seal of approval on his Son's entire life's work. **"If Christ has not been raised, our preaching is useless and so is your faith"** (1 Corinthians 15:14). If Christ's body is still dead, you are still in your sins. Your guilt has not been lifted. Your own body will never leave its grave.

But Christ has been raised. So are our hopes. "I believe in the resurrection of the body," we say in the Apostles' Creed. Do you believe those words? Those who do are forgiven and immortal.

Do it again

Pastor Mark Jeske

If only the task of mothering were a string of "one and dones." If only you needed to teach each life lesson to your kids just one time. If only every prayer for your children's well-being were answered immediately. If only.

The reality is that mothering is a marathon, not a sprint. The reality is that mothers often carry burdens for their children for many, many years and that they will need to pray long and repeatedly for the things they know only God can do for their dear ones. How our families need mothers with spiritual stamina!

Hannah wanted to be a mother more than anything in the world. She is a model for moms in the persistence of her prayer: **"In bitterness of soul, Hannah wept much and prayed to the Lord. . . . 'If you will only look upon your servant's misery and remember me, and not forget your servant but give her a son . . .'"** (1 Samuel 1:10,11).

That's just one of many reasons why we all owe such an enormous debt of gratitude to God for our mothers and to our mothers for pointing us to God. I will never know how often my mother prayed to God for me. But my life has so many blessings that I can be sure she prayed a lot. Thank you, Mom.

What have you done for me?

Pastor Mark Jeske

One of the things that hindered me from more enthusiastic thanks to my dad on Father's Day was that so much of what I owed him came to me unconsciously. When you are blessed to have a dad throughout your entire childhood, you don't realize that you are being trained in absolutely vital life skills: telling the truth, finishing a job, respecting and obeying authority, restraining your temper, and treating women with respect and tenderness.

Where you really notice the importance of good fathering is in its absence—a young man who is violent preys on women, can't hold a job, can't finish school, and can't obey orders. Or in a young woman who is not secure financially, not secure in her beauty, not protected from abusers, and is not able to wait for marriage to have sex and children.

Here's to all the fathers who stuck around, who went through the grueling years of raising and discipling their children. On Father's Day we salute you not only for what we can remember that you did for us but for the million things we can't remember but which have become part of our minds and hearts and behaviors. **"My son, do not forget my teaching, but keep my commands in your heart, for they will prolong your life many years and bring you prosperity"** (Proverbs 3:1,2).

____

____

____

____

____

An attitude of gratitude

Pastor Mark Jeske

"I'll be happy when I get _____" is a triple trap. For one, it keeps you miserable as you wait impatiently to be fulfilled. Second, wanting more never satisfies, even if you get your first wish, because you then want still more. Third, it cheats you out of the happiness with the wealth that you already possess.

Cultivating a thankful heart and thankful spirit are learned behaviors. You have to choose to be like that, because the attitude you're born with is one of selfishness, greed, and discontent. By nature we feel cheated, envious of others, and sullen at our lot in life.

Jesus calls us to a better way. He opens our eyes to the gospel of our free and full forgiveness, given to us at the cost of his death. He opens our eyes to our new and wonderful relationship with our heavenly Father, source of all good gifts. He opens our eyes to the great wealth we already have—treasures of possessions, friends, and family. Best of all, he promises that we are not only forgiven but immortal.

The gospel makes us optimists. It also invites us to overhaul our attitudes daily to be in line with our new status in heaven. **"Be joyful always; pray continually; give thanks in all circumstances, for this is God's will for you in Christ Jesus"** (1 Thessalonians 5:16-18).

____

____

____

____

____

About the writers

Pastor Mark Jeske brings the good news of Jesus Christ to viewers of *Time of Grace* in weekly 30-minute programs broadcast across America and around the world on local television, cable, and satellite, as well as on-demand streaming via the Internet. He is the senior pastor at St. Marcus Lutheran Church, a thriving multicultural congregation in Milwaukee, Wisconsin. Mark is the author of several books and dozens of devotional booklets. He and his wife, Carol, have four adult children.

Linda Buxa is a freelance writer, Bible study leader, and a regular speaker at women's retreats and conferences across the country. She is also a blogger for Time of Grace Ministry and the author of *Dig In! Family Devotions to Feed Your Faith*. Linda and her husband, Greg, live in Wisconsin, where they are raising their three children.

Diana Kerr is a certified professional coach, writer, and blogger on a never-ending chase for a life focused on what matters most. Her business and life's passion is all about equipping goal-oriented Christian women with the tools and truths they need to get unstuck and make the most of their time and life. You can find out more about Diana or read her motivational and transparent content on her blog at dianakerr.com.

Pastor Daron Lindemann is pastor at Holy Word Lutheran Church, a new mission start in Pflugerville, Texas. Previously he served Grace Lutheran Church in downtown Milwaukee, and Hope Lutheran Church in Irmo, South Carolina. Daron has authored articles or series for *Forward in Christ* magazine, *Preach the Word,* and his own weekly *Grace MEMO* devotions. He lives in Texas with his wife, Cara, and has two adult sons.

Jason Nelson had a career as a teacher, counselor, and leader. He has a bachelor's degree in education, did graduate work in theology, and has a master's degree in counseling psychology. After his career ended in disabling back pain, he wrote the book *Miserable Joy: Chronic Pain in the Christian Life* (2007, NPH). He has written and spoken extensively on a variety of topics related to the Christian life. Jason lives with his wife, Nancy, in Wisconsin.

About Time of Grace

Time of Grace is an international Christian outreach media ministry that connects people to God's grace through Jesus Christ so that they know they are loved and forgiven. The ministry uses television, print, social media, and the web to share the gospel with people across the U.S. and around the world. On the weekly *Time of Grace* television program, Pastor Mark Jeske presents Bible studies that are understandable, interesting, and can be applied to people's lives. The program is broadcast locally, nationally, and internationally on various networks, including ABC Family, which is carried by virtually all cable providers in the U.S. For a complete broadcast schedule, visit timeofgrace.org. Watch *Time of Grace* or visit timeofgrace.org, where you will find the program via streaming video and audio podcasts, as well as study guides, daily devotions, blogs, a prayer wall, and additional resources. You can also call 800.661.3311 for more information.